Abhishek Majumdar Collected Plays

Abhishek Majumdar Collected Plays

Dweepa
Pah-La
Djinns of Eidgah
Muktidham
9 Kinds of Silence

ABHISHEK MAJUMDAR

methuen | drama
LONDON • NEW YORK • OXFORD • NEW DELHI • SYDNEY

METHUEN DRAMA
Bloomsbury Publishing Plc
50 Bedford Square, London, WC1B 3DP, UK
1385 Broadway, New York, NY 10018, USA
29 Earlsfort Terrace, Dublin 2, Ireland

BLOOMSBURY, METHUEN DRAMA and the Methuen Drama logo are trademarks of
Bloomsbury Publishing Plc

First published in Great Britain 2024

Copyright © Abhishek Majumdar, 2024
Introduction © Sundar Sarukkai, 2024

Abhishek Majumdar has asserted his right under the Copyright, Designs and Patents Act, 1988,
to be identified as author of this work.

Cover design by Rebecca Heselton
Cover image: *Rocket Hole* © Rania Matar

All rights reserved. No part of this publication may be reproduced or transmitted in any form or by any means, electronic or mechanical, including photocopying, recording, or any information storage or retrieval system, without prior permission in writing from the publishers.

Bloomsbury Publishing Plc does not have any control over, or responsibility for, any third-party websites referred to or in this book. All internet addresses given in this book were correct at the time of going to press. The author and publisher regret any inconvenience caused if addresses have changed or sites have ceased to exist, but can accept no responsibility for any such changes.

No rights in incidental music or songs contained in the work are hereby granted and performance rights for any performance/presentation whatsoever must be obtained from the respective copyright owners.

All rights whatsoever in this play are strictly reserved and application for performance etc. should be made before rehearsals to Permissions Department, Bloomsbury Publishing Plc, 50 Bedford Square, London, WC1B 3DP, UK. No performance may be given unless a licence has been obtained.
No rights in incidental music or songs contained in the Work are hereby granted and performance rights for any performance/presentation whatsoever must be obtained from the respective copyright owners.

A catalogue record for this book is available from the British Library.

A catalog record for this book is available from the Library of Congress.

ISBN: PB: 978-1-3504-2366-4
ePDF: 978-1-3504-2368-8
eBook: 978-1-3504-2367-1

Series: Methuen Drama Play Collections

Typeset by RefineCatch Limited, Bungay, Suffolk
Printed and bound in Great Britain

To find out more about our authors and books visit
www.bloomsbury.com and sign up for our newsletters.

For my daughter Rai.

In memory of Dipali Majumdar and Elyse Dodgson.

Thanks to New York University Abu Dhabi, Division of Arts and Humanities.

Contents

Introduction by Sundar Sarukkai 1
Dweepa 7
Pah-La 63
Djinns of Eidgah 123
Muktidham 191
9 Kinds of Silence 255

Introduction

Sundar Sarukkai

Reading plays is not like reading other texts. It is not like reading novels or even poetry. Perhaps this is the reason why I find so many enthusiastic readers of fiction unable to read and enjoy plays. And even when plays are read, they are read with a different attitude. Theatre-makers read these texts differently, particularly in comparison to genres like novels and short stories. A director feels little qualm in rewriting dialogues or editing the text of the play to suit her production. It is only big names in theatre like Beckett who have the clout (now through his Estate) to insist that the productions strictly follow their text. Actors feel that they have a right to 'change' lines and words. In the name of adaptation, I have seen large-scale use of plays which have been changed to suit the interests and expertise of theatre-makers. For example, plays of Shakespeare are very often adapted into Indian languages and the adaptations take many creative liberties with the text. Such an attitude towards a text in the time of plagiarism-phobia says much more about theatre as an activity, as well as pointing to an inherent 'incompleteness' of these texts that arises from its form.

Such an attitude might seem to reflect the fact that the readers of these texts do not 'respect' the autonomy of the author. It might seem that the autonomy of the text/author of a play is always subservient to those who perform it. I often contrast this position to my attempts to get students to write collectively in my writing workshops. I find that sharing authorship, sharing the creative act of writing with others, is most difficult for students since they have been trained to believe in the absolute autonomy of the individual mind. In the midst of this strongly established belief about authorship that some would see as characterizing modernity, it is remarkable that authorship in plays continues to be dealt with ambiguously.

However, we can also interpret this action in another way, as one that gives its readers the freedom to do what they want with the text. It is not the author of a play who gives this freedom to the readers. It is the culture of theatre itself that produces this freedom independent of what the playwright might think about it. It is this character of freedom that permeates even the 'doing' of theatre, and it begins first with the act of reading the text. Even devised theatre challenges the privileged position of the author/maker. These acts are not the consequence of collaboration that is so essential to a performance; they arise primarily as challenges to each other's positions and beliefs. The doing of theatre arises from these provocations of challenges and freedom.

I begin with this observation about reading plays since this book is a collection of plays that will be read, first and foremost. The act of merely reading is rarely the ultimate aim of reading plays. The reader who reads it might be reading it for producing the play or for adapting it. Unlike a reader of a novel where, in general, there is no aim other than that of the pleasure of reading, a play is often read with this expectation of converting the text into another form. Thus, the written play is always incomplete – incomplete both in its form as well as in its reception by the reader. There is something else 'outside' the text that is needed to complete the text, both for the author and the reader. The author signals this by giving authorial directions and suggestions in the text. The author is essentially saying what must be done in the production of the play, thereby tacitly recognizing that the dialogic structure of the text cannot voice this absence by itself. Equivalently, reading alone cannot unravel the meanings of the text since it has the shadow-presence of the possible performance that accompanies it. Thus, there are many kinds of absences structuring a written play. In a deeper sense then, reading a play is to engage with the different 'levels' of invisibility that are present in the text compared to novels and essays, in general. This quality necessitates different strategies of reading plays.

Majumdar's plays are an excellent illustration of the presence of a complex layering of invisibility. Thus, they raise new challenges to a reader of his plays, whether the reader is reading them purely as a literary text or for potential use as material for a production. One of the most useful ways to understand the commonality among his many plays is to first understand the nature of the absences that are present in his plays. I will discuss his plays, with specific reference to the collection in this volume, in the framework of three types of invisibilities that animate his work: Language, Politics, Time.

While I pose this question of the invisible from the perspective of reading plays, it is important to note that for Majumdar, the theme of the invisible is an essential catalyst for his writing. As he writes in his book *Theatre Across Borders*, there are three questions that have influenced him throughout his journey as a theatre-maker. The first question is 'What is the invisible?'; Majumdar asks this question as he believes that theatre is 'about making the invisible visible' (pp. 10–11). The second question is 'What is a society?' and the third is 'Which patterns are beautiful?' (13). It is also important to note how his approach to theatre is deeply influenced by three performing traditions. These are (1) Ramlila (the performance of Ramayana, culminating in the victory of Rama over Ravana), (2) the influential theatre personality Habib Tanvir and his group, and (3) Bengali theatre. What were influences when he was growing up have transformed into an ideal type for comparison even now: he notes that when he directs/performs, he imagines how all those three traditions would have done it.

One can clearly see that, right from the beginning, a sense of politics has been essential to the plays Majumdar has written. It is a kind of politics that is not entirely moored in the 'modern', since the notion of 'tradition' too plays an important role in his theatrical journey. He himself notes that tradition is present in modernity for him, and the three influences mentioned above all come with their own world of traditions. The capacity to engage with tradition within modernity also allows him to deal with plays set in the past with contemporary sensibilities. *Muktidham*, a play set in eighth-century India, is a good example of a play set in a historical time, capturing the growing conflict between Hindus and Buddhists, but resonates with imageries of the present Hindutva movement in India. So it is not just theatrically presenting/recreating events of the past but is a way of engaging with past events as points of origin of contemporary events. The political operates at different levels in this text, as in the play *Pah-La*. In *Pah-La* it is obviously about the Chinese repression of Tibetan people but this is again presented through a mix of historical tropes. The politics in this is quite clear and it is not restricted only to the Chinese aggression. It is on the broader politics surrounding the idea of non-violence, and the possibility of non-violence in the face of violence. As he writes in his book, the question that is at the centre of this play is this: 'What is the future of non-violence?' (95). The powerful play *Djinns of Eidgah* is explicitly political in that it deals with the politics of Kashmir, a world that is very much in the forefront of the imagination of India. Both *Pah-La* and *Djinns* draw upon the voices and experiences of the oppressors as characters, but do so not to present multiple viewpoints but to find a voice to speak about their own internal contradictions. In an essential Buddhist sense, a philosophy that attracts Majumdar, these plays are about searching for the possibility of a middle path. For example, the possibility of finding non-violence has to be in the midst of violence, not in a world that is completely bereft of violence. *The Island* was influenced after he saw the eminent film director Girish Kasaravalli's film *Dweepa*. The play arose as a tribute to it and drew upon his own training to be an environmentalist. As Majumdar pointed out in a personal conversation, all of his plays are a mix of the personal, political and the philosophical. It is interesting to note that religion is one domain that has deep relations to each of these three domains. It is not surprising therefore that Majumdar's plays often go back to themes surrounding people's beliefs and the reflections of these beliefs within an institution called religion.

Religion has a literal relationship with the invisible, but also has deeper social and institutional invisibilities associated with it. Just as religion seems important to him as a playwright, so too his concern with the theme of language. Majumdar points out that, when he wrote *Muktidham* in 2017, he 'had to write five kinds of Hindi in it to mirror that reality', the reality of eighth-century India. In the context of this volume, which has both plays written in English and those translated into English from Hindi and Bangla, it is important to recognize his engagement with the theme of language in writing plays. Writing in English is political and sometimes the political is made visible, although many times it remains invisible as something that is taken-for-granted. Language itself cannot be universal for Majumdar. English in India is not the same as English outside the country – by this, I do not mean that the structure of the language is radically different but only that the invisible world of language that surrounds the 'legible' language is different in these different contexts. English in India is fraught with questions that do not arise in other contexts. His decision to focus more on writing plays in other languages was related to the politics of English theatre in India, the kind of audience it had, and the nature of the themes they dealt with. Language becomes an important part of theatre-making for him since he believes that 'people watch English plays differently'. This was particularly true for humour; in a private conversation he suggested that the same audience watches the performance of humour in different languages differently. There is also the power of privilege that enters English theatre. He pointed out that in India, knowing English was enough to be seen as an actor but that was not so in other languages. There is a cultural, traditional and philosophical specificity to each language that becomes part of any theatre produced in a place like India, an essentially multilingual place, and a multicultural haven. Thus, English cannot be deployed casually in the construction of theatre in India, if theatre is essentially grounded in the political as it is for Majumdar. However, at the same time, English is also the language that he engages with in writing and directing plays in other countries. I want to suggest that his awareness of the politics in the use of English in the context of India influences his 'play' with English even for plays set outside the Indian context. This awareness influences both the form and content, if not directly, at least on a subliminal level.

In this collection, one of the plays was originally written in Hindi, another in Bengali. Although the shift to writing in Hindi and Bengali is shaped more by the world inhabited by English speaking audiences, actors and writers, Majumdar is not taking the next step of claiming that English cannot capture the cultural worlds of the people and traditions he writes about, a contentious point some Indian-language writers have promoted. However, it may seem that this position that English is incapable (or at least incomplete) in its capacity to express fully the idioms of a society can be inferred from his comment on *Muktidham*. When he notes that he had to write this play in five kinds of Hindi 'in order to mirror that reality', he seems to acknowledge that English's failure is perhaps in not being able to mirror the reality of a complex multilingual society. But what kind of a failure can this be? Does the problem reside in the language per se, in the fact that the languages don't 'belong' to the performers, or that they don't 'belong' to the cultures that are represented in the play? The question of language too is a political one in India and we have to see Majumdar's plays as one element of this politics.

The politics of English is primarily a response to the written text, as a language in which a text is written. Even in a cosmopolitan city like Bangalore, a city that has enabled Majumdar to establish his theatrical practice, and where there is a comparatively more robust English theatre, the politics of language continues to stake its claim. Many Indian-language theatre-makers are uncomfortable with English theatre, if not outright dismissive. There are many reasons ranging from the thematic interests of the 'English crowd' to the kind of audience that typically comes for this theatre. It is true that a particular class of people tend to be the dominant viewing class of this theatre. Thus, theatre in English does not, for the most part, attract a larger egalitarian crowd across class and caste. But this does not necessarily mean that plays in Indian languages attract a large crowd. In fact, the viability of 'serious' theatre (in contrast to 'commercial' theatre) in Indian languages is a serious problem.

The experiment with multilinguality that characterizes Majumdar's plays is present even in plays written exclusively in English. It is another aspect of his engagement with layers of invisibilities in his plays. While much can be written about this aspect, I will limit myself to one observation regarding the idea of language itself in theatre. It is that language in theatre consciously transcends verbal language. While it is true that language is more than the verbal component alone, in theatre this is an essential quality. That is, language in theatre – theatrical language – has the verbal only as its subset. The other elements of theatrical language too mirror multiple realities of these cultures. Here is where the politics associated with translation makes itself visible. Translation understood as movement from one verbal language to another does not capture the full complexity of the act of translation in theatre. There are other forms and other acts of translation that have to occur simultaneously on stage. The explicit presence of other languages and their translation into English makes us aware of the presence of translation. In such a situation, we should also become aware of other kinds of translation that always happen with theatre. One way this appears in performance is through the contexts of various subjectivities that inhabit Majumdar's plays – the subjectivities of the place, people, events, characters, of languages themselves, and, most importantly for him, the subjectivities of space and time. The subjectivities of space and time can be an interesting discussion in themselves. For example, consider the role of time in Majumdar's plays. Time can be seen as a 'character', sometimes visible but sometimes not, in his plays. It has an enduring presence perhaps in all his plays. Making this explicit, he notes in his book, 'At the heart of every good play, whether set in the future or not, lies an argument for the future' (160).

These actions are those that make theatre possible. Time has a deep relation with the idea of movement and travel. Re-emphasizing this connection, he notes, 'In a way, the entire act of theatre-making is a way of travelling. To another reality. Only to reveal what we really are deep inside' (6). What is the reality that theatre really reveals? The reality that theatre reveals is always more than the reality that the text of the play reveals. But a playwright has to find a way to condense this larger theatrical reality within the limitations of a written text, in the hope that it will be discovered in its performance, and will emerge in the coming together of its many subjectivities.

Politics is intrinsic to Majumdar's conceptualization of theatre itself. Theatre-making is a 'way of travelling' in order to reveal realities of the inner human subject through engaging with the realities of the outer. It is this approach that offers a new dimension to how we understand his plays. His plays, in general, have been explicitly political in the sense that they deal with what are seen as political issues. *Djinns of Eidgah* is dominantly about the politics of Kashmir, *Pah-La* the politics of Tibet, *The Island* the politics of environmentalism, *Muktidham* the politics of Hindutva, *9 Kinds of Silence* the politics of war. On reading these plays, one can perceive these political themes right on the surface. But the politics works much deeper in these performances. For example, *9 Kinds of Silence* is not just about a particular imagery of conflict but is as much about the politics of speech and the constant, irreducible tension between language and silence. The fact that this is played out between a mother and son offers more metaphorical readings of the matriarchal relationship between language and silence, as well as between power and silence.

Moreover, politics too gets transformed in the space and time of theatre. Themes and stories in his plays are not 'political' like a story, a novel or even a newspaper report. Just as theatrical language is different from language, so too is theatrical politics different from the politics of the world. This politics arises in the act of performance, in the way audiences perceive and receive them, in the way governments and other agencies attack them. Such responses have not been new to the plays in this volume. There have been attempts to close down some performances of these plays, the playwright has been attacked by motivated groups, and pressure has been mounted on groups to stop these productions. It might seem, then, that the governments and other groups are against the explicit politics in these plays. But, in reality, their fear is more. They realize that the power of theatre, more than that of pure texts alone, is the capacity to discover our own inner realities through our experience of outer realities, as Majumdar describes. Theatre has this power to transcend a mere presentation of reality, of merely being a 'mirror of reality' to being a mirror of the self, our-selves. Street theatre foregrounds this performance of bringing the self before each member of the audience, and it is not surprising that one of the influences on Majumdar has been different forms of Indian theatre that all have some connection to 'street' theatre. Unlike fiction, where the imagination of the character is produced within the minds of readers, plays embody these imaginations and place them on stage, to recreate what the viewers could have imagined and could not have imagined also! The performances of these plays are not mere representations of some events but are an invitation to the audience to enter the stage, to be an invisible presence on the stage.

I believe that this is one way to interpret Majumdar's own claim of the processes that lie behind the writing of his plays. In the writing of his plays, research is an important component. This field research involves spending significant time talking to people in depth, from different perspectives. And doing this is not only difficult but can prove to be hazardous, especially as seen in his accounts of his field research in Kashmir, China and Tibet. But Majumdar points out that all these in-depth interviews are not merely to gather information that goes into the play. He is looking for something else altogether: 'What I am looking for is not information, I am looking for shared presence' (95). What is this shared experience? Between the actors, between the team that produces the whole play, between an individual in the audience and the actors, between the audience as such and the actors, or between the members of the audience? To extrapolate Majumdar, I would say that reading plays like the ones in this book should be seen as an attempt to find a shared presence between the imagination of the playwright, the events and drama of the play, and the reader. The task of the reader is to find strategies that will produce this shared presence, not just look for particular narratives and for particular events. Once this is done, there is a possibility that it will shine a *stage light* on our inner self. If these plays can achieve that, there is nothing more that a playwright like Majumdar can ask for.

Reference

Majumdar, Abhishek. *Theatre Across Borders*. London: Methuen Drama, Bloomsbury, 2023.

Dweepa (The Island)

Translated to English from Bangla by Bhaskar Chattopadhyay

A tribute to Girish Kasaravalli's film by the same name and to Susmit Sen's composition 'Depths of the Ocean'

The play was supported by the Boell Foundation for its research

Dweepa first premiered in Kannada, Jayshree Kambar's translation, on 30 October 2015 at Ranga Shankara Theatre Festival, Ranga Shankara, Bangalore, India. Produced by Rangashankara as part of the annual theatre festival 2015.

Director and Playwright	Abhishek Majumdar
Assistant Directors	Venkatesh Prasad, Surabhi Vasisht
Sets	Vijay Benacha, Balakrishna
Costume	Surabhi Vasisht
Visual Design and Film	Vandana Menon
Music	Vasu Dixit and Bindhu Malini
Projection and Music Execution	Bhamini N.
Lights	Niranjan Gokhale
Makeup Design	Ramakrishna Kannarpadi
Makeup	Surabhi Vasisht
Production Interns	Sathwik N., Heena Sharma
Production Manager	Venkatesh Prasad
Man	Raghunandan Seshanna
Woman	Sunita M. R.
Moidul	Sriharsha Grama
Morris	Deepak Subramanya
Moinak	Venkatesh Prasad

Characters

Attendant, *attendant in a circus*

Man (M), *a man, used to work in a bookstore, played the role of Hindu deity Shiva in a local play and gets blown to an island in the Bay of Bengal after a storm*

Moidul, *Flight Officer of Bangladesh Air Force, pilot of the helicopter in a joint India-Bangladesh-USA rescue mission*

Moinak, *Commander of Indian Air Force, highest-ranking officer in a joint India-Bangladesh-USA rescue mission*

Morris, *Wing Commander of US Air Force, member of the three-man rescue team in a joint India-Bangladesh-USA mission*

Old man chewing paan, *one of the four old men in a circus*

Old man drinking alcohol, *one of the four old men in a circus*

Old man smoking pipe, *one of the four old men in a circus*

Old man taking snuff, *one of the four old men in a circus*

Woman (W), *a woman, used to work in a bank, played the role of Hindu deity Kali in a local play and gets blown to an island in the Bay of Bengal after a storm*

Scene One

We see a stage, half buried in the sand. It has been blown away from a coastal town in a violent storm and has finally collapsed on an island. There are a few broken stage lights strewn around. A few trees. Sand. Footprints of turtles on the sand. The **Man**, *wearing a tiger skin, just like Lord Shiva – lying around in one corner. The* **Woman**, *dressed like Kali Maa, sits up and looks around. Her bloody red tongue is sticking out, much like that of the deity. With some effort, she takes off the tongue prop and looks at the* **Man**. *Then she looks at the turtle tracks.*

W Wake up . . . wake up . . . wake up! See here. It seems they tried to come back last night. (*The* **Man** *doesn't wake up. Instead, he stretches his limbs and grunts.*)

W *Baap re baap*! What a storm! Trees and houses, huts and plants – all destroyed, everything gone. How can you sleep in all this?

M Mmmm . . .? What? Where can I get a cup of tea, a double-roti and an omelette?

W See? See? You men are all the same. The only thing you can think of is food. You don't remember who you are, you don't remember your name, your age, class, clan, education. You are on an island with a woman, and you don't even remember your relationship with her. But you wake up in the morning, and what do you think of? Tea! And omelettes! Huh!

M (*irritated grimace*)   Oh ho! Stop making a fuss. I remember everything . . . (*yawns again*) everything!

W Really?

M Yes, yes . . . all I ask for is a cup of tea and a few biscuits, and you start shouting at me – at ME! Emperor Nicholas – the sole heir of the kingdom . . . and you dare. . . . (*Looks around and comes to a sudden stop.*)

W Wait a second, wait a second – WHO? Nicholas?!! Nicholas? I knew it! It's worse than I thought! Everything is destroyed in this blasted storm, and who am I stranded with on this island? A crazy idiot! And not just *any* idiot! What memories! What imagination! All dressed up like Shiva and says he is Mr Nicholas! Huh!

M Oh, shut up! I remember everything . . . I remember . . . I remember language. See? Here I am speaking to you. I remember words.

W My foot! Tell me – who am I?

M You . . . (*Looks up at her.*) You are a woman!

W A woman? Woman who?

M (*shrugs*)   Woman. Mother. One who gives life. Or . . . or . . . Life partner. Or Grandmother. Or maid . . . or . . . by the way, you look great in that Kali dress. (*Smiles.*)

Scene One

W A-ha-ha! And have you seen what you yourself are wearing? Now tell me, who am I? How am I related to you?

M To *me*? That . . . I don't know.

W What an intelligent man I have met! Says I am a woman! Huh!

The **Man** *looks here and there.*

M What place is this?

W Now he's talking.

M You . . . (*Finds a broken mirror and looks at it.*) Oh maa! Is that . . . *me*? What happened to me? Who am I?

W Ah! Now sahib is waking up finally!

M It's not funny. What's the matter? What is going on?

W Do you remember last night?

M Last night? Yes, I remember last night. There was a play being staged in the neighbourhood, for Shiv Ratri – we were acting, you and I. I was playing Lord Shiva. I looked down at you from the skies and said – 'If you don't stop that stupid dance, I'll come down to earth and destroy everything. I kept telling you, and you kept ignoring me, and I kept telling you, and you kept dancing . . . so I gave you one last warning and jumped down from the ramp . . . and then . . . .

W And then . . .?

M (*dreamily*) And then . . . there was a storm . . . it came and it blew everything away. It seemed the skies opened up and let all the rains out. It rained so hard! (*Suddenly looks at the* **Woman**.) But you have to admit, I gave a *fasclaas* performance!

W Who are you? And where was I? Are you talking about a past life or something?

M I remember the storm . . . around the middle of the second act. The entire island began to shake. We were so terrified . . . .

W You mean on stage?

M No, in reality. The neighbourhood pandal was shattered. Oh! The trees and plants were all uprooted, and were flying in the sky here and there. Yes. . . . I remember . . . .

W Please, I beg of you. Look here now see? Do you see?

M See what?

W Right here, don't you see? Footprints!

M Oh . . . yes, yes! Turtles?

W Yes, turtles! A hundred years old. Two hundred perhaps. They have been coming here for thousands of years, to lay eggs. Right here. They are born here, and they die here.

M So? Why should I care?

W What do you mean 'why should I care'? How are they coming here this year? The island is not where it used to be. Don't you get it? Our town, and the villages around it – all blown away in the storm. And we were blown away too, and we reached this island. This must be the Bay of Bengal.

M What's that got to do with the turtles?

W Remove your foot.

M Hain?!!

W I said lift your foot from the ground.

The **Man** *lifts his foot and looks down.*

W See here? Turtle tracks. They are going back . . . .

M (*perplexed*) Yes, so?

W (*excited whisper*) It means one can find one's way back from this place!

M You mean the *turtles* can find their way back?

W Off-ho! If the turtles can, we can too.

M How can you be so sure?

W Of course! Is there anything that any creature in the world can do that human beings cannot?

M (*shuts his eyes and begins*) Well, there's a tiny animal on the Galapagos Island . . . millions of them, in fact . . . .

W (*interrupts*) But not in Bengal, right?

The **Man** *shakes his head and says 'no'.*

W So, if the turtles can find us, perhaps other human beings can find us too?

M Correct. But what if they don't look for us? After all, how many days have we been here?

W I don't know.

M What do you mean you don't know?

W I mean I don't know.

M *Dhur shaala*! How are you related to me?

W I'm not sure.

M Hain! Mother? Sister? Aunt? Girlfriend? Wife? Who are you? Or, is it possible that you are Maa Kali herself? (*Smiles.*) What's your name?

W I don't know. I remember more than you do, but I don't remember my name.

M But it seems we know each other from before the storm.

W Yes, I think so too.

M *O baba*! So, here we are, marooned on a remote island thanks to a *pralay* that has wiped the rest of the planet away, without any memory, and we are waiting for turtles? This is like science fiction!

W What nonsense!

M I remember now! I used to work at a bookstore. Books, yes books. There used to be this . . . this thing called books. (*Looks around.*) I don't see a book around here though.

W A book? What is a book?

M (*nods his head*) Now I understand. This is why we are stuck in this place *baada*. All because of science fiction. I mean think about it . . . When did science fiction become literature, huh? And when did Football become a subject of poetry? Did Sarat Babu, Bankim Babu create literature based on Science? Or Crime?

W Who are you talking about? Who are all these people?

M One second. . . . I'll explain everything. . . . I remember now . . . .

W Oh! You remember these people? But you don't remember me? You men!

M So many things got tossed around in the storm, why isn't there another human being in sight?

W Yes, no one.

M Has everyone run away? What about our audience? We had an audience, right?

W They must be all dead.

M Dead, and gone.

W Yes, or else we would have seen someone. What a storm! What rains! They must have died by the hundreds, poor things. And all the *loot-maar* oh!

M *Loot-maar*? In the middle of a storm?

W I bet you don't remember anything other than . . . that . . . what's the name of that thing? Ah yes, book.

M Yes, you could say that. By the way, there's this book called *Robinson Crusoe*, you know . . . .

M Shut up, don't talk nonsense. Stop fooling around and think.

M Think about what?

W What do we do now?

M Well, we have to rebuild everything. Start from the beginning. Think about it . . . what if no one finds us? We don't even know if anyone is looking for us. In fact, we don't even know if anyone else is alive. And all this excitement and optimism about the turtles . . . let me tell you about a British explorer named Charles Darwin, who said in a book called *Origin of Species* that . . . .

W   Shut up! One more word about books and I swear I'll hit you on your head.

M   But one thing is there, we both remember the Shiva-Kali story.

W   It's a thousand-year-old story, how can we forget it so easily?

M   Arrey no, not that. I remember it because I had seen a few pictures of them in a boo. . . . (*Glances at the* **Woman** *and shuts up quickly.*)

W   So, we need to rebuild this planet? Very well. Let's start with food. What shall we eat?

M   No, let's start with relationships. How are you and I related?

W   What good is a relationship without food?

M   We can get all the food in the world. But what do we do once we get food? Who gives food to whom? And how much? Will you give me your food, or will you snatch my food away? Will I share my food with you? These are important questions. Without the answers to these questions, food is useless.

W   Alright then, I'll be your husband. And you be my wife. I faintly remember these two relationships.

M   Yes, me too.

W   Me husband, you wife. OK?

M   OK. Hundreds of books have been written about husbands and wives . . . .

W   One more word about books, and I'll break your face.

Brief pause.

W (*extends her neck*)   Clear?

M   Clear.

W   *Khabardaar*!

M   Alright.

W   Now follow the turtle tracks and keep searching. They must be coming from some far away land. Remember, one turtle, four legs.

M   Darwin said . . . .

W (*clenches her teeth*)   One tight slap . . . .

The **Man** *curls up and shuts his mouth.*

W   Go now. If you see another human being, blow this whistle. I'll come when I hear the whistle blow. In the meantime, I'll go and search for food.

M As you wish.

W Go.

*The **Man** begins to leave.*

W (*calls out from behind*)   Listen . . .

M Yes please?

W Who was Nicholas?

M Huh?

W You were talking about some Nicholas when you woke up. Who was he?

Brief pause.

M I don't know. I'm sorry, I made a mistake. Shall I go now?

W Go.

*As the **Man** leaves, the **Woman** stares after him.*

Scene Two

*Commander **Moinak**, Flight Officer **Moidul** and Wing Commander **Morris** are out on a search operation in a helicopter. The sound of the rotor is heard first, and then we see the helicopter. **Moidul** is seen flying it, with **Moinak** beside and **Morris** behind him.*

Moinak   Lower, lower . . . take it lower.

Moidul   If I take it any lower naa, it'll become a boat.

Morris   Push down on the throttle, push it . . . nonsense!

Moinak   Does the Bangladesh Air Force have a tradition of arguing with senior officers?

Moidul   No sir. But then, it doesn't have the tradition of sailing in a helicopter or flying in a submarine either.

Morris   What's that? Over there?

Moinak   Where? Where?

Moidul   What are you showing us, honey? It's such a huge ocean, how will we understand if you say 'over there, over there'?

Morris   You talk too much, Moidul. Had you been in our US Air Force, we would have bitch-slapped your ass to hell.

Moidul   Sir Morris, the pilots in your Air Force – do they get threats like this while flying? The joystick is in my hands, can you see? This is not the US Air Force sir, this is a Bangladesh Air Force helicopter. We can start a revolution in mid-air also!

Moinak Calm down, both of you. What is it that you saw, Morris? Point it out clearly.

Morris Over there, Commander Moinak, over there.

Moinak *Arrey*, over where?

Moidul Joint Operation – my ass! Ei je, *Dada*, please hurry up. The fuel in the tank is from Bangladesh.

Morris Oh my God! People are dying, a whole village from West Bengal has been washed out into the sea down there. And look at this stingy asshole going on about his fuel. To hell with your fuel! All you Bengalis are . . . .

Moinak Beg your pardon?

Morris Not you sir, I was talking about him.

Moidul Do you know what the population of Bangladesh is? You want us to sacrifice two week's rations of ten East Bengal citizens in order to save two West Bengal citizens?

Morris That call is not yours to take. Is this an Air Force or a grocery store? Shut up and fly the damn thing.

Moidul You haven't told us yet what is it exactly that you saw?

Moinak I think we should focus on the job. We should put all our attention to the task at hand.

Moidul Don't mind sir, you're a higher-ranking officer, but why is it that you Indians always say everything twice?

Morris THERE! There it is . . . the wreckage.

Moinak Lower, lower . . . take it lower. Down we go . . . further down.

Moidul Sir!

Moidul *starts taking the helicopter lower.*

Moinak Looks like something, let me see.

Moidul Morris is a Bengali.

Morris That's right sir, *hami Bangali ache*.

Moinak Oh, I see! Jolly good!

Moidul Why so much English, sir? That too in air? Everyone here understands Bangla. Please.

Morris I'm an Intercultural Officer. Back in America, we usually tend to discuss such issues as Internationalism, Interculturalism, Interpsychology, Intersexuality . . . .

Moidul And you think in my country we can't go beyond Intermediate? Racist bastard!

Moinak Uff! Don't flare up at everything, Moidul. Let's try and take a good look at what Morris Sahib is showing us.

Moidul *Dhur shaala, baaler chaal*! Where did I get stuck? They told me there would be a joint exercise for a couple of hours, and then music and fun for six hours. And then they send me to look for two Indians in the middle of the sea! *Chhyahh*!

Moinak Does the life of a fellow human being mean nothing to you? Is human life . . . .

Moidul Sir, say it only once!

Moinak Alright, alright. Is human life not valuable at all?

Moidul Two Bengalis worth so much?!! Tell me honestly, if this was not a joint exercise, would you have cared to search and rescue people from the two affected villages? Do you know how many people die every day on the streets of Dhaka?

Moinak That doesn't look like wreckage!

Morris What IS that? It's so beautiful!

Moidul You don't know?

Morris No.

Moidul *Jaah-babba*! It's from your country, and you don't know?

Morris From my country?

Moidul Yes. You said you want to create Disneyland in the middle of the ocean! Our government ran here and there and sanctioned the project. And then you came and started doing a lot of *hullah* . . . .

Morris What nonsense? It must be a Russian or Chinese project. If we had to set up Disneyland, why would we do it *here*?

Moidul Arrey, that is the question sir, that is the question. Why do you always do everything here – that is very difficult to say.

Morris Push the throttle down.

Moidul Sir.

Morris Our data says we are right on the path of the MH370.

Moidul Really? And what is that path?

Morris The data from INSAT said that if we were to draw two curves with the Andamans as the origin point – one towards Kyrgyzstan, the other towards the southern end of the Indian Ocean – then we should find the aircraft somewhere within this perimeter. We are headed right towards that area.

Moidul West Bengal and East Bengal – both these places come directly under any kind of perimeter around the tragic accident sir, what can we do?

Moinak True. What can one do if the magnetic poles get all messed up?

Morris   A famous study conducted at Harvard has found that the entire subject of the magnetic poles changing is just a myth, or insignificant, at best.

Moidul   Sir, let me tell you something. All studies conducted by any university of your country always say the same thing – that any earthquake, any big flood, any volcano and any alien attack can only happen in New York, and a young American man shows courage and daring by rescuing his American girlfriend, and saves the world in the process. Everything else is insignificant.

Morris   You shut up and do your job. Here, sir . . . look at these INSAT data . . . .

Moinak   Yes, let me see?

Morris   See? There's no trace of this island in the satellite images. It simply shouldn't exist.

Suddenly, a jingle starts playing.

Morris   This . . . God damn it . . . why can't I cancel it . . . damn these ads!

Moidul   Oh, advertise? Advertise of what, sir?

Morris   I don't know. Keep quiet.

Moinak   You see this heat wave, moving down this way, like a conveyor belt? If this were to suddenly change direction and start moving upwards, then all hurricanes and magnetic poles will switch directions too.

Moidul   Tell me honestly, are you two really searching, or are you making me go round and round just like that?

Morris   Hasn't sir told you to push the throttle all the way down? What the hell is wrong with you? It seems like you are driving a rickshaw. Why are we crawling for the last two hours?

Moidul   Sir, if you don't know which direction to fly towards, then what's the use of flying fast?

Morris   You guys from the subcontinent – how can you be so insensitive? Are you even human?

Moidul   I'll throw you out.

Morris   What?!!

Moidul   *Allah-kasam*, I'll push you out of the helicopter.

Morris   Sir, are you not going to say anything to this insolent assho –

Moidul *grabs* **Morris** *by the neck and almost pushes him out of the flying helicopter.*

Morris   What are you doing? Sir . . . help . . . help!

Moinak   Ah-ha! What the hell is going on? Listen here . . . Moidul . . . don't . . . .

Moidul   Arrey, don't worry, Morris. Moinak sir will not say anything, I know. He is scared of Musalmans!

Moinak   Morris, say sorry. Apologize. Quickly!

Morris   Apologize for what?

Moidul *lowers him a little more.* **Morris** *is now dangling dangerously from the helicopter.*

Moidul   Waah, American ego, waah! Listen *shonamoni*, don't apologize for yourself, apologize for your country!

Morris   Sorry, sorry. . . . I made a mistake . . . it won't happen again. *Hamake maap khariye dao.*

Moidul *pulls him back into the helicopter.*

Moidul   See sir? All a game of language!

Morris (*trembling*)   I . . . I'll have you sk-skinned . . . .

Moinak (*breathless, panting, scared to death*)   Can we have some calm please?

Morris   I'm trying to save two of your fucking Asians, with you two fucking Asians in your fucking Asian helicopter, and you're trying to fuck with me?

Moidul   We are searching for Asians because of you Americans only.

Morris   Oh, come on! I mean, really, come on! Are you kidding me? You're blaming us for this incident? Isn't that a bit too much?

Moidul   Not at all. The weak always blames the strong . . . it's natural.

Moinak   Please, I sincerely request you. Let us all focus on the work at hand.

Moidul   After all your research and big big studies, you'll finally say what my old *Dadijaan* used to say – 'Whatever you do, everything is in Allah's hands'.

Another ad jingle starts to play.

Moinak   Isn't there any way to disable this?

Morris   Technically, yes, it can be done. But that would slow down the data download speed.

Moidul   Whatever button they ask you to press, you keep pressing that, or else they will call you *fataak se*. Last time, when I was searching for that lost aeroplane naa, your INSAT sold me one big box of electronics, from Malaysia. Till date, I don't know what exactly they do.

Moinak   We'll find it. That island. We have to find it, we most certainly do. Or else, we'll lose face.

Morris   Yes, we gotta find it. Or else, I won't get my bonus in the next appraisal.

Moidul   If we find it, very good. If we don't, what can we do? Everything is in Allah's hands. We are just . . . insignificant!

Scene Three

Back to the island. We hear the shrill sound of a whistle.

W (*with whistle in hand*)   Shocked! I am shocked by your foolishness!

M   Sorry.

W   Eat less tonight.

M   Why?

W   Punishment.

M   Means?

W   Punishment means punishment, that's all.

M   I remember the word, but not the concept.

W   You make a mistake and then you have to repent for it.

M   But I will repent on my own.

W   And what if you don't? That's why, punishment.

M   But I'm telling you I'll do it.

W   *Achchha*? How?

M   I will . . . think.

W   That's not good enough for me.

M   Then what?

W   I will punish you. Whatever I like, or need, I will take away.

M   But that would hurt, no?

W   Yes, it will hurt YOU.

M   Yes, that is what I am saying.

W   Yes, so you'll not do it again next time. Whatever I tell you, you'll listen. Whatever I ask you to do, you will do it.

M   I understand.

W   Very well. Now start cutting these tender coconuts.

M   I still don't understand what my mistake was.

W   Why did you blow your whistle just like that?

M   I didn't blow it just like that!

W   You didn't? What is this? Did I ask you to blow the whistle when you see this?

M   You asked me to blow the whistle if I see something.

W   Something important . . . or some incident . . . not a useless glass box.

M   But you can see far away objects with this. I saw you from over there, it seemed you were standing right here. And the sea . . . far away. Big waves, crashing down, becoming smaller and smaller as they come closer . . . .

W   This is called a machine.

M   If I put my eye on this end of the machine, I can see from the other end.

W   What will we do with a machine . . . will it take us back where we came from? No more arguing with me.

M   No, I thought it might be something useful.

*The **Woman** throws a stone at the **Man**.*

M   Arre! What did I do. . . . I am only saying . . . .

*The **Woman** gets up, walks up to the **Man** and slaps him hard. All quiet.*

Pause.

W   Open your shirt.

M   Hain?!!

W   Open it . . . open it quickly.

*The **Man** looks scared, takes off his shirt.*

W   Give it to me.

*The **Man** hands over his shirt to the **Woman**.*

W   You will not get this till I think you have learnt your lesson.

M (*sheepishly*)   Alright.

Pause.

M   I am feeling shy.

W   Very good.

M   If I open my shirt, why does that make you so happy?

W   It doesn't matter that you open your shirt. What matters is that you will open it when I ask you to, and again wear it when I ask you to . . . THAT is important.

M   I understand . . . .

W   You will walk when I ask you to . . . stand still when I ask you to . . . .

M   How sweet!

W   You like it?

M   Yes, I like it.

W But a punishment is not something you like.

M But it seems it will be fun . . . and fantastic!

W You want to sleep with me?

M Yes, I want to.

W But not just when you want to.

M No, no. . . . I understand. This relationship is quite nice actually!

W Yes, quite nice.

M You want to sleep now?

W No, not right now. Now, I want to drink tender coconut water.

M And then?

W And then I'll sleep when you don't want to.

M With me?

W Who else?

M Man is the only animal who wants a master. Someone to tell him what to do, when to do . . . someone to punish him? I feel so happy, I can't explain it to you. But . . . what happens if I don't listen to you?

W God will punish you.

M Who is that?

W You don't remember anything at all, do you?

M I'm the wife, remember?

W That's true. Wives are not supposed to remember anything.

M Yes, and even if we remember, we are supposed to act like we don't remember.

W If the wife is intelligent, the husband doesn't like it at all.

M Really? Then, let's say I don't remember.

W You do, or you don't?

M I don't.

W God is . . . someone . . . who claims to know everything. A smartass, hard-dick, fucked up piece of shit, with an oversized ego . . . people say he is the one who created everything.

M What do you mean 'everything'?

W Everything – trees, plants, water, clouds, rain . . . everything has been created by him only.

M I don't understand. Do these things need to be created?

W Absolutely. Everything needs to be created. Where do you think they came from? Just because you're dressed up as Shiva, you only know of the tale of destruction. But there's the creation part also. That is managed by other gods.

M What about your . . . your intense desire to keep me under your feet, does this also come from God?

W If I don't get the coconut water in two minutes, I'll make you run around naked on the island.

M I see . . . .

W If you don't listen to me, God will skin you alive.

M He is on your side, is it?

W Yes.

M Why?

W Because I am the husband.

M So, God is on the husband's side?

W God is always on the stronger side.

M I see! So . . . so . . . God is on the storm's side, not on man's side, correct?

W You could say that, yes.

M And that's why our deaths are inevitable?

W Yes, of course.

The **Man** *hands over the tender coconut to the* **Woman**.

M Oh! Then what's the point of listening to you and doing as you say?

W *Arre dhur* . . . idiot! God will make life miserable for you later, not now.

M Later? Later when?

W After death.

M How sweet! I like this concept of 'now' and 'later' – tell me more about it.

W You see that big wave over there . . . far away? That's now. It'll come here later.

M Who is going how far – is that the concept of time?

W No. . . . I don't remember . . . .

M There's a book on this subject . . . but I suppose you'll hit me on the head if I talk about that . . . .

W A-ha! So, you do remember, hain, *chaandu*?

M I have experienced all kinds of violence.

W Of course. You're a man after all, it's quite natural for you to understand violence. God is also a man.

M Really?

W Absolutely. So, we were talking about time . . . .

M Yes . . . time?

W See the wave is coming this way . . . but there're a lot of things happening in the meantime, right?

M Yes, for example we are drinking coconut water.

W Right, or for instance, that bird just flew from here to there . . . .

M Yes.

W So, while the bird is flying from here to there, how much coconut water we drink – THAT is time.

M But . . . what about the waves?

W Well, look at it like this . . . now the wave is over there, the bird is over here and the coconut is in your hand. And later, the wave is over here, the bird is over there, and the coconut is in my hand.

M Does God drink coconut water?

W A lot.

M So, why will he punish me?

W Because I'm saying so.

M Very well.

W But not now . . . later.

M When the wave comes here, then?

W No . . . after death. After several such waves, after several such birds, after several such coconuts . . . .

M I see . . . so, after I die, he sort of becomes my husband?

W You could say that, yes.

M This accident . . . has he done this?

W Yes.

M Why? What have we done?

W It's difficult to say. For example, why would I punish you – that's not easy to say. Now, be afraid of me.

M How do I do that?

W By showing your devotion.

M And if I don't?

W If you don't, then after death, God will put you in a pot of boiling oil with lots of chillies and cook you for a thousand years.

M *Babbah*! This God had got quite a bit of imagination!

W God is the source of endless imagination! Where do you think the storm came from?

M I think I finally understand. God is on your side . . . if I don't listen to you, then cooking in boiling oil . . . devotion to you is devotion to God . . . am I correct?

W More or less.

M I found some turtle footprints.

W More?

M Yes . . . both coming and going . . . on the other side of the island.

W They are coming but they are not laying eggs?

M No, I didn't see any eggs.

W That's it . . . that's the end.

M The turtles' God, and our God – are they the same?

W Yes.

M So, if the turtles don't lay eggs, then God will punish?

W God WILL punish, but it's difficult to say WHO he will punish.

M Trees, plants, rivers, oceans – everything has a God?

W You ask too many questions.

M You don't like it?

W I like it actually. Having an answer for everything is a sign of power and strength. So yes, trees, plants, rivers . . . they have Gods too. But they don't know that they have Gods.

M And we know?

W Yes, we know.

M I see!

W What if they never lay eggs again?

M So, what?

Pause. Suddenly, stormy winds begin to blow.

W What a hopeless day! Neither did anyone find us, nor did we get any information on how to start a new life – a life where there will be no more storms. (*Looks up at the sky.*) It seems we are going to die here.

M Storm? Again?!! God is coming down again, is it? Or is someone playing Shiva again?

W I don't know who is coming, who is not. But once again, we'll forget everything.

M Husband-Wife – can't we draw a picture of this?

W Yes, of course, we can.

M If we can remember this relationship, then at least we won't get into it again.

W Why, what's wrong?

M Well, we became husband and wife, but God is not happy.

W That's because you couldn't make ME happy.

M Shall we draw a picture of God too?

W There's no picture of God. He is everywhere, he is in everything.

M Then what happens tomorrow?

W Everything is getting destroyed again.

M Again . . .?

W Everything is flying around.

M But didn't we have a dialogue in the play that whatever we do, Shiva only threatens to punish us, he never actually comes down?

W Now-a-days, he comes down quite often. Four times a day!

M *Bojho thela*! Now . . . there's way too much of everything.

W That's what we have always wanted.

M Now he comes daily. Soon, five of them will come together.

W Do you want to sleep now?

M Sleep with you? Yes, I want to.

W I like to sleep. The body – it's everything . . . .

M That's right. God has given us this body.

W If tonight is the last night, then to hell with trees and plants and turtles. . . . I want to die in my sleep . . . .

M Come here . . . .

W I'm your husband . . . you come here . . . .

The apocalyptic storm rages on. Darkness.

Scene Four

An eclipse-like darkness is descending upon the island. The **Man** *and the* **Woman** *are seen lying next to each other. It is evident that they are seeing a bad dream. While they are in the dream, several turtles are seen coming near the beach from the waters and turning back. Suddenly, the* **Man** *and the* **Woman** *wake up with a start.*

W   If they lose their way in the dark, will we be able to show them the path?

M   When the apocalypse comes, it seems we can't even sleep in peace. I am dreaming of a man – a sleeping man – lying on the banks of a deep ocean. No words, no worries. And all kinds of slithering snakes and reptiles are rising from the depths of the ocean.

W   And in my dream I see shadows . . . different shapes and sizes, all around me . . . shadows of people. I can clearly see their forms and faces . . . but I can't seem to recognize any of them.

M   As the snakes and reptiles emerge from the water and come towards me, I begin to lose my memories . . . and they seem to understand that I'm losing my memories . . . and they seem unwilling to live with a man without memories . . . they are coming, but they are refusing to lay their eggs. They are staring at the sky. They won't give up. They are looking at me and smiling . . . smiling. Creatures of the deep . . . and yet, they are killing themselves by drowning in those waters. And as they die, I'm losing my memories . . . one by one.

W   I am in love . . . deep love. . . . I drown myself in love. They say all dreams are sexual in nature . . . except the ones about sex. In my dream, I'm seeing a huge turtle tear my clothes apart . . . and trying to drag me into the depths of the sea . . . where a hundred other turtles are waiting for me . . . waiting to surround me . . . molest me . . . make me fulfill their wildest desires.

M   They say all dreams are sexual in nature . . . except the ones about sex.

W   What a nasty sound they make when they all scream together . . . a sound that is creasing the moon . . . they have me in their grip today . . . they are saying . . . do you want to know what the planet is? Why this storm? Why the rains? Why the clouds? Come, we'll show you, *saali haramzaadi*!

M   I'm soaring in the sky like an ancient bird . . . picked away and left floating in the sky by a clan of wingless birds. I wonder how they fly. They have hair on their bodies, and glasses on their eyes. They wear nail-polish, and hold a hammer in their hands. They are saying they have nailed a man called Jesus to a piece of wood so that he can't go anywhere. They are saying – You think you are God? We will teach you a lesson now, *saala*!

W   So much noise all around.

M   Hundreds of ancient drums . . . beating.

W   But why are we losing our memories? What a strange nightmare!

28 Dweepa (The Island)

M They are flying . . . and chanting . . . .

W There's nothing called space, right?

M Right, nothing . . . .

W No space, no Halley's Comet, no Antarctica, no Big Bang . . . *baada, dhoper chop*!

M Now, we'll fuck you, *harami*. We'll show you who's the boss.

W Nothing is real. There's nothing in reality. Nothing . . . except this moment.

M Do you see it now? Yes, this is the planet. Everything else is ours. And then . . . and then . . . .

W And then they laugh again . . . those scary screams all over again . . . they'll eat me now, I know . . . and before they swallow me, they'll do things to me . . . things I can't even talk about . . . .

M 'Now, you feel ashamed, *naa haramzaada*? Come on now . . . sleep . . . sleep with your mother's sister. Everything is yours, it's all about you, right? Now see what it feels like.' And then they drop me from up there.

W They drag me to the bottom of the ocean, and tell me 'come on now, get on your knees and pull up your ass. Why *gandu*? You feeling scared now?'

M What filthy language! What nasty things they are doing to me!

W You think civilization is your father's property, huh? I'll show you civilization now.

M Here, take more, and more. What else do you want to see, tell me?

W I . . . .

M Who am I?

W Who are you, tell me?

M Who are you?

W You're selfish . . . that's who you are. . . . But that's not all. You're a cruel and dangerous animal.

M Your cruelty is wrapped around memories.

W You have an infinite power to forget . . . you often forget that you are not really yourself.

M You're an inventor. You've invented God. You've invented religion. You've invented science, happiness, hope, war, colour, race, knowledge, *mukhshuddhi, alpana* and even funerals. Now face the consequences.

W I prize my own cruelty, I really do.

M Now face the consequences. This doesn't end here, this will never end . . . until you do.

W Destruction is the end, destruction will spare you. But we'll keep you alive, under water, under our feet.

M We'll keep you alive, high up in the skies, as a whore of the birds.

W All dreams are sexual in nature *saala* . . . .

M . . . except the ones about sex.

Scene Five

Moidul *is seen lying on one end of the island. The parachute is lying nearby. He is wearing the uniform of Bangladesh Air Force. In his left hand, he is seen holding a small open bottle with a soapy liquid inside. In his right hand is a small wired handle with a circular aperture at its end.* **Moidul** *dips the handle in the soapy liquid, looks up at the sky and blows bubbles into the air.*

Nearby, the **Man** *wakes up from his sleep. He sees* **Moidul** *and tries to wake up the* **Woman**.

M Wake up . . . wake up, *Didi* . . . look, it seems we have a visitor . . . a distant relative.

W Aah! What are you doing? Let me sleep.

M Please . . . wake up. There are some strange round round things coming out of his mouth. Where are we, *Didi*?

The **Woman** *wakes up, irritated.*

W Who? What *Didi*? . . . What the hell is happening, huh? You're travelling in a bus, and you can't even sit straight?

M What are you saying, *Didi*? See, look here . . . .

The **Woman** *walks up to the* **Man** *and looks at* **Moidul**.

W Oh maa! Where did the bus go?

M Bus? What bus?

W There used to be a thing called a bus. It used to run around on top of people.

M Look there . . . he is our distant relative, no?

W *Joi Shiv Thakur*!

M *Arre dhur Shiv Thakur*! See (*Brings a notebook and shows it to the* **Woman**.) . . . See this notebook . . . do you remember anything?

The **Woman** *looks at it carefully.*

W Oh maa! Yes . . . of course (*Giggles.*) I'm Kali?

M Yes!

W How do I look?

M *Arre dhur*! What am I showing you? *Didi* . . . oh *Didi*? Look here . . . .

W Are we brother and sister today?

M Yes, you're the elder.

W Baah! Very good! Brother-sister . . . what a beautiful relationship! I remember, even Gods used to have brothers and sisters. For instance, Ram's brother was Lakshman.

M Gods don't have sisters.

W Is that so?

M Do you see the man?

W Arre! That's Keshto!

M Keshto? Who is Keshto?

W He used to work at our home. He was good with tools and repairs . . . sometimes he used to go to the market and get the groceries . . . he even used to tie plaits on my hair . . . if required, he used to drop me at school . . . . yes, I remember Keshto . . . clearly. (*Yells out.*) Keshto . . . *ei* Keshto! Keshto . . . *arre ei* Keshto!

Moidul *is startled, looks behind him.*

The **Man** *and the* **Woman** *are running towards him screaming 'Keshto! Keshto!' at the top of their voices/*

Moidul Stay away! Stay away from me I say!

W Stop saying rubbish! (*In a sing-song voice.*) I know who you are!

Moidul Me?

M These green shirts . . . whose are they?

Moidul I . . . I don't remember . . . .

W A-ha-ha-ha! He doesn't remember! As if he's fallen from the sky!

Moidul Fully correct! I have fallen from the sky only . . . trying to save the *Kurma Avatar*.

M Who is that?

Moidul The whole world is balancing on the back of a . . . *ei ki bole* . . . turtle. That turtle's name is Kurma Avatar. And that Kurma Avatar has called me. So, I came. But . . . this box . . . it's saying something Commander, Commander . . . .

M *Khabardaar* Keshto! Don't pay any attention. This is my *Didi*. *Pranaam kor*!

Moidul *Didi pranaam*!

W *Pranaam*! Why are you blowing this soap water in the air?

Moidul   To call the turtles, *Didi*. The turtles are very old animals, so when they see new new things, they are very excited.

M   But why are you calling the turtles?

Moidul   They are all children of Kurma Avatar. They will take me to their mummy.

W   Look, Keshto, we are also looking for turtles only, OK? But the turtles are not coming anymore. And even when they come, they are not laying eggs. They have realized something . . . something that we haven't. Now come on, I want you to repair this island a little bit. I was looking for a good hardworking young fellow, it's good that you came.

Moidul   Meaning?

M   Meaning, I'll give you one tight slap. Stop fooling around and get to work.

Moidul   What work?

M   Build a house.

Moidul   But . . . I am alone . . . and I don't know how to . . . .

M   So, learn.

W   Yes, learn. And then do it. If you don't do it, then who will do it? We can't do all these repair works!

Moidul   Am I . . . am I a slave?

M   Of course! *Didi* remembers clearly . . . one storm after another . . . she forgot everything . . . but as soon as she saw you, she recognized you. Last time, when she was dressing up as Maa Kali in the neighbourhood play on the night of Shiv Ratri, you were the one who fixed her bloody red tongue. Isn't that right, *Didi*?

W   Absolutely!

Moidul   What if I rebel? I . . . I don't remember anything like that . . . .

W   Look, you are getting a relationship almost free of cost, so take it. Later, after the *pralay*, when you will have to wander around without a relationship, then you'll go mad.

Moidul   But. . . . I think I came searching for the turtles.

M   *Shaala*, do you want to look for turtles, or do you want to build relationships and survive, huh? If you live alone, you will die, idiot.

W   Think what will happen if we don't care about you, if we don't give you food? Or if we torture you?

M   Several books have been written on this subject. There was a man with a small beard called Stalin. He has said that power and influence make a man, and everything else is civilizational bullshit.

Moidul   But does that mean that you will do nothing and I'll do all the hard work?

M   You have to work hard. There's no other way to survive. Mankind is dying because we are too soft, and the planet is too cruel. It's taking out all its frustration on us.

W   Yes, man is a cruel animal, living in a cruel world. Take me for example. Before the storm came, I used to work in a small bank in a small town. Very ordinary life. But the day I played the role of Kali in a neighbourhood play, I realized what life is!

Moidul   Really? What is life?

W   Life is cruel. As soon as you see a turtle, you kill it and eat it. Then more turtles will come. And we will follow them and go back home. We'll eat their flesh and keep walking on their shells. Till we reach home. Man is the ultimate animal. The reason all the other animals are alive is because man is right there at the top. We must never forget that man is on top of the turtle, the turtle is not on top of man.

Moidul   You . . . you are giving me a relationship? Tell me – what do I have to build?

M   Build a machine. Something that lets us hear faraway voices. So that we know if anyone is alive on earth.

Moidul   Alright.

Moidul's *walkie-talkie creaks.*

Morris   Hello Moidul . . . Alpha calling Moidul . . . Moidul come in. Are you there? Come in . . . .

The three of them look around, startled.

Moinak   Alpha calling Moidul. Are you there?

W   You built the machine so quickly? Aren't you a slave? You are so wise! Slaves don't have wisdom. Break it, break it now . . . .

Moidul   As you wish.

Moidul *starts breaking the radio. After a lot of effort, the three of them smash and tear the radio apart. But the sound keeps cackling from the radio.*

M   You can build it, but you can't break it? *Shaala dushahoshi*!

Moidul   I can, I can. . . . I'm breaking it . . . .

M   Didi, look what I found. (*Drags Shiva's trident and Kali's sword to the place, both props.*)

W   Weapons! Where did you find them?

M   Must have been flying around in the storm. Perhaps someone used them in ancient times.

W   But what will we do with these?

The voices of **Moinak** *and* **Morris** *calling out for* **Moidul** *seem to spread out through the skies, it's not coming just from the radio anymore.*

W *Maar shaala ke*! Punish him!

M *De maar, de maar*! Teach him a lesson.

*As the **Man** and the **Woman** start punching and kicking **Moidul**, he continues to try and break the radio. But the more he breaks it, the louder the sound becomes. The **Man** and the **Woman** tear **Moidul**'s clothes apart. Out of breath, they plonk down in one corner. Then they throw the weapons towards **Moidul**.*

Moidul Where did you find these?

M I told you naa – someone left them behind, and I found them.

Moidul But these belong to a circus. Back home, we poke caged animals with these weapons. You have found these lying around. Which means there will be a tiger also nearby. What happened to the animals in the storm?

W Tiger? Yes, there used to be a thing called a tiger. Not in our neighbourhood, but it was there nearby.

M Jim Corbett wrote about tigers. Kill a tiger, chop off its head and then put up the head on the wall. or on top of a door. Tiger was created for this only.

Moidul You are too cruel!

W You want me to hit you with this *trishool*? You're a slave, so talk like a slave. *Shaala haramzada*!

Moidul *Aapa*, don't mind, I'm telling you good things only. You see in the circus, within the cage, a man whips the tiger and the tiger obeys him. If you're not cruel and brave, how would you tame a tiger? I'm calling you brave.

M Now get back to work. Build a machine that will tell us if there are people outside this island.

W Yes, like the one you broke just now.

Moidul So many animals in the circus. They must be very brave.

W Big big intellectuals live in the circus, you know that? Circus is the ultimate stage of human civilization.

Moidul And what if the animals escaped in the storm?

M If they escaped, then they escaped. We are human beings, we will catch them by their tails one by one and thrash them. You mind your own business . . . bloody slave.

W See if there's anyone else in the world. We want that machine, or else . . . .

Moidul I'm afraid.

W You should be.

M We want that machine before the next storm comes. We are brother and sister – our relationship is fantastic. We can kill for each other.

Moidul But, *Aapa*, we have to look for the Kurma Avatar.

M So, look for it. Let us know when you find it.

W We will change the world with our own hands – the world that has been balancing on top of the turtle's back since ancient times. We will change the times.

M Much before the end. Till the next end comes, we won't have to remember anything.

W *Shaala*, we will eat everything we get. We will snatch it and eat it. Enough is enough . . . no point being soft anymore. I want it. . . . I want it . . . .

M I want it too. . . . I want this island . . . .

Scene Six

Moinak *and* **Morris** *are seen in the helicopter. Several hours have passed after the storm. They seem exhausted. Their clothes and unkempt hair bear evidence to the fact that they have been toiling for several hours now.*

Moinak (*speaking to the Ground Control over the comm. system*)   No . . . no sir. . . . I don't know how he fell off. (*Pause.*) I understand, sir . . . of course, sir . . . of course, it's a sensitive matter. I am sorry, sir . . . we'll see what we can do. Wing Commander Morris is here with me . . . yes, sir . . . ok, sir . . . over and out.

Both of them seem agitated. They try to calm down and continue to fly the helicopter for sometime.

Moinak   You did it on purpose, didn't you?

Morris   Look here, sir, you are a senior officer. But please don't talk nonsense.

Moinak   Or else you'll push me out?

Morris   I'm serious as hell, sir. This may very well be a Joint Operation, but the rules in the book state that all officers involved are expected to maintain the decorum and follow the procedures as mandated by their respective forces. I'm sure I can expect basic etiquette from you, sir?

Moinak   You throw a man out of the helicopter in the violent storm and then you dare to teach me about decorum? Bastard!

Morris   Mind your words, sir. Everything you say is being recorded by the Black Box.

Moinak   I want everything to get recorded, damn it. When we land, I'm going to check the Black Box myself, and then the recorded evidence will tell everyone what you did to Captain Moidul.

Morris   Me? What did I do to him? The three of us were in this helicopter. And then there was a big hurricane. And one of us, in fact a pretty ordinary pilot – pardon my saying so – tried to catch a glimpse of God knows what down there, and he fell off.

Moinak   He fell off, did he? Just like that? And you think I didn't see you take off his seatbelt?

Morris What the fuck! I took off his seatbelt because he asked me to take it off. God knows why. And what about you? You were sitting right next to him. I could point a finger at you.

Moinak Stop being an ass, will you? We were in the middle of the storm – who do you think flew this thing?

Morris You? All by yourself?

Moinak Of course, who else? Can this helicopter be flown by two people? Idiot! Moron!

Morris There! There you go, happily breaching the protocol again.

Moinak Fuck your protocol!

Morris May I remind you – our ships are patrolling the waters down there.

Moinak *looks at* **Morris** *with a surprised look on his face.*

Moinak What? What the fuck did you say?

Morris Stop abusing me, I warn you.

Moinak What the fuck did you say . . . tell me again?

Moinak *raises a hand to hit* **Morris** *on the head.*

Morris Don't you dare put that hand on me, I'm warning you. Our country's ships are down there on the sea.

Moinak Bastard! Bloody swine! You multiply like bed bugs and send your ships to all parts of the world, and you think that's enough to scare me? How dare you? Have you seen yourself in the mirror? Asshole! YOU are warning ME?

Morris You're going to be a billion and a half, and you tell me that we multiply like bed bugs? (*Scoffs.*) When the guy was falling off, all you could think of was to save your own life, isn't that true?

Moinak Son of a bitch, in case of an emergency, even in a commercial aeroplane, they advise you to help yourself before helping others. Haven't you heard?

Morris Then why the sudden soft corner for the man, huh?

Moinak Taking care of one's own safety is not the same as pushing someone out of the craft. If we don't find him, we will both face court-martial, keep that in mind.

Morris You may be court-martialed. They won't lay a finger on me.

Moinak Oh no, don't worry about that – I'm an Indian after all. If I go down, I'll drag you along with me.

Morris Protocol is protocol. Why don't you understand what's going on around here? Is this your first international project?

Moinak *is silent.*

Morris (*smiles*)   A-ha! Now I see! And all the while, you really felt for the man. Indians are all about aspiration, after all. You even love your mothers because of your image. Tomorrow, if four movies claim that loving your mother is old school and orthodox, you'll throw her out of your house.

Moinak   We're running out of oil. We can't keep flying for long.

Morris   Perhaps we should go back to base.

Moinak   I won't go back without the man. I have at least that much humanity left in me.

Morris   Indeed? And how will your humanity help you if your fuel runs out?

Moinak   Do you see this? Oh God! Look! (*Suddenly points towards a dial in the control panel.*)

Moinak *and* **Morris** *fiddle around with the control panel for some time. They keep saying 'Hello, hello' into their radios, trying to reach Ground Control.*

Morris   Turn it around, turn it around. What just happened?

Turns the helicopter around.

Moinak   Hello, hello, Control Room, hello!

Morris   Give it to me . . . .

Moinak   I'm on it. You try to communicate with the American base.

Morris   Hello, hello, Control Room, hello! Shit! What happened to this? Take it down, further down . . . .

Moinak   Can't take it any lower. Perhaps I should try taking it higher and see.

Morris   OK, try, let's see.

Moinak   What on earth is going on? I've heard this sort of things happening over the Bermuda Triangle!

Morris   Nothing happens over the Bermuda Triangle. That's all a load of crap people say. All these fucking things happen only in Asia. God, I shouldn't even have come here.

Moinak   What nonsense? Did we go and plead with you to come here? You go everywhere and try to be a smartass, and . . . .

Morris   Do you know that for every flight of an American aeroplane or helicopter, Bangladesh gets paid $10,000?

Moinak   But that doesn't mean that you'll throw a Bangladeshi pilot overboard?

Morris   OH, FOR CHRISSAKE, I DIDN'T THROW HIM OVERBOARD! IS THAT BLOODY CLEAR?!! (*Pause.*) Now, please try and find out what's wrong. If we can't communicate with anyone, we won't be able to figure out where we are, or where we are going. Even the radar isn't showing anything. I don't want to die in Asia!

Moinak   Don't worry, my friend. Let's not mark the oceans by Asia, Africa etc. Think of everything as the Pacific or the Atlantic etc.

Morris   What does international protocol say?

Moinak   About what?

Morris   Hang on a second . . . hang on . . . let's take a look at this handbook. I'm sure it must say something about this . . . everything is mentioned in handbooks.

Moinak   Exactly what protocol are you looking for?

Morris   What if we go outside the radar's range? What do we do then? What does the protocol say?

Moinak   Just chant 'Hari Bol, Hari Bol'. There's nothing else to do. Chant 'Hari Bol' and keep trying.

Morris   All kinds of protocols are mentioned here. Tell me something – exactly whose protocol should we follow now?

Moinak   What do you mean?

Morris   See, this says – 'Protocol by highest officer' – so that's you. And then, 'Protocol by largest representation in the exercise' – which is me. And finally, 'Protocol by host vessel' – as in this helicopter, which belongs to Bangladesh. Now what do we do?

Moinak   Whichever is the most convenient for you, whichever gives you mental peace.

Morris   What a strange and . . . and stupid thing to say! What if I die? Here? In Asia? What if I drown down there? What a strange guy you are! (*Starts crying. Whimpering in the beginning, and finally bawling away.*)

Moinak *looks at* **Morris** *and continues to fly the helicopter.*

Moinak   I'm sure we'll have fuel for another half-an-hour of flight time. Don't worry. Please don't cry.

Morris   Why should you care? You're only interested in rising through the ranks and reaching the top. Me. . . . I've come here for my country. What if something happens to me?

Moinak   You are already at the top kid. How much higher can you go? Don't cry. An Air Force pilot shouldn't sit and cry . . . makes me restless. Come here . . . .

Morris (*still weeping*)   Uncle, uncle. . . . I'm just a kid . . . just a little boy. Please help me.

Moinak   Yes, yes . . . let me look for Captain Moidul for some more time, and then, I'll take you home, alright?

Morris Uncle, uncle . . . please take me home . . . don't let me die for that Bangladeshi fellow . . . uncle, uncle please.

Moinak The protocol says you can't cry. No sweetheart. If the civilians come to know, they'll make fun of us . . . HELLO . . . HELLO . . . HELLO . . . IS ANYONE THERE? . . . .

Morris *is still weeping,* **Moinak** *flies the helicopter.*

Moinak Just a little bit more . . . we'll look for him, alright? Try doing something in your life for someone else, for a change. Who knows, you may actually like it.

Scene Seven

Return to the island. **Moidul** *is in a cage. The* **Woman** *is standing outside the cage, surrounded by several turtle shells. At The* **Woman**'s *command,* **Moidul** *is coming out of the cage and going into the cage, again and again. The* **Woman** *seems to have aged by several years. She seems tired and restless. She is seen killing turtles with a stick.*

W No one . . . no one came. (*Pause.*) Maybe it doesn't matter if we get lost? Such a large planet! So much science, so much wisdom! And we are being washed away from an island into the ocean, and no one came to know? Tell me, who sent you? Tell me, or I'll skin you alive.

Moidul Listen, you are mistaking. I am also in the same situation like you. I don't know why I came here. Maybe I am just like you only. Then, you started shouting circus-circus. I didn't get any circus, but in the end, I got this cage. Somehow, I pulled it till here, and see, you locked me only.

W Why aren't these turtles dying? Are they part of some ancient tribe? What is it that they know and we don't?

Moidul Bring me out . . . just once. Just unlock this door, Maa Kali. . . . I'll find out and let you know.

W If I unlock the door, you'll run away.

Moidul Even if I run away, where will I go? You are saying as if I have lots of places to go.

W If we have to live here forever, I'll break your hand.

Moidul Hain!!! Why are you blaming me for that?

W Who do I blame then? Wear these glasses now . . . here, hold them (*Hands over a pair of eye-testing glasses. There's a box of lenses next to her.*) This one a-a-and this one. Which one is better?

Moidul What is this?

W An owl. Must have belonged to someone. Has come to this island in the storm.

Moidul Can't see anything.

W Oh . . . and now?

Moidul This is worse.

W Turn it . . . turn it.

Moidul Yes, a little clear now.

W Cylindrical power, that's why.

Moidul You don't remember your father's name, but you remember cylindrical power?

W How do we know what we remember, why we remember? Tell me what you see?

Moidul Ocean

W Clear?

Moidul Almost

W Do you see a ship?

Moidul No

W Boats? Any human beings?

Moidul No. But I can see many turtles.

W I see. What are they doing?

Moidul They are going back.

W What do you mean?

Moidul Can't see too far.

W Take this, take this . . . and put it on . . . what do you see now?

Moidul They're all going back. You take a look?

W Why should I look? If I have to do everything myself, then what's the difference between you and me? And if there's no difference between you and me, then how will we rebuild the planet?

Moidul I don't understand . . . .

W I want to go home. Rebuilding the planet is not easy. I can tolerate everything, but starting from scratch – no – it's an unnecessary, fruitless exercise . . . all rubbish . . . people used to say . . . we'll bring in changes . . . we'll bring new times . . . we'll do this and that . . . everything is a game of ego. Smartasses. Why are the turtles going back?

Moidul I don't know . . . perhaps because you're catching them and killing them one by one?

W How did they know beforehand that I would kill them?

Moidul   That I don't know. Give me one more pair of glasses and I'll tell you.

W   Alright.

Moidul   I can see a bit more clearly with this one. But I still don't understand why the turtles are going back. Turtles are said to be old, ancient animals. Perhaps they survive so long because of such instincts and intelligence?

W   If they are intelligent, why would they lie at my feet, hammered to death? It means I am more intelligent.

Moidul   No, that's because you are holding the stick. Will you please let me out? I don't understand why I'm inside this.

W   Because you are crazy.

Moidul   Crazy? Why should I be crazy?

W   You went looking for a circus, came back with a cage – this itself is a sign of craziness. There's no place for crazy people, criminals and education in a civilized society, in fact these can prove to be quite dangerous. A society that strives to develop must always keep their crazy people, criminals, teachers and students locked in cages.

Moidul   Why?

W   Civilized people will not be able to see them, and so, they'll not think about them. They'll stay at a comfortable distance and society will prosper.

The **Man** *enters the scene, with several other dead turtles of different sizes.*

M   *Didi*, see how many more I got?

W   Very good. We'll eat them.

Moidul   Listen, brother, please let me out. I'm feeling very restless.

M   If we let you out, how will the others learn about the punishment for not doing their work properly? What do you say, *Didi*? Am I not right?

W   Absolutely right! I asked him to look for a circus, *Babu* brings an empty cage!

Moidul   What do you mean 'others'? There's no one else here.

M   Maybe there's no one now, but there will be others.

W   As in, there could be others. Or perhaps they are around, but we don't know about them. If they see that a slave is not being punished, then they would dance on our heads. (*Kills another turtle.*) *Dhur*! They won't even die with a single blow.

M   He looks sweet in those glasses! (*The* **Man** *and the* **Woman** *smile.*)

W   He has cylindrical power . . . (*Smiles.*)

M   Really? (*Increases in intensity.*)

W   What is cylindrical power?

M   I don't know (*Continues laughing.*)

W   But he has it (*Continues laughing.*)

M   Cylindrical . . . cylindrical (*Continues laughing.*)

Moidul   Laugh, *Didi* . . . laugh as much as you want to. But remember, that brother will take your life one day.

M   I'll give you one tight slap if you talk nonsense. (*Laughs as he says these words.*)

Moidul   I'm a slave, that too locked in this cage. Even if I get out, I'll remain your slave. But he is not your slave. One day, when he gets the opportunity, he will kill you. And he will take away everything on this island.

M   What will I take? What is there to take on this island? If you talk rubbish again, I'll push you into the water.

Moidul   See? He is saying what is there on this island, see? He is already talking about poverty.

W   Why will my brother kill me?

Moidul   Look at history. If you remember it. I remember my past more than I remember my present. History says that brothers have taken more lives than slaves.

M   He's talking all nonsense, *Didi*.

Moidul   I think we will have to live here only . . . and if we die here, then no one will understand who died where . . . .

M   *Shaala*! You are going on and on and on. (*Enters the cage angrily.*)

W   What are you doing? Come out, come out of there.

M   No, I won't. I'll kill this slave today . . . how dare he . . . .

W   I said come out of the cage.

M   Don't raise your voice at me. How dare he insult me? And you also are listening to him silently.

W   Come out of there. (*Screams.*)

Moidul   No . . . why would he listen to you now? He is a cruel animal after all!

The **Man** *enters the cage and starts hitting* **Moidul**. *He drags him out and continues to hit and kick him.*

W   Stop . . . stop, I said. What are you doing? We will have to do all the work if the slave dies.

M   Don't try to lecture me on what to do, what not to do.

Moidul   Trust me, *Didi*, this fellow will lead you to trouble. This brother-frother is all rubbish.

M   One hundred and eighty turtles I killed today. Now I want to kill a man. *Shaala*, you think this is a joke?

W   If you kill him, I'm warning you, I won't do any work.

M   You won't do any work? Do you think I'm crazy? You think all of this is a joke? And you can do whatever you like? Who is the man on this island – you or me? Or is it the slave?

W   I . . . let me explain . . . .

M   To hell with your explanation . . . you think you are the only one working hard? And I'm just fooling around? I kill turtles the whole day, then look for footprints, then sit down and stare at the sea . . . and what do I get? Screams and yells at the end of the day.

W   I'm becoming very angry now.

M   I'll rip your clothes and make you run naked on the beach, understand?

W   Who are you? What's wrong with you?

M   This fellow is going on talking rubbish . . . why aren't you scolding him?

W   I scolded him.

M   Is that how you scold someone?

Moidul   I can see the future quite clearly with these glasses . . . if you have cylindrical power, you can see the future.

M   I'll show you the future, *haramzaada*!

W   Don't you raise one finger at him, I'm warning you.

M   You . . . you . . . you think you can tell me what to do, what not to do? (*Charges at the* **Woman**.)

W   Don't try to scare me . . . don't . . . .

The **Man** *tugs at the* **Woman***'s shirt in sheer rage, and rips a part of it off her body. All quiet.*

Pause.

M (*in a composed manner*)   I may not remember anything else, but I do remember a man's place in the society, understand?

Pause.

W   Moidul . . . kill the bastard!

Moidul   Excuse me?

The **Woman** *pulls off the remaining portion of the shirt from her body.*

W   When civilization lies in these clothes, then there's no reason left to remain civilized anymore. Kill him . . . kill him now!

The **Woman** *pounces on the* **Man**. **Moidul** *also starts hitting him.*

M   What are you doing? What did I do? I did whatever the rule says. This is what the rule is. What is this? You . . . both of you will die . . . you can't live in this world without a man.

*The **Woman** takes the **Man**'s head in her hands and crashes it against the corner of the cage. The **Man**'s head gradually turns all bloody. But the woman doesn't stop, she continues to hit the corner of the cage with the **Man**'s head. After some time, the **Man** collapses on the ground.*

Moidul *and the **Woman** sit in silence.*

*The **Woman** looks at the **Man**'s body, takes off his shirt and puts it on herself.*

W   You're a slave, don't forget that, so behave like one.

Moidul   Alright, *Didi*. (*Enters the cage and locks himself in.*)

W   What do you see through the glasses? What is the future like?

Moidul   Bright, *Didi*! The future is very bright! I see a bright future, and a fantastic circus!

Scene Eight

*A circus tent. Four old men sitting inside. The first one chews **Paan**. The second one takes **Snuff**. The third one smokes a **Pipe**. The fourth one drinks **Alcohol** from a glass. An **Attendant** rushes inside and looks at the old men.*

Attendant   *Arre, Dadu*! Will you please go behind the curtains? The circus is about to start. Why are you sitting here?

Pipe   What? What circus? Who watches circus shows these days?

Alcohol   No elephant, no tiger . . . even the parrots and Russian artists are also not there. Is the public stupid that they will come here? Is this 60 or 90?

Att.   This is 30, *Dadu*. If you drink any more, you'll die. And listen, the public comes or doesn't come – but we have to practice. You are the ones taking care of this world, otherwise now-a-days, everything is doomed.

Paan   That is true, well said. Smart . . . smart fellow. We are everything. Where would the world have been if there was no circus? God knows from where we came flying and dropped here.

Alco.   Really, where from?

Snuff   No . . . can't remember . . . *baal* can't remember . . . no.

Pipe   But there was a big storm in the middle of a circus show.

Alco.   I still shudder to think of it . . . .

Att.   *Dadu*, please start the rehearsal. If someone finds this island, and you mess up the show, then the public will give us a nice thrashing.

Snuff   Topic? What's the topic today?

Att.   Storms. All these storms are coming again and again . . . .

Snuff   What? A circus show on storms?

Att.   Arre, *Dadu*, so many storms, one after the other . . . on land and over sea, in the skies . . . everything messed up . . . what if the public wants to see a circus on this matter?

Pipe   How can a circus be on a 'matter'? Nonsense! Circus is like circus pure entertainment . . . fun, dance, jumping around, lions and tigers etc.

Alco.   See what the bourgeois is saying, see . . . haven't you seen Marxist circus? *Haramzaada*! You are smoking on your pipe and saying the public will sit and watch people jumping around and you reactionaries will do whatever you want?

Pipe   Among the four of us, you're consuming the most precious thing, understand? The 180 millilitres that you drink everyday – who pays for it, your daddy? So much debate and thinking on the resources of the planet and manual labour . . . but when it comes to actually doing something, ZERO!

Att.   *Dadu* I'm blowing the starting whistle.

Snuff   Both of you are in bad politics. Just breathe. Inhale, exhale. No politics. Circus and politics are totally different.

Alco.   Everything is politics, brother . . . a baby comes out of its mother's womb and calls her maa, even that is politics. Politics is /

Paan   One more quotation and I'll spit on your face.

Att.   *Dadu*, here's the whistle. (*Blows a horn and then stands in the front with a big smile on his face.*) Ladies and gentlemen, welcome to the 'Firefly Circus'. Those of you who are still alive, you drop all your work to come and see our circus, to laugh and play with us, and to see some remarkable feats that are impossible for ordinary people to achieve. It's quite possible that you too were engaged in your own activities, but then a violent storm blew you away and dropped you on this island! Earlier, circus shows used to feature lions and tigers, bears and elephants and parrots, but.

Paan   Hey you! If you speak so much in the practice, what will you do in the real show – speak all day?

Att. (*whispers*)   *Dadu*, side please? (*Smiles.*) Firefly Circus is proud to present before you – 'Dare Devil Dadu'. They can entertain you with their stories – starting from the discovery of fire, to last night's storm. In the olden days, this used to happen in schools, but since the schools have started their monkey and bear dances, we have taken up this responsibility ourselves. The principal topic of discussion for tonight is these storms, the ones that come again and again. Our *Dadu*s will now dissect and analyze the topic for your entertainment.

Pipe (*pushes the* **Attendant**)   Go on now, get out of here . . . and where's the ring of fire? How will I make my entry? Light it, light it now.

The **Attendant** *switches on the lights on a big ring, and* **Pipe** *Dadu jumps through the hoop. The* **Attendant** *holds the 'ring of fire' up.*

Pipe All these storms that you see . . . the sea levels rising . . . these are all because of the Asians.

These Asians have started all this nonsense. *Baaler chaal*, we've started making so many things from safety pin to mustard oil that the planet is *ekebaare chude laat*! We are telling them again and again – do less, produce less, eat less, wear less – but these *chutias* just don't listen. They don't even have basic social etiquette – *maagir baccha*. I jump through fire and swear by Maa Kali, only this island will survive at the end. Because on this island, people have very poor memories, and therefore there are hardly any Asians here. These Asians have very little brains but very strong memories. As long as there are Asians in this world, the planet is bound to get destroyed. If we want to save the planet, we will have to drown the Asians, every last one of them.

A gong is struck, and amidst a thunderous applause, **Pipe** *Dadu walks up to the* **Attendant** *and takes the ring of fire from him.* **Paan** *Dadu takes a run-up and jumps through the hoop. He comes and stands in the front.*

Paan Did you listen to what Lord Hardinge said? Let me tell you what this planet is – it's a reflection of God. So much philosophy all around, and you have a problem with my philosophy? As long as God exists, mankind will also exist. But God is a little angry with us. Because we are doing whatever we want. We're eating pigs, we're eating cows, we're giving unlimited freedom to women. You tell me, isn't it natural for God to lose his mind?

God is not happy with any religion, not ANY of them. Jesus Christ got nailed to a piece of wood, but he couldn't save mankind. Five times every day we yelled Allah Allah, but we couldn't really keep the women under control. Ram, Shiva, Hanuman – we called them Gods but didn't really do anything substantial. It's quite natural for God to be furious.

God exists everywhere. In the waves, in the coconut tree, in the frog in the well, in the baby turtles, everywhere. If God becomes angry, everyone becomes angry. That is why these unnecessary problems are happening.

I've crossed the ring of fire and I tell you – pray, pray to the almighty, perform rituals, nail people to crosses, read the *namaaz* eighteen times a day, do a little bit of dieting and always, always keep your mothers and sisters and aunts under strict control. otherwise, the future is doomed.

Horn. Applause. **Alcohol** *Dadu jumps through the ring of fire.*

Alco. Everything is nonsense! Fraud and hype, created by the scientists of the world! Science is like the Draupadi of the modern man. You can do whatever you want, whenever you want, with Science. Scientists have only one agenda – scare people and get paid to scare them. They sit on piles of money and say – the world is coming to an end, and it's all because of us. *Baada* did we kill the dinosaurs? Did we create the continents?

They say scientists will save us from catastrophes. Had there been so many continents without catastrophes? Had there been this planet without catastrophes? Catastrophes are bound to happen – no one can do anything about it . . . .

Rest Now this is too much . . . .

Alco. Oh shut up all of you! You and your cheap addictions! All you can say are cheap things. You expect everyone to drop what they were doing and go home and listen to the scientists and get scared? While the scientist babus will fly around in jet planes from one continent to another and scare people?

Science is saying that it is because of us that there are so many violent storms happening on this planet. It says we are warming up this planet.

I jump through fire and ask you this – was the planet never warm before? All nonsense, huh! All this is just a way of making money, I tell you. Where is it written that nature will continuously move towards a finite equilibrium? Perhaps nature itself is nothing but an elected catastrophe?

Snuff *Dadu's turn, jumps through fire.*

Snuff So much discussion, so much debate! Bangla will drown, *Ingrej* will drown, all animals and birds will die. If we don't act today then after a hundred years our grandchildren will burn, or they will be forced to live on Mars . . . .

All I want to say is that man wakes up in the morning and doesn't care about what happens in the evening, and you think he will care about what happens a hundred years later? Man doesn't know his next-door neighbour, doesn't listen to his mother, in fact, what is his relationship with himself?

A man who goes through his entire life trying to find acceptance for himself, a man who spends his childhood trying to mould himself like his father, you think that man cares about the future?

If nature exists outside us, then to hell with the skies, the rivers, the oceans and the trees . . . and if nature exists within us, then let me ask you – is the storm inside us, or outside? I've jumped through the fire and this is what I have to say –

If no one comes to watch the circus, very well. We don't even know who we are. Who is watching whose performance? Is the tiger performing for us, or are we performing for the tiger? If the world is somewhere outside of us, then so what if we can't save the world? And if the world does need saving, then how is man expected to save it?

If I am not Nature, then perhaps there's nothing called Nature. And if I am Nature, then all we need to do is to save ourselves. The rest is all a farce, just a show. As the circus is, so am I. And as am I, so is Nature.

Scene Nine

Moidul *and the* **Woman**. *They have grown old now.*

W God, please bless me. Please save me from my troubles. Please give me the eternal strength to rise after I fall – like the sun and the waves. Dear God, you, the nameless, faceless stranger, the first charioteer of the world, the first father, the first Aurangzeb, please, please free me from this island, please.

Moidul Aah, *Mamoni*, what are you doing?

W *Bapi*, is that you?

Moidul Can't you see I'm doing my calculations? Don't disturb me.

W *Bapi*, I'm offering a heartfelt prayer to God, asking him to take us back to our old house again.

Moidul I can see that, but right now, I'm working with very complex mathematics. If my calculations go for a toss, I'll break your bones and bury you in the sand.

W *Bapi*, whenever you sit down with your calculations, why do you always turn so violent?

Moidul *Mamoni*, this daily nonsense of yours about God, why is it that you always start it when I'm sitting down with my work?

W What is it that you are working on today, *Bapi*?

Moidul Today, I'm trying to calculate the diameter of Heaven, sweetheart.

W *Fasclaas*! But what is Heaven, *Bapi*? And how do you know it is round?

Moidul Heaven is an island, where people who never slept with others go, after they die.

W So, you mean, no one goes to Heaven?

Moidul Some people do, but very rarely. And that's why Heaven is more expensive, and round.

W Why round, *Bapi*?

Moidul There's a man named Chitragupta, who sits in Heaven and maintains a detailed calculation of the good and bad deeds of all the people in the world.

W So?

Moidul So, if you do a bad deed then the centrifugal force of the deed will push you away from Heaven. And if you do a good deed, then the centripetal force of the deed will pull you towards Heaven. If both these forces are applied on you, then you'll keep circling the centre of Heaven forever.

W I'm scared, *Bapi*.

Moidul Why?

W Too much Mathematics!

Moidul Don't be scared of Mathematics, sweetheart, be scared of God. Mathematics just explains the game, but remember, it's God who is playing the game.

W   *Bapi*, didn't you say you are a Musalman?

Moidul   That's what I thought.

W   So?

Moidul   Allah doesn't have an image. So it's difficult to put him in an equation.

W   So, will we go to Heaven?

Moidul   I don't know. But we want to.

W   When will we go somewhere, *Bapi*?

Moidul   Don't act like a sissy girl, sweetheart. Look at your skin, it's all wrinkled. And you're asking stupid questions like a little girl. 'When will we go?' Leave me alone with my calculations.

W   But, *Bapi*, you are my *Bapi*.

Moidul   Oh God!

W   I mean, my father . . . my guardian.

Moidul   For now, yes.

W   Then why are you hurting my prayer?

Moidul   I'm not hurting your prayer, I'm asking you to pray in silence. Talk to God as much as you want to, but please do it in silence . . . .

W   Bapi, what're the calculations like?

Moidul   Complex, lots of factors to consider.

W   What factors?

Moidul   For instance you take the vector position of mankind, then apply statics and dynamics on it, consider the torque of the planet, and then when you intersect the parabola and hyperbola of Karma, at exactly that point, you rule out uncertainty, and solve the equation with a Chi-square and ANOVA chart.

W   *Baap re baap*! Seems very difficult, *Bapi*?

Moidul   If I would have said the entire thing in Bangla, my teeth would have fallen off.

W   *Bapi*, are you angry with me?

Moidul   Not exactly the way you think.

W   Then how?

Moidul   Heaven is round, earth is round, life and death – everything is round. Isn't this becoming a little too simple to understand?

W   I'm asking you – why are you upset with me?

Moidul   Because if you wouldn't have been around, I'd have left this place.

W   How, *Bapi*?

Moidul   I wouldn't have had to worry about you anymore.

W   But you've almost destroyed the entire island worrying about me, *Bapi*?

Moidul   What else could I do, dear? You'll need a lot of things to secure your future. Who will give you those things?

W   My dear *Bapi*, my sweet *Bapi*! So, my future is responsible for the destruction of this island?

Moidul   Of course! Why should I care? I can very well go to Heaven and play centripetal-centrifugal quite happily. But you . . . what will you do?

W   *Bapi*, how did we grow so old? Have we been living on this island for a long time? And the story of that Shiva-Kali play – is that true?

Moidul   Must have been a long time. When we are alive, we don't get to know how time flies by. I have to do so many things for you. But you're ruining my calculations . . . .

W   Accha, what is the diameter of Heaven?

Moidul   Quite small . . . between 1 to 1.5 millimetres.

W   So small? How will we all get into Heaven then?

Moidul   We don't have to enter it. We only have to revolve around it.

W   But still, how do we revolve around something so small?

Moidul   It's possible, quite possible. Everyone has to climb on everyone else's shoulders, quite manageable.

W   *Bapi*, isn't anyone ever going to find us?

Moidul   I don't know. . . . I can only calculate the diameter. . . . I can't predict the future, dear.

W   Then what's the point of calculating the diameter?

Moidul   I'll kill time. I've already created everything for you, now I can afford to kill time.

W   What did you create by breaking this island, *Bapi*?

Moidul   Language, Mathematics and God . . . now go live a comfortable life.

W   How, *Bapi*?

Moidul   How? We'll play around with these three things. Whatever happens, we're not turtles, so we will not live forever. Do you see how the turtles are writhing all around us? They are not allowed in Heaven. So, they will live here forever. They'll come, they'll go, they'll lay eggs.

W   What do I do now?

Moidul   Pray.

W   Should I ask God to make everything better?

Moidul   No, ask God to let you have a good time.

W   That dead man over there . . . aren't we going to bury or cremate him?

Moidul   No. The turtles are eating him, let it be.

W   This time, can I be the mother?

Moidul   Alright . . . .

W   Come . . . come close my baby . . . .

Moidul   Maa, maa go!

W   Come, put your head on my lap and sleep.

Moidul   Maa, have we grown old?

W   Not exactly. Compared to the age of the earth, you are just an infant.

Moidul   Maa go. . . . I really love you for destroying the island.

W   I did it for you my darling. But I won't be able to carry on anymore.

Moidul   But there's nothing else to do, Maa.

W   Don't talk like a fool. If you can't do anything, how will you live?

Moidul   Look, we're doing just fine! Killing turtles and eating them . . . so many turtles, so few human beings . . . we'll eat and live.

W   A long time ago, I used to live on an island.

Moidul   Yes. . . . I understand.

W   There used to be a lot of people there. I had a small job also.

Moidul   You've told me. You were doing something with that man one day, right?

W   Yes, a play. We're acting as Shiva and Parvati.

Moidul   And then, a storm came . . . right?

W   Yes . . . and we came here . . . .

Moidul   And since then, a new storm comes every day, and we have to start from the beginning every time . . . correct?

W   Who knew God could be so cruel? Did Shiva and Parvati know? Did the people in our village know all these years? They know a lot . . . .

Moidul   We also destroyed everything on this island, Maa. Did we know?

W   But we did it out of love, dear. I did it for you. Does a good intention have no value at all?

Moidul I'm not sure. . . . I think so . . . or perhaps not . . . .

W What do we know, baby?

Moidul You tell me, you are my mother.

W That's only till the end of the day. Tomorrow, I'll be something else.

Moidul Yes, tomorrow we'll be something else.

W Do you hear that, baby?

Moidul Yes, it's the sound of that machine again, coming from the sky.

W It means there are others too. I think they're looking for us.

Moidul Why aren't they able to find us, Maa?

W I don't know. Perhaps we'll never be found.

Moidul Really? You think so?

W Had they not found us by now otherwise?

Moidul They are coming back. If we can hear them, why can't they hear us, Maa?

W Because they are far away . . . far, far away . . . .

Moidul But we have invented all three once again – Language, Mathematics and God.

W They've done the same.

Moidul They've invented that machine also, Maa.

W That machine must be the same thing   . . . if we live for a couple of thousand years, we will also invent a machine like that . . . it's all about those three things dear – Language, Mathematics and God. . . . (*Both look towards the sky.*)
Even if they come, I won't go. Will you?

Scene Ten

Moinak *and* **Morris**, *still flying. They have grown old too.*

Moinak How many days have we been roaming around?

Morris Must be three or four days.

Moinak (*laughs*) Looking at you, it seems it's been ages. I want to eat *Batasha* and water. I want to take water from the fridge, mix it with sherbet, sit down in the veranda of my house and sip it slowly.

Morris We can't find them 'cos you're not focusing on the job.

Moinak I want to take my little daughter to the fountains in the evening. I want to scold her when she touches the water from the fountain. (*Laughs.*)

Morris Hello... hello... Control Tower, why aren't you responding to us?

Moinak I want to go back. I'm scared to look down. I want to live in the sky.

Morris Hello... hello... Control Room, I have a serious patient with me....

Moinak You know, Morris, when that little darling of mine grows up, I want to take her around the world. I've seen the world from the sky. I think the world is beautiful, amazingly beautiful. How did you grow so old, Morris?

Morris Hello, Control Room? The pilot from India has gone bonkers, or maybe he's smoked a lot of pot! Hello will you please tell me the coordinates?

Another ad starts.

   Ad: *What do you want to see in the skies? A new book, documentary, aunty chats, gossip about your mother-in-law, or a whole new dance? You choose, we deliver. Your favourite program. And an attractive gift voucher from Motilal and Motilal and Motilal and Motilal and so on and so forth.*

Moinak I don't believe in God. Do you?

Morris Hello, Control Room? Can you cut out these ads, please?

Moinak Does God want us to go around in circles? God has spared the cane and spoilt the child. (*Laughs.*) You're a Christian, aren't you? I want to take my little girl to the church. If she grows up with a single religion, what will happen to her, Morris?

They say it's all our doing... the storms, the hurricanes, the earthquakes, the apocalypse... they say WE created them, it's all our fault. Is that possible? Nature has never given us any assurances. Nor has it ever agreed to dance to our tunes. Then why this angst? This... this terrible desire to take revenge?

Morris Hello sir... sir... please send a couple of American ships. This guy is mumbling all kinds of scary shit. Sir, please get me out of here.

(*To* **Moinak**.) Commander Moinak? Commander Moinak? Sir, you're a higher ranking officer, sir. What do I do if you go batshit crazy at such a crucial moment, sir? Please, for God's sake....

Moinak I want this, I want that, for my little darling. I'll catch a couple of fishes from the sea, go back to my home in town, sit down in the yard with her and listen to her talk. That's all I want.

Morris Our fuel is almost gone.

Pause.

Morris Are you listening to what I am saying? Our fuel is almost gone. Why are we flying around in circles over this vast ocean? What are we looking for? We won't find anything down there.

Moinak You want to turn around and go back?

Morris We don't have any other choice, sir.

Moinak   We haven't found anyone, Morris. But I still have a strange comforting feeling.

Pause. **Morris** *looks at something closely.*

Morris   Look there, sir . . . there. SIR! SIR! Look there . . . those are people . . . look sir . . . .

Moinak   Where? Where? I don't want to land.

Morris   We've been looking for them for ages, and now we have found them, and you are saying you don't want to land?

Moinak   Who are they? Are they people? Are they also lost, like us?

Morris   You've hurt your head, haven't you?

Moinak   Land the helicopter softly. . . . I'm warning you.

Morris   Yes, sir . . . sure, sir. . . . I will, sir . . . .

Moinak   How will they recognize us?

Morris   The way we recognized them.

Moinak   We've flown over this island several times, why haven't we seen anything before?

Morris   I'm taking her down, sir. Remember, if we go up and down too much, the chopper will sink.

Moinak   Alright, I understand.

Morris   Hello . . . hello . . . yes, sir . . . yeah, we found them . . . landing now . . . sorry . . . sorry, what? Why? Why? (*To* **Moinak**.) Take her up, sir, take her up. (*Back to the radio.*) What's that, sir? What did you say? Abort mission? But why?!!

Moinak   Up and away she goes, up and away into the great beyond. I want to take my little girl to space.

Morris (*in the radio*)   Sir, what the hell is going on? What are you saying? Is this a game?

Moinak   How do we find those who want to get lost?

Morris   Sir, I don't understand. You said the mission was critical. And now you're asking us to abort. Why?

Moinak   I've heard there are quite a few warm air currents in the sky, sweetheart, so cover yourself. I want you to be able to see everything down below.

Morris   I don't know which Air Force you're giving this order from, but whoever is giving it, please ask him to reconsider.

Moinak   Hello, hello, sir this is Commander Moinak speaking. That's right, sir, yes. We spent our whole life looking for it, and now all of a sudden, you're asking us to let it go?

Morris Of course we can come back, sir. In fact, our fuel is almost down to zero. So, it's good if we come back. But . . . are we going to let it go just like that?

Moinak What do you mean the area of interest has changed? Focus area? In galactic warfare? Are you watching a lot of Hollywood films? Do you think we've fooling around in the sky? You think this is child's play?

Pause.

(*Furiously.*) I'm making you upset? Really? Let me tell you something – YOU are making me upset! Yeah, yeah, go right ahead and court martial me. You think this is a joke?

Morris I still don't know which Air Force you are from. And honestly, I don't even care anymore.

Yes, I'm here. No, I don't want it. . . . I don't want your promotion, and I don't want your medal. You can take your medal and shove it up your ass! Fuckers!

Year after year, I've been seeing only the ocean. I haven't slept, I haven't eaten . . . .

Moinak Three hours? Who said it's been three hours?

Morris Over the ocean, three hours is equivalent to a whole era. The ocean is huge, it has a vast extent. In all its glory, it's staring us in the face right now, as we are staring back at it. The only difference is – the ocean is three times as large as the ground. And you. you think you can look into a 4×4 screen and understand the ocean?

Moinak Interest has changed? Let it change. We'll not come back.

Morris We'll live in the skies . . . forever . . . .

Moinak When we want to, we'll dive into the waters below.

As they say this, they start taking off their respective Air Force uniforms.

Moinak We'll do whatever we wish to.

Morris Whatever we want.

Moinak The ocean is not anyone's father's property. We'll die in the waves, we'll die in the sky, or in a deep chasm . . . but we'll not die locked up in a stupid room.

Morris Let everything get crushed to bits . . . we won't search, we won't return . . . .

Moinak We won't do anything . . . the ocean has taught us . . . we won't do anything.

Morris Nothing. It's not necessary. It's a vast ocean. You and me? We're nothing!

Moinak We're so small, so insignificant! How can we harm the ocean?

Morris Over and out! Now we can breathe in peace!

Moinak Well? Shall we land?

Morris   Sure, if we want to.

Moinak   But where?

Morris (*smiles*)   Wherever we want. We're the kings now. This is all ours!

Scene Eleven

Sound of the waves crashing. Lots of turtles all over the stage. And amidst them, **Moidul** *and the* **Woman** *are seen sitting. They are old and wrinkled.*

W   The notebook says we've covered all relationships . . . how old are we now?

Moidul   No, no. There are still so many relationships left – friend, aunt, uncle. There is no end to it, actually . . . .

W   Do you remember the end? How did everything begin?

Moidul   Yes . . . the play on the night of Shivratri. I used to work at a bookstore, and I was playing Lord Shiva. You used to work in a bank and you played Maa Kali.

W   And then the storm came, right?

Moidul   I think so. I told you – if you don't stop dancing, then the world could end.

W   But were you there? I thought the other man was there. You came later.

Moidul   Yes, I came later, but I remember what happened before. It is not necessary to be at a spot to remember everything about it.

W   But they were all waiting . . . and did he come? the one they were waiting for?

Moidul   And when he came, what did he do?

W   Do you remember this cage?

Moidul   Yes, I brought it from the circus.

W   Where did so many turtles come from?

Moidul   They came from the water . . . they have found the place again . . . now they will find us too.

W   Will we go?

Moidul   Where?

W   Will we go back? To where we came from? What if it happens again?

Moidul   Storm? We will not go and watch that play, that's all.

W   How can we not go? We can't change the past.

Moidul   But we are talking about the future . . . not about the past.

W   I think the world is really resting on a turtle's back.

Moinak *and* **Morris** *enter the stage.* **Moinak** *is dressed as Lord Shiva,* **Morris** *as Maa Kali.*

Moidul You think so?

W Yes. Just see . . . there are so many of them . . . much more than us. Do you think they remember everything?

They start the play.

Moidul The sun is setting. One more day is coming to an end . . . .

W You and I have somehow become one. Don't you feel that?

Moidul Yes. It seems. . . . I am a wave, I am the water, I am the sun . . . rising and falling.

W I'm the night, I'm the day, I'm a turtle, I'm a tree . . . as if I'm everywhere.

Moidul Maybe that is why we could not find the relationship.

W How is the sun related to the ocean? Aunt? Uncle? Slave?

Moidul I can understand now – so many people waiting for that God – I know why he comes every day now.

W Why?

Moidul He wants to know if we are still waiting for him or not.

Meanwhile, **Moinak** *and* **Morris***' play is in full swing, accompanied by background music. Their lips are moving, but we don't hear their voices.*

W When he didn't come, then we waited for him. Now he comes every day, so we don't remember anything . . . .

Moidul There is nothing to remember. See . . . how the whole world is waiting for the sunset?

W Yes (*smiles*) . . . it's beautiful!

Moidul Even if they come for us, we will not go . . . .

W No. (*Pause.*) . . . I have a feeling, you know?

Moidul What feeling?

W Even now, somewhere, everyone is waiting for that creature.

Moidul Really?

W Yes, and WE are that creature.

Moidul We?

W Yes . . . you and I . . . .

Moidul How?

W   We don't go anywhere . . . but then we are at one with the sun, the sea, the sky . . . that means we go . . . every day we go. They see us every day.

Moidul   Let us set now . . . we will rise again . . . .

W   Yes . . . .

The sound of the waves. The sun is setting gradually. They sit and watch the sun set.

Pause.

Morris   If you don't stop dancing right now, I'll come down to earth . . . and I'll bring a storm with me . . . .

Moinak   Come, I want to see your storm . . . come . . .

Storm. Music. Black out.

Glossary

Achchha – Bengali. Really (surprised expression)

Allah-kasam – Urdu. Swear to God

Alpana – Bengali. Ritual drawing to adorn houses during auspicious occasions in Bengal

Andamans – Andaman and Nicobar Islands is an archipelago of India consisting of 571 islands, at the junction of the Bay of Bengal and the Andaman Sea

ANOVA chart – a statistical table

Aurangzeb – sixth Mughal Emperor ruling vast parts of India between 1658 and 1707 CE

Baada – Bengali. Colloquial slang for the male genital organ. Used as an expletive

Baal – Bengali. Pubic hair. Used as an expletive

Baaler chaal – Bengali. Expletive

Baap re Baap – Bengali. Expression of astonishment

Babu – Bengali. Gentleman

Bankim Babu – Bankimchandra Chattopadhyay. Bengali writer

Bapi – Bengali. Endearing word for Father

Batasha – Bengali. Sweet made from hardened sugar and jaggery

Bay of Bengal – part of the Pacific Ocean near the Bengal region

Bermuda Triangle – also known as the Devil's Triangle, a loosely defined region in the western part of the North Atlantic Ocean formed by connecting Miami, San Juan and Bermuda. Urban legend suggests a number of aircraft and ships have disappeared in the region under mysterious circumstances

Big Bang – a theory of astrophysics that describes how the universe expanded from an initial state of high density and temperature

Bojho thela – Bengali. Unexpected burden. Expression of frustration

Chaandu – Bengali. Sweetheart (sarcastic)

Chhyahh – Bengali. Expression of disgust

Chi-square – a statistical test

Chitragupta – Hindu mythological character. Assistant to Lord Yama, deity of death and justice. Chitragupta is considered to be the record keeper of virtues and vices of mortals during their lifetime

Chutia – Hindi-Bengali. Idiot. Used as an expletive.

Cylindrical power – also known as astigmatism. A condition in which the shape of the cornea or the lens of the eyes become irregular in curvature

Dada – Bengali. Elder brother

Dadijaan – Hindi-Urdu. Grandmother

Dadu – Bengali. Grandfather

Dhaka – capital city of Bangladesh

Dhoper chop – Bengali. Bullshit. Total lie

Dhur – Bengali. Expression of disgust

Didi – Bengali. Elder sister

Draupadi – Hindu mythological character from the epic Mahabharata

Dushahoshi – Bengali. Audacious

East Bengal – eastern part of the undivided Bengal province in British ruled Indian territories, known as East Pakistan between 1947 and 1971. Now known as the south-Asian country People's Republic of Bangladesh

Ei ki bole – Bengali. Expression of confusion

Ekebaare chude laat – Bengali. Totally fucked up

Fasclass – colloquial Bengalilicisation of First Class

Fataak se – Hindi. Fast. In a flash

Galapagos Island – a volcanic archipelago in the Pacific Ocean, a province of Ecuador. Its isolated terrain shelters a diversity of plant and animal species, many found nowhere else. Named after the giant turtles that call it home

Gandu – Bengali. Expletive connoting a stupid person. Asshole

Halley's Comet – a short-period comet visible from Earth every seventy-five to seventy-nine years

Hamake maap khariye dao – Bengali. Please forgive me

hami Bangali ache – Bengali. I'm a Bengali

Hanuman – Hindu mythological character, a monkey-faced god, follower of Ram. Worshipped as a god of strength and devotion. He is one of the sons of the god of wind, Lord Pavana

Haramzaadi / haramzaada / harami – Urdu-Bengali. Bastard. Used as expletive

Hari Bol – Bengali. Hail Lord Hari/Vishnu

Hullah – Bengali. Ruckus

Hyperbola – a mathematical expression, defining a type of smooth curve lying in a plane

Ingrej – Bengali. Colloquial expression for an Englishman

INSAT – acronym for the Indian National Satellite System. It is a series of multipurpose geostationary satellites launched by ISRO for telecommunications, broadcasting, meteorology, and search and rescue operations. Commissioned in 1983, INSAT is the largest domestic communication system in the Indo-Pacific Region

Jaah-babba – Bengali. Colloquial expression of surprise, disappointment, etc.

Joi Shiv Thakur! – Bengali. Hail, Lord Shiva!

Kali Ma – Hindu mother goddess of destruction and death, wife of Shiva according to some scriptures

Khabardaar – Bengali. Caution

Kurma Avatar – incarnation of Lord Vishnu as a giant turtle. Second of his ten incarnations or avatars. According to Hindu mythology this avatar holds the earth on its back

Kyrgyzstan – officially known as the Kyrgyz Republic, a landlocked country in Central Asia, lying in the Tian Shan and Pamir mountain ranges

Loot-maar – Hindi. Chaos, loot, pandemonium

Lord Hardinge – a British diplomat and statesman who served as Viceroy and Governor-General of India from 1910 to 1916

Lord Shiva – Hindu god of dance and destruction, husband of Kali according to some scriptures

Maagir bacha – Bengali. Born of a whore

Maar – Bengali. Beating

Mamoni – Bengali. Endearing term for a woman, especially a young girl

MH370 – Malaysia Airlines Flight 370 was an international passenger flight operated by Malaysia Airlines that disappeared from radar on 8 March 2014 while flying from Kuala Lumpur International Airport in Malaysia to its planned destination, Beijing Capital International Airport in China

Mukhshuddhi – Bengali. Palate cleanser

O baba – Bengali. Expression of astonishment

Paan – Bengali-Hindi. Betel leaf. Common local palate cleanser

Parabola – a mathematical expression, defining a mirror-symmetrical u shape

Parvati – Hindu mother goddess. One of the incarnations of Kali, daughter of Himalaya mountain (Parvat) and wife of Shiva according to Hindu mythology

Pralay – Bengali. Apocalypse

Pranaam – Sanskrit. Hindu way of showing respect. A form of Namaste

Ram – Hindu mythological character, protagonist of the epic Ramayana. Widely worshipped in India as an incarnation of Lord Vishnu

Robinson Crusoe – a novel by Daniel Defoe, first published in London, 1917

Saali – Bengali. Sister-in-law. Used as expletive

Sarat Babu – Saratchandra Chattopadhyay. Bengali writer

Shaala/saala – Bengali. Brother-in-law. Used as expletive

Shiv Ratri – Hindu night-long festival celebrating Shiva

Shonamoni – Bengali. Darling

Torque – a measure of the force that can cause an object to rotate about an axis

Trishool – Sanskrit. Trident. Indian weapon

West Bengal – western part of the undivided Bengal province in British-ruled Indian territories, known as the Indian state of West Bengal following Indian independence in 1947

Pah-La (Father)

Research supported by Foundation for Universal Responsibility of
HH The Dalai Lama, written for the Royal Court Theatre with support
from Reimagine India, Arts Council England

Pah-La first premiered on April 3, 2019 at Royal Court Theatre, London, UK.

Original Cast and Crew

Director	Debbie Hannan
Designer	Lily Arnold
Lighting Designer	Jessica Hung Han Yun
Composer and Sound Designer	Tom Gibbons
Movement Director	Quang Kien Van
Constable Gaphel	Paul Chan
Deng	Daniel York Loh
Deshar	Millicent Wong
Dorjee/Ling	Gabby Wong
Pema	Zachary Hing
Rinpoche/ Man with the stick	Kwong Loke
Tsering	Richard Rees
Jia	Tuyen Do (This role is not in the current draft)

Pah-La has been translated to Tibetan by Lhakpa Tsering and directed by Harry Fuhrmann and Lhakpa Tsering in 2022.

Cast and Crew of Tibetan production

Director	Lhakpa Tsering
Co-Director	Harry Fuhrmann
Writer	Abhishek Majumdar
Producer	Saatvika Kantamneni
Stage Manager and Light Designer	Yael Crishna
Deshar	Kalsang Dolma
Dorjee	Tenzin Yonten
Tsering	Tenzin Wangchuk
Pema	Youngkyar Dolma
Deng	Lhakpa Tsering
Rinpoche / Man with a stick	Tsering Bawa
Ling	Tenzin Pema
Gaphel	Tenzin Lhundup

Musicians

Male Musician	Nyima Dhondup
Female Musician	Tenzin Passang

Characters

Constable Gaphel, *male, late 60s, Tibetan. Constable from the village, works for the Chinese authorities*

Deng, *male, late 40s to early 50s, Han. Communist Inspector of the PRC*

Deshar, *female, early 20s, Tibetan. Training to be a Buddhist nun, Tsering's daughter*

Dorjee, *female, late 20s, Tibetan. Training to be a Buddhist nun, Deshar's friend in the Buddhist nunnery*

Ling, *female, 30, Han. Constable at the Lhasa Central Prison. Helps Deng interrogate Deshar*

Man with a stick, *male, late 60s, Tibetan. Stranger on the school ground*

Pema, *male, 12 years old, Tibetan. Shepherd village boy, Tsering's student*

Rinpoche, *male, late 60s, Tibetan. Head of the Buddhist monetary*

Tsering (Ngabo), *male, early 60s, Tibetan. Ex Chushi Gangdruk Commander. Pema's teacher, Deshar's father*

Prologue

As the audience walks in butter lamps are lit on stage.

Act One

Scene One

A room in a nunnery in eastern Tibet. Two beds, a place to pray and some books. Late evening. It's snowing outside.

Deshar *is wearing a soldier's shirt on top of her robes.* **Dorjee** *is wiping blood off* **Deshar***'s face. It is slightly swollen.*

Dorjee   You stole it!

Deshar   I asked for it.

Dorjee   He said no.

Deshar   He was in the shower.

Dorjee   You asked him while he was in the shower?

Deshar   Yes. It is our shower.

Dorjee   But he was inside it.

Deshar   So, I asked him from outside!

Dorjee   May I take your clothes please?

Deshar   They are bringing more uniforms for all of us.

Dorjee   You are insane!

Deshar   Aaah . . . (*In pain as* **Dorjee** *presses too hard.*)

Dorjee   You have a cut.

Deshar   He hit me.

Dorjee   Deshar. You broke his jaw!

Deshar   He was threating.

Dorjee   Deshar, he is a Chinese soldier. You are a Buddhist nun.

Deshar   So? I wasn't violent or anything.

Dorjee   DESHAR . . . YOU STOLE HIS CLOTHES, YOU LEFT HIM STRANDED IN THE COLD IN A COLD TOWEL AND YOU BROKE HIS JAW!!

Deshar   Look.

Dorjee   What.

Deshar *opens her fist which was closed so far.*

Dorjee   What is it?

Deshar   Inner molar. (*Laughs.*)

Dorjee   Inner . . . what . . .

Deshar   Here. touch it.

Dorjee *touches it.*

Dorjee   It's a . . . TOOTH!

Deshar   Inner molar. Third from left. (*Pause.*) Third from inside. (*Laughs.*)

Dorjee   Their commander is coming in two days to examine the nunnery and here you are breaking their teeth.

Deshar   They cannot expel me. I did the best in class.

Dorjee   They are not expelling nuns for bad results, Deshar! It's not the Education Board.

Deshar   Aaah . . . gentle, Dorjee, gentle. My god you are so aggressive for a nun.

Dorjee (*unable to contain her laughter but trying to*)   You . . . you broke his . . . inner . . . inner. (*Looking at* **Deshar**.)

Deshar   Molar. Third from inside.

Pause.

His mouth was open.

Dorjee   You hit him with his mouth open. (*Bursts out laughing.*) There is blood downstairs. In front of Rinpoche's room

Deshar   I am the one bleeding. (*Shows her small wound.*)

Dorjee   You have a scratch. He has a broken jaw and a missing tooth. When Rinpoche finds out /

Pause.

Why did you want his clothes?

Deshar   What did they say at lunch time?

Dorjee   They said, their commander will be here in two days, in the new train and that they will give us re-education.

Deshar   And?

Dorjee   And those nuns who are not needed in the nunnery will be sent away.

Deshar And??

Dorjee What?

Deshar This does not make you angry?

Dorjee I sometimes don't believe you are the top of your class, Deshar.

Deshar I asked him from outside the shower.

Dorjee What?

Deshar Sir . . . what are you going to do with me if you take me away?

Dorjee and **Deshar** *laugh.*

Dorjee Why did you do that?

Deshar The Buddha is for sarcasm.

Dorjee Sarcasm is nonviolent. (*Laughing.*)

Deshar But what did he do?

Dorjee What?

Deshar He said (*pretending to be him:*) 'We will parade you in soldier's fatigues and make you sing for the motherland' and then he laughed like a hyena.

Dorjee Like a what?

Deshar *still pretending to be the soldier in the washroom, emulates a horrific laugh which she calls laughing like a hyena.*

Dorjee Then?

Deshar Then I said: (*Being herself but overdramatic.*) Sir, then I'll just take your clothes right away and follow the path of liberation.

Dorjee *laughs.*

Deshar 'If you touch my clothes, I will have you thrown out on the first day the commander arrives'. (*Does his laugh again.*)

Dorjee And so, you broke his tooth!

Deshar (*still enacting*) No, he came out like this and I was standing here with my face covered. I was going away, when he walked out of the shower and kicked me and I, out of sheer reflex –

Within this time, **Rinpoche** *is at the door.* **Dorjee** *has spotted him and is standing with her head down while* **Deshar** *is lost in her story.*

Landed an elbow to the left of his (*showing his face*) and as he fell, I plucked his tooth and said (*she enacts plucking his tooth*) 'my brother, I am sorry you will not bite me. I am sorry brother, I can't wait for re-education . . . I want your clothes right now' . . .

She is laughing as she notices **Rinpoche**. *Stands up abruptly. Looks at* **Dorjee**. *Tries to take the solder's shirt off. Stops. Bows down with folded hands.* **Rinpoche** *looks at her.*

A beat –

Scene Two

Tsering's *house.* **Pema** *(12 years old) is sitting next to him.* **Rinpoche** *and* **Deshar** *are standing. Still Snowing outside.*

Tsering (*to* **Pema**)   Everything that's circled.

Pema   Teacher Tsering, but everything is circled! (*Pause.*) I mean /

Tsering   What's your language, Pema?

Pema   Tibetan, Teacher.

Tsering   What kind of Tibetan?

Rinpoche   May we /

Tsering   I am with a student. You may help yourself to some tea.

Rinpoche   I am sorry but /

Tsering   It's there. The girl knows.
(*Beat.*) Yes, Pema. What kind of Tibetan?

Pema   Our kind Teacher.

Tsering   Everything circled is Mandarin.

Pema   Teacher . . . but . . . this word here /

Tsering   It's used like Mandarin. You cannot use every language the same way, Pema. You lose your language, you lose who you are, what you are and most importantly, why . . . (*Looks at* **Rinpoche**.) Why you are. You understand?

Pema *looks at* **Deshar**. **Deshar** *makes a funny face at him. He giggles.* **Tsering** *looks at* **Deshar**. *She pretends to be serious and so does* **Pema**.

Tsering   Yes. How can I help you?

Rinpoche   Have her back. (*Pause.*) For a few days.

Tsering

Rinpoche

Tsering   I did not send her.

Rinpoche   She has broken the rules.

Tsering   Of?

Rinpoche Of the monastery. We have to set up a disciplinary . . .

Pause.

We have an inspection.

Tsering So?

Rinpoche We cannot have undisciplined nuns in the monastery.

Tsering What did she do?

Rinpoche She was violent?

Tsering *looks up at* **Rinpoche***.*

Rinpoche She hit a Chinese soldier and stole his uniform.

Tsering You mean she was unruly. For a moment I thought she fought for something.

Rinpoche They will expel her and many others if we are seen as violent.

Tsering Fighting for freedom is not violence. Misleading people is. (*Pause.*)

Rinpoche Commander Tsering, there have been many self-immolations in Tibet. In our region not a single one. We can preserve this place of learning if the Chinese see us for being for what we are.

Tsering Self . . . self-immolation. People burning themselves. (*Pause. Says a prayer.*) This is our destiny. To burn ourselves.

Pause.

Rinpoche We can save our great school, Commander. We need your help.

Tsering Not my problem. (*Beat.*) Pema. (**Pema** *and* **Deshar** *keep making faces at each other and reacting to what the elders are talking about.*)

Pause.

Tsering You, girl . . . come here. Sit.

Deshar *comes and sits next to* **Pema***.*

Tsering Why is this sentence incorrect?

Deshar *looks at it again.*

Deshar

Tsering You can't. (*Pause. Looks at* **Rinpoche**.) Because, Pema, in Tibetan languages verbs come after objects. And in Chinese usage it's the other way around. You get it?

Pema Yes, Teacher Tsering.

Tsering No . . . you don't. And neither do you (*at* **Deshar**) and nor will you. (*At* **Rinpoche**.) Because, deep deep inside, all of you have become Chinese. Your mind is in Mandarin and you are just using Tibetan-sounding words.

Rinpoche   They are children, Tsering.

Pause.

Tsering   Re-education, is it? Is that what the Chinese are calling it?

Rinpoche   Yes. They want to reduce the number of nuns in the monasteries.

Tsering   No. They want to save resources. That's what we are for them. Costs. (*Pause.*) And they are coming by the train, isn't it. Look at the village, gearing up to celebrate the one day when this train will stop here. Idiots.

Rinpoche   We do not have violence in our culture, Tsering.

Tsering   Culture. (*Laughs.*) We were warriors, Rinpoche. You are confused between culture and theology. These words have meanings. They are not sounds you make every morning, while doing the Kora.

Rinpoche   The monastery needs her to be out for a week. We have our hands full already.

Tsering   She left on her own. I have my hands full too.

Pause.

Rinpoche   I don't want her to be expelled.

Tsering   You have destroyed her ability to judge right from wrong.

Rinpoche   She ran away. From you. We found her.

He looks at **Deshar**.

Rinpoche   It's for the village, Tsering. It's a site of great learning. Do you deny that?

Pause.

The village needs it.

Pause.

Tsering   If she makes one mistake, I will leave her at your gates myself.

Pema (*loudly*)   SHE WILL STAY HERE.

Looks down.

Rinpoche (*with folded hands*)   Thank you . . . Thank you, Commander Tsering.

Pause.

Tsering (*to* **Deshar**)   You can sleep in the shed outside. No contact with the students. I don't want you to fill their brains with the fluff you are learning.

Deshar   Yes, Teacher Tsering.

Pema   I will bring her the food, Teacher.

Tsering   No, you won't. I will. You won't meet her, see her or talk to her for this week . . . Is that clear? (*Pause.*) Is that clear?

Deshar and Pema   Yes, Teacher Tsering.

Rinpoche Thank you.

Tsering I am not doing this for you. I am doing this for the village. (*Pause*.) I heard you have some prayer rituals to bless the train.

Rinpoche Yes. We have been asked.

Tsering By?

Rinpoche The authorities.

Tsering And what does His Holiness say about the Beijing–Lhasa Express?

Rinpoche He says it's just a vessel. It's not good or bad. It depends on how it's used and what it brings.

Tsering (*laughs*) A vessel! A vessel, he says! A vessel that brings in the beast in its entirety is just a vessel! 'Just'. Unfortunately, His Holiness only knows one meaning of the word 'just'. The one about fairness is lost on him.

Scene Three

Late night. **Pema** *and* **Deshar** *on a mountain.* **Pema** *looking at the sky through a small telescope. There is some snow but it's not completely covered in snow.*

Pema OOOOOO . . . Where did you get it?

Deshar Tashi brought it.

Pema From?

Deshar Beijing.

Pema I want to be an astronaut when I grow up.

Deshar *laughs out aloud.*

Pema Look, that's an astronaut.

Deshar (*pretending to be serious*)   Where?

Pema There . . . on that star. It's a new spaceship.

Deshar What's a spaceship?

Pema A spaceship is the Yak on which astronauts go far.

Deshar How far?

Pema To another world. Look . . .

Deshar Is that a Yak?

Pema That's a spaceship. I will be the first Chinese on a star beyond that bright star.

Deshar Chinese?

Pema   Tibetan. I mean Tibetan

They hear the train. **Pema** *looks at the train in a distance through the telescope.*

Pema   Actually . . . I think, I will be an engine driver.

Deshar   Oh. (*Laughs.*) Why?

Pema   Look at the train.

Deshar *looks.*

Deshar   Beautiful. I have never seen it this closely. Is that a place to eat?

Pema   Yes, it's called a dining car.

Deshar   How do you know?

Pema   Dolma's father has been on it. He told me.

Deshar   Wow . . .

Pema   Show.

Pause.

I'd like to be a waiter. Look at his uniform.

Deshar (*playing him. Taking the telescope and looking through*)   Wow . . . see the engine driver's uniform. Here.

Pema   Yes. On second thoughts /

Deshar   Yes, I think you will be a good engine driver.

Pema   Yes. It's quite a fast train. I think I'll do a good job of it. How far is it?

Deshar   Very far. It's a good telescope. There's a shepherd out at night.

Pema   Where? (*Pause.*) Oh yes, there.

Deshar   I think his sheep are beautiful.

Pema   Show me . . . Yes, he has so many.

Deshar   They are climbing up quite quickly, isn't it?

Pema   Yes.

Deshar   He is really brave to go out at night.

Pema   You think he is braver than the engine driver?

Deshar   And the waiter, and the astronaut.

Pema   Actually. I think /

Deshar   You are already a shepherd, Pema. (*Laughs.*)

Pema (*smiles*)   Yes.

Deshar   So, what do you want to be when you grow up?

Pema   I want to be this.

Deshar   No improvement?

Pema   No. Why can't I be this? I like this.

Deshar   That's because you haven't seen the world outside.

Pema   I just did. I saw it, and I think I am fine.

Deshar   You don't want to move ahead?

Pema   I am ahead.

Deshar   If the Buddha thought like this, he would never have become the Buddha.

Pema   The Buddha did not have a telescope.

They laugh.

Deshar   What if they don't let you be who you are, Pema?

Pema   Who?

Deshar   The Chinese.

Pema   Will they not let you be a nun?

Deshar   They want all of us to be like them.

The train passes by with a loud sound. They look at it.

Pema   It's beautiful.

Deshar   And yet.

Pema   And yet, I want to be a shepherd and you want to be a nun. (*Laughs.*)

Pause.

Deshar   I don't know. I really don't know what I want to be.

Tsering *appears.*

Silence.

Tsering   Pema. Come here.

Pema *goes running to* **Tsering** *and stands next to him apologetically.* **Tsering** *slaps him hard. He falls.*

Deshar   I am sorry . . . I am really /

Tsering   Did I grant you permission to take him?

Deshar   No . . . no . . . I am really sorry /

Tsering   Did I ask you to leave the house and join a nunnery?

Silence.

Tsering You go when you want, you come back when you want, you do whatever you feel like and I am the poor father, is it?

Deshar Pah-la, I am sorry, I /

Tsering I fought for this country, Deshar. And His Holiness called my movement off by turning non-violent one day. And the whole world just forgot about us. I brought you up, by myself, with everything I could and you just left.

Deshar You killed Amahla.

Pause.

Tsering What?

Deshar You killed her.

Tsering No, Deshar, I gave her dignity. She was going to leave me, and go away to meet His Holiness with my baby in her arms, across these mountains. She was fleeing her home to seek the blessings of a man who called off our only chance of independence.

Deshar So, you killed her.

Tsering

Deshar You shot her.

Tsering I shot her? Who said I shot her?

Deshar The villagers. Everyone knows.

Tsering She was brought back, raped and dying in an army truck. You were lying on the floor of the truck.

Deshar And then you shot her.

Tsering They said I could only save one of you, Deshar. Your mother asked me to shoot her.

Pause.

WE . . . we, your mother and I, saved you, Deshar.

Pause.

Deshar That's not what everyone says, Pah-la. That is not what people believe.

Tsering I don't lie, Deshar. There is no one more Buddhist than me in the world.

Deshar But people /

Tsering People believe His Holiness wants independence, Deshar, when he himself has announced the middle path. People believe what they want to believe.

Deshar You should have saved her. I was an infant.

Silence.

Tsering You know what the real problem with Tibet is, Deshar? (*Pause.*) It's not the Chinese. It's our children. They grow up to be delusional.

Deshar

Tsering Spare this boy. Go back to the nunnery.

Deshar

Deshar You . . . you are a cynical, old, angry man, Pah-la! You will make him like yourself.

Tsering Come, Pema . . . we do not need to stand here and listen to this.

He begins to walk away.

Deshar You killed her, Pah-la . . . (**Deshar** *breaks down.*) Everyone knows you killed her, Pah-la. (*She falls down and starts crying.*)

Pause.

Tsering (*goes back to her*) You will never ever call me that. Is that clear? Your mother died. I am sorry. But she was born in Tibet. And in Tibet, your mother's death, your father's anger are not the only things hindering your salvation.

Silence.

Deshar

Tsering And you will never ever come close to this boy.

Silence.

You don't know what you want to be isn't it? Isn't that what she said?

Pema

Tsering What?

Pema Yes . . . yes, Teacher Tsering

Tsering Go back. Get re-educated. Get humiliated by the Chinese soldiers and keep hoping that the Dalai Lama will reappear one day and make everything alright. This delusion is what you ran away for, isn't it?

Deshar I ran away from you. You killed my mother.

Pause.

Tsering If you don't know who you are, living in Tibet, you will never know who you are. It's much easier to be a Buddha than to be an ordinary Tibetan in this world.

He takes **Pema** *and walks off.*

Scene Four

Rinpoche *and the nuns of the monastery alternately light and blow out butter lamps. They chant as they engage in this ritual. A brilliant light on stage with the glow of 100 butter lamps and, at any point of time, most lamps are lit while no lamp is lit long enough. The continuous play of the temporality of fire and life is played through this ritual.*

Sound of the train. As the train arrives closer, the nuns and **Rinpoche** *turn to look at the train. As the train arrives at a high speed, the lamps go off. Darkness.*

Scene Five

A giant Buddha statue.

The prayer room and main classroom in the nunnery.

One chair which **Constable Gaphel** *has placed.* **Deng** *is looking at the statue. Next to it are Buddhist scriptures and also materials for prayers.*

Rinpoche *is looking at* **Deng**.

There is a flipboard next to the chair.

Deng   How much does it cost us, Rinpoche?

Rinpoche   Sorry?

Deng   How much is this Buddha statue for? What is the damage to the common taxpayer, such as myself?

Rinpoche   1,400 years, Commander Deng. The taxpayers of this country have got a really good bargain.

Deng (*smiles*)   No one. Absolutely no one can defeat Buddhist monks at rhetoric.

Rinpoche   Blessings of the Buddha.

Deng   I love your sense of humour.

Rinpoche   One wants to smile. The Buddha laughed a lot.

Deng   The Buddha. THE BUDDHA . . . must have been a great fundraiser.

Rinpoche   On the contrary, it was a cultural revolution.

Deng

Rinpoche *smiles.*

Deng   How is it that the cultural revolution spared these relics? Chairman Mao must have really liked them.

Pause.

Rinpoche   Would you like some tea?

Deng   Thank you. I am at work.
(*Pause.*) One of your nuns hurt a soldier.

Rinpoche   I am sorry.

Deng   Is this what you . . .

Rinpoche   They are like my family. I apologize on their behalf.

Deng (*laughs*)   I have a daughter. We don't raise children with violence.

Rinpoche   How old is your daughter?

Deng   Eight.

Rinpoche   Aah. May the Buddha bless her.

Deng   Because of you people I won't see her for months.

Rinpoche   Why is that?

Deng   Can't bring her along.

Rinpoche   No, you can't. Her mother?

Deng   Died two years ago. I raised her myself.

Rinpoche   May the Buddha bless you and give you peace.

Deng   If we can do this soon.

Rinpoche   You shall have our complete cooperation, Commander. May you be with your child at the earliest.

Pause.

Deng   Is that your trunk?

Rinpoche   Yes.

Deng   What is in it?

Rinpoche   You may take a look.

Deng   Nothing personal I hope. (*As* **Deng** *walks to the trunk to examine it.*)

Deng *opens it. It's empty.* **Deng** *shows it to him.* **Rinpoche** *smiles.*

Deng   Where are the contents of this?

Rinpoche   It's an empty box.

Deng   Where is the stuff that was in it?

Rinpoche   Gave it away.

Deng   When?

Rinpoche   Over this lifetime.

Deng Gaphel . . . Please search the room.

Rinpoche *smiles at* **Gaphel**. **Gaphel** *bows*.

Deng We have Tibetans working for the motherland.

Rinpoche Surely. Gaphel-la, (*to the* **Constable**) just put back everything in its place, please.

Especially the scriptures.

(*To* **Deng**.) We are short of people, as you know.

Deng I think that you are far too many, to be honest. These scriptures. How old are they?

Rinpoche Thousands of years.

Deng New books?

Rinpoche Several.

Deng Who writes them?

Rinpoche Scholars. Monks and nuns.

Deng What are they about?

Rinpoche The mind.

Deng The mind?

Rinpoche Yes, all of Buddhism is only about one thing. The mind.

Deng And?

Rinpoche And?

Deng Separatism? False history?

Rinpoche I'm afraid not. We are yet to find our political teeth.

Deng (*to* **Constable**) Nothing?

Constable Nothing, Commander.

Deng Why did you give everything away?

Rinpoche I gained a little, very little knowledge. It left no place for things.

Deng So, what are the pillars of your education?

Rinpoche The 'what' of our education?

Deng Pillars . . . foundation, principles? What do you teach . . . about the mind?

Rinpoche Pillar. (*Pause.*) To see the world for what it is.

Deng And which is?

Rinpoche It's in our mind. Isn't it?

Deng

Rinpoche It is. In our mind.

Deng This chair. It's here.

Rinpoche Yes, in a way.

Deng In what way?

Rinpoche In the way, that I first have to perceive of myself in my mind, and then perceive of this chair through my sense of 'I'. That if 'I am here' then there is a chair. Surely.

Deng If you are here then it is here. But it costs money. It costs taxpayers' money to get this chair here. Or is the money too in our mind?

Rinpoche In a way, it is actually.

Deng So, while shepherd and nomads in your village starve to send the monastery food and blankets, you question whether the things they are giving you are really here or not? This is your education?

Rinpoche

Deng This Buddha statue, it costs a few thousand Yuans.
These robes, they cost us money. This monastery is not running on your mind, it's working on labour and money.

Rinpoche That is true as well. Just like the police force is.

Deng Oh . . . the police force. The police force protects. What does the monastery protect?

Rinpoche What does the police force protect?

Deng People. Common people.

Rinpoche From?

Deng Other people.

Rinpoche Why?

Deng Why?

Rinpoche What does it protect *exactly*, in people?

Deng Their life.

Rinpoche Which is?

Deng Their happiness, their well-being, their way of life.

Rinpoche I am really glad, Commander Deng. It seems like you and I have the same job.

Pause.

Deng Your people need re-education.

Act One, Scene Five

Rinpoche   I see.

Deng   Your knowledge is of no use to the common man. People cannot be starving while hundreds of monks and nuns sit in monasteries and debate whether they are really here or not.

Rinpoche   People have never starved in Tibet. They have, however, in mainland China.

Pause.

Deng   I am not here to play word games with you.

Rinpoche   I was merely clarifying.

Deng   We do not discuss economics with monks!

Rinpoche   Why?

Deng   Because you consume material and look down upon the material condition.

Rinpoche   We do not look down upon any condition. On the contrary, the Buddha pushed for land reforms.

Deng   I am a soldier, not a monk. I don't wake up every morning and debate.

Rinpoche   Hmm . . . and we are not even wondering who really needs the re-education.

Pause.

Deng   Constable.

Constable Gaphel *turns the flipchart.*

Deng   So, these are our five major pillars of re-education. The education of those who were denied it when they were young.
One. Opposition to Separatism.
Two. Unity of Tibet and China.
Three. Recognition of the Chinese Government-appointed Panchen Lama as the true Panchen Lama.
Four. Agreement that the Dalai Lama is a political terrorist dressed up in the garb of a religious man and that he is destroying the unity of the motherland.
Five. To agree that Tibet was never and shall never be a separate country and it is in fact an integral part of our beloved motherland.

Rinpoche   Excellent.

Deng   Do you agree?

Rinpoche   With?

Deng   The five pillars.

Rinpoche *goes closer to the flipchart.*

Rinpoche   Too many nouns, unfortunately. My entire training is in verbs.

82   Pah-La (Father)

Pause.

Deng   You need to include these pillars in your morning assembly. Every day.

Rinpoche   The nunnery will not do any such thing.

Deng   Then you will have no nuns to teach.

Rinpoche   This is a school of philosophy, Commander Deng, not a shop in downtown Beijing. There is going to be no bargain.

Deng   Well, in that case, your students will need to put up with some harsh re-education.

Rinpoche   May the Buddha make us see each other's views.

Deng   May the Buddha stop breeding separatists.

Rinpoche   There are no separatists here.

Pause.

Deng, *signaling to* **Constable Gaphel** *to go out and bring someone.*

Tense silence between **Rinpoche** *and* **Deng**. **Deshar** *is brought in. She stands in a corner and bows to* **Rinpoche**. *She is angry.*

Deng   I suppose we know who this girl is. (*Silence.* **Gaphel** *hands him a file.*)

Deng   Deshar Tsering. Daughter of Ngabo Tsering. Commander, Chushi Gangdruk. Trained in Colarado by CIA. (*Pause.*) No separatists?

Rinpoche

Deng   Constable Gaphel. Do we have any other information about her father?

Gaphel   No . . . no, Commander

Deshar   He has nothing to do with me. I am not his daughter.

Rinpoche   Deshar!

Deshar *looks down. Sobs.*

Rinpoche   You can go to your room.

Deshar   I am sorry. I am sorry, Rinpoche.

Rinpoche   You may go. We can speak /

Silence.

Deng   Perhaps you can help us understand if we need re-education or not?

Rinpoche   She is a young nun. Her education is not complete. Let her go.

Deng   I thought she is one of your best. (*Looking at the file.*)

Rinpoche   Yes.

Act One, Scene Five 83

Deng If she answers our questions satisfactorily, we will let everyone stay here and there will be no re-education. (*Pause.*) Alright?

Rinpoche Deshar, you may /

Deng You may not, Deshar, if you want to give a chance to your sisters to stay.

Deshar (*looks up at him sternly*) Ask.

Deng The Buddha meets a blacksmith. The blacksmith works eighteen hours a day to make a living. The Buddha asks for his tools in return for salvation. What should the blacksmith do?

Pause.

Deshar The blacksmith should not have to work eighteen hours a day to make a living. If, despite knowing this, the Buddha asks for his tools, the blacksmith should break every bone in the Buddha's body.

Pause.

Rinpoche Go, Deshar.

Deng The blacksmith had two children, out of whom one died due to an illness that could not be treated. There is one building in the village which is the monastery of the Buddha. The blacksmith goes to the Buddha and pleads for a hospital while his second child is unwell.

The Buddha insists on the importance of Salvation and wants to keep the monastery. The blacksmith gathers other people in the village to plead but the Buddha still does not hear them. He keeps insisting on the monastery and makes the case for Salvation, what should the blacksmith do?

Deshar The blacksmith should start a revolution. Overthrow the Buddha and take over the monastery.

Deng (*looks at* **Rinpoche**) Well . . .

Looks at **Deshar**.

Deng Good. I must meet your father before I leave.

Deshar One day, a man steals the blacksmith's clothes. He wears them and roams around the neighbouring towns and villages, claiming to be a blacksmith by the day but by the night destroying every house that gave him shelter. Soon he claims that every house is his and that all of them are one without any difference whatsoever as long as the similarity is in their allegiance to this blacksmith who actually is not a blacksmith at all in the first place.

One day the imposter enters the blacksmith's house, tries to throw him and his family out, breaks the altar of their god, belittles everything else they had in their lives and the blacksmith and his family are asked to now prove to the imposter that they are loyal imposters and he is the original blacksmith.

The real blacksmith still has his tool in his hand and is mighty good at using it. What should the blacksmith do?

Pause.

Rinpoche   Deshar go in. Now!

Deng *comes close to her.*

Deng   Do I sense a streak of violence? Did you get it from your father or is it part of monastic education nowadays?

Deshar (*makes a fist holding herself back*)   What should the blacksmith do?

Pause.

Deng (*to* **Deshar**)   Re-education starts tomorrow. For everyone.
I am not staying away from my child to put up with the insolence of others.

Pause.

Deng (*to* **Rinpoche**)   There is a contradiction in your education.

Rinpoche   Which is?

Deng   You are not sure whether you are here or not, but you are absolutely sure that Tibet is yours.

Pause.

Rinpoche   There is one in yours as well.

Deng

Rinpoche   You are protecting people from yourselves. (*Pause.*)

Deng (*loudly*)   Re-education starts tomorrow at 4 am, Constable. Let us show the master and his nuns, who is here and who exists only in their minds.

Scene Six

Montage of the next three days and nights

The same room as Scene Five.

The Buddha statue is present. In front of it many more chairs as the nuns are being brought in, told to write, learn, repeat. They are made to read newspapers and mark lines. They are asked to stand up and sing the National Anthem.

They get exhausted but are being brought in over and over again.

Scene Seven

Same room. Three nights later. Nuns are sitting exhausted, in a corner. **Rinpoche** *is on the floor lying in front of the Buddha statue with his eyes shut. There are* *newspapers strewn around.* **Deng** *is walking, picking up newspaper after newspaper and looking at them.*

He looks at **Rinpoche**.

Deng   There isn't one who has marked anything in green. Not one.

Looks around.

For three days and three nights we are here. In other nunneries, we have done this in two days and moved on. Just mark everything you believe in green. What is the problem? What are the nuns in this nunnery finding so hard to believe?

Deshar   The newspapers are yours. They are lying.

Deng   And you? Do you not understand that all your sisters here will be expelled if the re-education is unsuccessful?

Deshar   If it is successful, there won't be any need to expel us. Feed him.

Rinpoche   I am fine.

Deng   You, you have taught them to disbelieve. In Sera, Drepung, Ganden monasteries we have had many who we have been able to save. But here, your influence is complete. Total!

Rinpoche   I don't know how you forced others. It makes me proud to see that here, the truth is not compromised . . .

Pause.

Deng   Dorjee.

Dorjee *stands up in panic.*

Deng   Please bring it.

Dorjee *remains standing.*

Deng   Where is it? (*Loudly.*)

Dorjee *pulls out a folded photograph.*

Deng   Can you please let your sisters and your master know what it is? Now.

Dorjee (*tentatively*)   It's a photo.

Deng   Of?

Dorjee *remains quiet.*

Deng *looks at her.*

Dorjee   His Holiness the Dalai Lama.

Constable Gaphel *immediately bows.* **Deng** *looks at him. He stands up.*

Deng   And it was found in?

Dorjee *remains quiet.*

Rinpoche I gave it to her. When her brother died. For solace.

Deng Do we not know, in this country, it's illegal?

Pause.

Deng Nun Dorjee, you have your licence. You may leave this nunnery and be a nun elsewhere.

Dorjee *starts to cry.*

Deng You may leave. There is a train tonight. Take it and leave this place. This nunnery is shut.

He snatches **Dorjee***'s picture and tears the picture of His Holiness to bits.*

Dorjee *is in tears.*

Dorjee I need the money. I need the money, Rinpoche, I'll starve otherwise. (**Dorjee** *cries holding* **Rinpoche**.)

Rinpoche I understand. Keep this face in your mind. (*Showing the bits.*) Go . . . go, my dear.

Dorjee But where will I go, Rinpoche?

Rinpoche Take that train. It's a vessel, like His Holiness said. It won't make you less Tibetan or less Buddhist. Take it and go somewhere far. Search for the Buddha in you.

Smiles.

Looks at **Deng**.

Rinpoche So is our nunnery going to be closed?

Deng Since this is your education, (*looking at the newspapers*) I am afraid yes. We will break it and build a hospital.

Rinpoche May the Buddha bless you for building a hospital.

Silence.

Rinpoche It has already been /

Deng The demolition on the east side should begin any moment.

Rinpoche I thought you were bringing in equipment to build a road.

Deng To the hospital.

Rinpoche *turns towards the nuns.*

Rinpoche My dear children in the path of the Buddha. Leave. No licence can take away your quest from you. You may not be allowed in a nunnery again but the Buddha is within us. It is to be awakened. Leave.

Deng Everyone in a straight line. Leave the building.

Rinpoche *goes and sits next to the Buddha statue.*

Deng   Everyone in a straight line. leave the building.

Gaphel (*goes to* **Rinpoche**)   Rinpoche, master, please . . .

Rinpoche   Everyone in a straight line. Leave the building.

Deng   Leave.

Rinpoche *turns to face him.*

Rinpoche   I will go with him. Let the machines arrive.

Silence.

Gaphel   Master . . . please.

Deng   Leave.

Rinpoche *holds the Buddha's feet tightly and sits.*

Starts chanting Om Mani Padme Hum.

Gradually the nuns all come close to **Rinpoche**, *chanting Om Mani Padme Hum.*

Deng *looks at them. He hits* **Rinpoche** *with a baton and tries to drag him.*

Gaphel   Commander . . . I'll ask him, Commander . . . Rinpoche, master, this is good for everyone, please, please.

All the nuns chant louder. **Deshar**'*s eyes are open. Others have shut their eyes and are chanting.* **Rinpoche** *chants with his eyes shut and hands folded as* **Deng** *tries to drag him out with the* **Constable** *joining in trying to do it respectfully.*

Deshar *attacks* **Deng** *and hits him hard.*

Rinpoche (*loudly*)   DESHAR!!!

Everyone goes quiet.

Deng *is in severe pain lying on another side of the room.*

Rinpoche   Deshar. Deshar, my child. Stop!

Deng   I will bury this girl alive. Have I left my child to come here and take this shit from these / (**Deng** *is about to attack her in rage when* **Rinpoche** *comes in between and stops him with folded hands.*)

Deng *looks away.* **Rinpoche** *goes to* **Deshar**.

Rinpoche   You cannot . . . cannot hate him, Deshar. You cannot be a learned Buddhist scholar, and hate this man who is being cruel to you right now. He is a Buddha too. (*Pause.*)

We can lose this nunnery, we can lose our land, our language but, Deshar . . . we are this . . . (*Pointing at the Buddha.*) This is our path.

If we become violent, we lose everything.
My child you cannot, cannot hate.

Deshar *falls down crying.*

Rinpoche Leave, everyone. Leave. I am too old to now go out into the world. Let me go with my Buddha. Please leave.

Gaphel *is on the floor.* **Rinpoche** *goes close to him.*

Rinpoche I am at peace. Please leave.

Gaphel *sits with folded hands.*

Deng Constable, come here.

Constable *comes closer.* **Deshar** *is on the floor.*

Deng These people won't learn anything in this way. Disrobe this man before he dies at the feet of his god.

Gaphel Commander . . . I can't . . . we cannot disrobe him. He is a Rinpoche. He is one with the Buddha, we cannot . . .

Deng Are you denying orders?

Silence.

Rinpoche Do it, Gaphel-la. My clothes are not me.

The nuns chant Om Mani Padme Hum again. Loud.

Rinpoche May I teach my last lesson before you take my robes, oh Buddha.

Deng *walks away.*

Rinpoche (*looks at his students, hands folded*) The Sermon of Fire. Everything burns. Everything always burns, and the world is never the same. We never see the same mountain twice, or the same forest, for in our minds we are burning.

Have patience, let the fire of knowledge burn and the fire of hatred douse itself. Understand that everything changes and this too shall pass. Don't hate. Don't hate. I complete my teachings now. I hope what you are about to see does not make you hate this man and rather you can be compassionate towards his suffering that has led him here. May the Buddha be with you.

Rinpoche *goes and sits at the feet of the Buddha.*

Constable Gaphel *goes closer. He is unable to touch him.* **Rinpoche** *begins to take his robes off himself and handing them to* **Gaphel**. *As he gets disrobed, the nuns go away in a single line chanting.* **Deshar** *keeps looking at* **Deng**.

Scene Eight

A month later.

Snow all around. **Deshar** *and* **Pema** *next to the railway track.* **Pema** *has his telescope. A can of petrol is kept. Some wood to light a fire.*

Act One, Scene Eight   89

Pema *is looking through the telescope.* **Deshar** *is trying to light the fire with his help.*

Pema   That is . . . it.

Deshar

Pema   The last of the debris.

Deshar   They broke everything?

Pema   Yes.

Pause.

Pema (*looks at the sky*)   It took a month. Was a big nunnery.

Pause.

I come here every day. To wave at the train. Sometimes they wave back.

They smile at each other.

Deshar   Pah-la?

Pema   He has not stepped out since the monastery was broken.

Deshar   I thought he hated it.

Pema   Everyday he did the Kora. He has a picture of His Holiness hidden in the rice box.

Deshar

Pema   Do you hate something, sister?

Long pause.

Deshar   You?

Pema   Grammar.

They laugh.

Deshar   What do you hate about grammar, Pema?

Pema   It's a lot of work and I don't understand it.

Pause.

I think we hate that which we do not understand.

Deshar (*looking up at him surprised*)   Pema, you're a scholar. (*Laughs.*)

Pema   I told teacher Tsering the same thing in class the other day.

Deshar   You did?

Pema   He gave me sweets. The next day. But I knew he gave it to me for saying this, about hate.

Deshar   How?

Pema   How what?

Deshar   How do you know he gave you the sweets for something you said the previous day?

Pema   I understand things immediately. He takes a day.

Deshar *laughs.*

They light the fire by now.

Deshar   You go, Pema.

Pema   But I want to see the train.

Deshar   Pah-la will be worried for you.

Pema   He is teaching. He thinks I am in the barn.

Deshar   You have to stop lying, Pema.

Pema   I didn't hurt anyone.

Deshar   You lied.

Pema   One day a monk was roving in the forest, and a deer ran past him. Soon after, a hunter who was chasing the deer stopped next to him and asked about the deer. Is there truth in telling where the deer is, or is there truth in saving a life?

Deshar (*laughs*)   Truth is to tell where the deer is but yes morally the monk might as well lie.

Pema   Well, how can the monk tell where the deer is, sister? By the time he says it, the deer would have moved. No one knows where someone else is exactly. There is no truth that the monk can say.

Pause.

Deshar (*in awe of him*)   What are you learning, Pema!

Pema   Tibetan. (*He looks through his telescope.*)

Deshar *laughs. Looks at him in awe.*
(*Pause.*) It'll be here soon. (*Smiles.*)

Deshar   How far is it? (*She gets up.*)

Pema   Other side of two mountains.

Deshar   Let's have a race?

Pema   A race! You called me here for the race?

Deshar   I wanted to see you.

Pema   OK? (*Pause.*) Where are we racing to?

Small pause.

Deshar To the top of that hill.

Pema But we'll miss the train.

Deshar First horn we start running, by the fifth horn we need to get there. Whoever gets there first gets to go to the mastiff show in Kham.

Pema The Big Mastiff show?

Deshar Yes, the big one.

Pema But I want to see the train.

Deshar Or the Big Mastiff show?

Pema OK I'll see the train tomorrow.

Deshar Good decision.

Pema The first horn will be when it's one mountain bend away.

He looks.

Deshar Great.

Pema Don't be angry if you lose.

Deshar I won't be.

Pema You are always angry. Father and daughter.

Deshar *laughs*.

Pema If I win will you also get me sweets?

Deshar Yes. But you have to cross the top of the hill by five horns. Only then.

Pema Yes.

Deshar And don't turn back.

Pema Yes. Will you be angry if I turn back?

Deshar NO!

Pema Good to ask both of you. (*Laughs.*)

Deshar I am not like him.

Pema (*laughs loudly*) You are the same person, sister! His grammar is better. (*Pause.*) OK here it is.

Deshar How far?

Pema One more bend.

Deshar Pema . . . what is anger?

Pema I am going to win this race.

Deshar Do you know?

Pema   Anger is to run the race yourself but to hold it against me. (*He laughs.*)

Deshar   What?

First horn.

Deshar   What did you say?

Pema *has started running.*

Deshar   Tell Pah-la I love him.

Second horn. **Pema** *turns.*

Deshar   Don't look back.

Pema *runs. Third horn.* **Deshar** *pours petrol on herself. Begins to chant. Fourth horn. She lights herself. Fifth horn. She walks on the track. The chant fills the space. She lights herself. The train blows its horn incessantly.* **Deshar** *burns.*

Interval

During the interval the butter lamps are lit and are also available to be lit by audience members. The screen now shows names and pictures of all the martyrs who have self-immolated till the date of performance.

Act Two

Scene One

Lhasa Central Prison. Late night. **Ling**, *30, is with* **Deng** *on a chair.* **Deng** *is holding his head in his hands.* **Ling** *is comforting him . . . Polygraph room. Someone is tied on an interrogation chair. Connected to a polygraph machine. Not visible clearly. The screen shows eye dilation, heart rate and blood flow.*

Deng I need to leave.

Ling Did you ask, Commander?

Deng Yes.

Ling Next shift?

Deng They couldn't tell. Said I was needed here.

Ling Any other news? From other parents?

Deng I don't know. I don't know.

There is a loud alarm. Lights change. **Deng** *and* **Ling** *approach the person. She is* **Deshar**. *Now visible.*

Deng You received orders from his office in India?

Deshar

Deng Does she know?

Ling Yes.

Deng Why isn't she speaking?

Ling (*to* **Deshar**) The polygraph is on. Beep for lies, no beep for truth.

Deng Silence is registered as a lie. Manually.

Deshar *looks at* **Deng**.

Deng We want the truth. The truth.

Deshar

Deng Was it a telegram or a phone call?

Deshar

Deng Are you writing?

Ling Yes sir.

Deng Water.

Ling *makes* **Deshar** *drink water forcibly.*

Deng Who was it? Who asked you to?

Deshar

Deng Sing.

Deshar *feebly chants Om Mani Padme hum.*

Deng Five more protestors have been arrested this morning. An old woman was amongst them. She had his picture with her and was shouting separatist slogans. You know what will be done to her?

Deshar *continues to chant. The monitors keep showing changes in her levels but there are no beeps.*

Deng Three more nuns attempted self-immolation after you. One died. Two are critical. This much fire. This is what you've done.

Deshar *shuts her eyes tightly and chants.*

Deng Sing with me. (**Deng** *sings 'for the motherland'.*)

Ling *joins in.*

Deng What is the problem in singing. Sing!

Deshar *looks at him.*

Deng Sing or I'll wake everyone up and make them sing standing in the cold outside.

Deshar *feebly sings.*

Deng Louder.

Deshar *tries to sing louder.*

Deng Spit.

Deshar *spits on her robe.*

Deng Clean.

Deshar *cleans it with the cloth in her hand. She looks exhausted.*

Deng Who sent you orders to burn yourself?

Deshar

Deng Who are you praying to?

Deshar *keeps chanting.*

Deng Spit

Deshar No one.

The polygraph registers an answer with a green light. Does not beep.

Deng Sing.

Deshar No one.

The polygraph registers an answer with a green light. Does not beep.

Deng What, no one?

Deshar *looks at him . . . silence.*

Deng Water.

Ling *throws water on* **Deshar***'s face, makes her drink water forcibly.*

Deng You received a call from the hotline in the Kirti Monastery. There are reports.

Deshar

Deng Yes, or no?

Deshar

Deng You have to sign this and, in your voice, apologize for it.

Deshar

Deng No one just goes and burns themselves. It's painful.

Deshar

Deng So why would you? Did you get Independence? Did he come back? Are you insane or idiotic? What is it?

Deng*'s alarm rings.* **Deng** *and* **Ling** *sit in two chairs in the room facing each other taking a break.* **Deng** *immediately takes out his phone and checks.*

Deng No news from the school as yet.

Ling Neighbours?

Deng ⟨No. The school bus didn't come back.

Ling Why will anyone attack a school?

Deng Why will Tibetans attack anyone?

Ling Your daughter, sir . . .

Deng They won't hurt children. It must be a rumour. She must be at a friend's for safety.

Ling Yes, sir.

Deng*'s phone beeps. He looks at a message in horror.*

Ling Commander?

Deng It's her school? It's on fire!

Deng*'s alarm rings. They walk back to* **Deshar***. Splash water on her face. She wakes up.*

Deng (*now even more disturbed. Looking at his phone over and over again*) The exact words, were in which dialect? Were they his words or translated? Who received it?

Deshar

Deng You attacked me in your nunnery. I didn't even touch you.

Deshar *folds her hands, in apology.*

Deng I should have had you arrested, then and there. I should have buried you in the rubble as well.

Deng I won't ask you again. I need you to confess to who made you do it.

Deshar *is heard chanting under her breath.*

Deshar (*in pain*)   Pah-la

Deng What? What did you /

Deshar My father . . . My father . . .

Deng (*takes out his phone, shows* **Deshar** *Liu's picture*)   Here . . . here . . . look at this. This is Liu my daughter.

Deshar *tries to say her name feebly.*

Deng Liu . . . I said Liu.

Deshar *prays silently for her.*

Deng Don't pray for her. She is alive.

Deshar *opens her eyes. Looks at him and prays again.*

Deng Stop it . . . I said.

Deshar *continues to pray.*

Deng Stop it . . . I said . . . just stop it.

Deshar *stops and opens her eyes.*

Deng Ling.

Ling Sir?

Deng Separate her hands. Make her stop praying for my daughter.

Ling Sir?

Deng Do it.

Ling *tries to hold* **Deshar***'s hand. Then her finger. Part of it crumbles and falls.* **Ling** *throws up.* **Deshar** *screams.* **Deng***'s alarm rings.*

Deng *begins to splash his face with water and* **Ling** *sits in her chair holding herself from throwing up more.* **Deshar**, *in pain, sits and chants on her chair.*

Deng I will burn each one of them here till I know who attacked the school.

Ling The protest is largely non-violent, sir.

Deng They attacked a school! A school with children. Theirs and ours. Do you /

Ling Whoever did should not have, sir.

Deng I'll burn every one of them alive.

Ling You need to find your daughter, sir.

Deng When will I go? These bastards have erupted on the streets after her burning.

Ling She is the first of the nuns, sir.

Deng So, they can burn children, is it?

Ling No, Commander. They cannot. (*Pause.*) We don't know who did it.

Deng Shut up, Ling! Will you just shut up!

Bell rings. Lights change.

Deng *pours petrol on* **Deshar**. *Gives a matchbox to* **Ling**.

Deng I won't ask you again. I need you to confess to who made you do it.

Deng Burn her.

Ling Sorry what . . .

Deng Yes, burn her. Again.

Ling Sir?

Deng They are uncivilized savages . . . burn her.

Ling *is frozen.* **Deng** *is looking at her. The phone rings.*

Deng Comrade . . . yes, comrade . . . (*Closes his eyes.*) Yes, comrade.

Every cell is full. No, comrade, we can have more. They are, after all, criminals. For the motherland. (*Keeps the phone.*)

(*Pause.*) Two young Tibetan boys were trying to self-immolate at the gates of the prison! It's like you have started a festival of fire!

Deshar *folds her hands. Is in tears. Praying.*

Deng I'll make you speak. And the polygraph will not let you lie.

Deshar *can be heard chanting feebly. Green light on polygraph.*

Scene Two

Later at night. In **Deshar**'s *room.*

Deshar *is lying down.* **Ling** *walks in with medicines. Looks at the medicines that are lying next to her.*

Ling Seven tablets, three ointments, and two bottles of saline . . . why are you not taking them?

Deshar *opens her eyes and looks at* **Ling**.

Ling   Here. This is what you have.

Silence.

Ling   Is the bed comfortable?

Deshar *nods and continues to pray.*

Ling *takes out some pills and pours a glass of water. Walks up to* **Deshar**.

Ling   Open.

Deshar *keeps her mouth shut.*

Ling   Open . . .

Deshar *does not open her mouth.*

Ling   It will hurt if I force them down your throat.

Deshar *looks at her. Shuts her eyes again and continues to pray.*

Ling   OK . . .

She takes the pills herself, starts popping them into her mouth one by one. After two she drinks some water.

Deshar *opens her eyes and looks at* **Ling**.

Ling *pops some more. Fills her mouth with pills.*

Deshar   Don't.

Ling *is about to drink water.*

Deshar   (*trying to be loud in a feeble voice*)   DON'T

Ling *puts the glass to her mouth,* **Deshar** *moves her hand to snatch the glass away from* **Ling**'s, *the glass and her beads fall on the floor.* **Deshar** *immediately bends to pick up the beads and collapses on the floor.*

Ling   Deshar!

Ling *holds* **Deshar**'s *head in her hands.*

Silence.

Ling   Up . . . get up.

Deshar *tries to get up holding* **Ling**. **Ling** *tries to lift her but fails.* **Deshar** *is unstable and falls again.*

Ling *sits down exhausted on the floor and* **Deshar** *takes her beads and continues to count beads and pray.*

Ling   I am bad with suffering.

Deshar *looks at her.*

Ling I said, I am bad with suffering.

Deshar Those pills . . . can kill you.

Ling Someone has to take them. They need to be consumed.

Deshar I won't.

Ling Then I will.

Deshar I can't have your murder on my head.

Ling And I can't have yours.

Deshar You are a prison guard.

Ling You . . . a criminal.

Deshar I caused no harm to anyone.

Ling You can speak. More than a few words.

Deshar I didn't burn my tongue.

Ling You have been silent through the interrogation.

Deshar I have nothing to say.

Silence.

Ling People are on the streets in your name. Facing guns and water cannons in your name.

Deshar I don't know why.

Ling You did it.

Deshar I . . . I burnt on a railway track. To show the world that your train comes with its share of fire.

Ling *slowly goes towards* **Deshar**, *tries to lift her again.*

Deshar *gets up with great effort and sits on the bed.*

Ling I have been on duty for a week. Day and night. Please don't make this difficult.

Deshar I don't want to heal.

Ling I can kill you. You know that.

Deshar Yes.

Ling But you want to die.

Deshar *remains quiet.*

Ling *starts to take out medicines from the box again.*

Ling It's the new world order. Criminals who want to die. The ultimate challenge of law and order. How do you punish those with a death wish.

Here . . . open your mouth. I promise I will have to take all the pills otherwise. Right here in front of your eyes.

Pause.

Deshar May I ask you something?

Ling Yes

Deshar The commander. He has an insanity in his eyes. Something that was not there before.

Ling His daughter is missing.

Deshar Missing?

Ling Their school has been attacked.

Deshar By?

Ling Tibetans. (*Pause.*) By a mob.

Deshar Tibetans . . . Tibetans attacked a school?

Ling A mob did. Every revolution has its mob.

Deshar *closes her eyes and prays.*

Ling Do you realize what kind of sin are you accumulating? In just this week, there have been eighteen arrests just in the women's cell for self-immolation, and eight we couldn't even save. You . . . you are responsible for all this.

Silence.

Deshar *closes her eyes.*

Ling You really want me to believe, that out of the blue, a month after your nunnery was broken, that to build a hospital, one day you suddenly realized the plight of the Tibetan people and burnt yourself?

Deshar I burnt long ago. In my mind. In the mind, is where it matters. (*Pause.*) And the re-education. What is that? What kind of education disrobes one's teachers, insult's one's companions, destroys places of education . . . I had no other choice.

Ling And now you feel like talking?

Silence.

Deshar In the interrogation, he was threatening. I am not afraid of threats. I am talking because you are . . .

Ling *takes out an ointment and gently applies it on* **Deshar***'s legs.* **Deshar** *does not move. They look at each other.*

Deshar You are struggling.

Ling What do you want?

Deshar What do you want?

Ling I don't want anything. Just heal and go. Get out. If you heal, this insanity will stop.

Deshar You don't like the sight of burnt people.

Ling *gets up and looks at* **Deshar** *in surprise.*

Ling I am touching your wounds, nun Deshar. Don't dismiss the benevolence of the ordinary. Put yourself in my shoes. Three nuns died on the chair today. In front of my eyes. Just out of burns. I saw the torture of Tibetan men whose back was broken with steel boards. You think this is easy? Is it easy for us?

Deshar Then why are you doing it?

Ling Orders. The men were reactionaries.

Silence. She applies the ointment again.

Deshar I don't understand.

Ling What?

Deshar How do you know they are burning in my name?

Ling They are carrying pictures.

Deshar Of?

Ling Yours and the Dalai Lama's.

Silence.

Deshar Buddhism forbids /

Ling Doesn't Buddhism forbid killing oneself?

Deshar *is silent.*

Deshar You are pure.

Ling Everyone is pure. People don't need to burn themselves to prove it.

Deshar I did not do it on anyone's instructions.

Ling *remains quiet. Keeps applying the ointment and dressing her wounds.* **Deshar** *keeps looking at her.*

Deshar I did not receive any orders from His Holiness' office or the monastery. I just lit up. I did not burn. And everyone else is becoming this light, in these times of darkness.

Silence.

Constable Ling . . . I promise, on the Buddha. I did not /

Ling *is about to slap* **Deshar** *but stops herself. Hits the wheelchair instead.* **Deshar** *screams.*

Ling   Couldn't you have said this in the bloody interrogation room? At least this, the polygraph would have recorded it. I could have saved you.

Deshar   My denial would not mean a thing.

Ling   How do you know? Are we maniacs? We interrogate 800 people every year . . . do you realize 800 at least on that chair. We need to change the chair every month, because it breaks! Do you believe we cannot tell when someone is telling the truth and when someone is not?

Deshar   I burnt my body, to present my mind. There was no other way.

Ling   I can't change your mind. Have the pills. Heal your body.

Deshar   Let me die. I will pray that it heals your mind.

Ling   Deshar, I don't know what will happen to you and me. But the truth is that Han and Tibetan children are growing up together now. They cannot be burning in a school for the differences of their previous generations.

Deshar   Our children have no choices. My father fought against all the odds to raise me by himself.

Ling   Your Pah-la has been arrested today. He is in the prison next door.

Silence.

Deshar   I don't mean anything to him. Let him go.

Pause.

Deshar   Ling.

Ling   Yes

Deshar   Why does the commander not go to find his daughter?

Ling   He cannot. The Party won't let him.

Deshar   And you?

Ling   What?

Deshar   Will it let you?

Silence.

Ling   Are you going to take the pills?

Deshar   Is it going to make you less angry?

Ling *gives* **Deshar** *the pills.*

Deshar   If I die, will it stop?

Ling   What?

Deshar The arrests and the torture?

Ling If you tell the truth, it will.

Pause.

Deshar The Truth. To a machine that believes silence is a lie.

Ling Every god has his rules. Yours believes the truth is fire. Mine believes falsity a beep.

Deshar I will speak.

Ling Here.

Deshar *takes the medicines.*

Deshar Have you seen him?

Ling Whom?

Deshar Pah-la.

Ling Every father whose daughter is in a prison cell looks the same. I might have. But I can't tell. I can't tell anymore.

Scene Three

Inspector **Deng**'s *office.* **Tsering** *is standing next to a chair. Constable* **Gaphel** *is in the room.*

Gaphel Water?

Tsering (*looks at him in surprise*) Hospitality?

Gaphel *keeps some water in front of* **Tsering**.

Gaphel Are you OK, Commander?

Tsering Beads?

Gaphel I am Buddhist.

Pause.

Gaphel

Pause. **Tsering** *looks at* **Gaphel** *carefully.*

Gaphel I was with you, Commander Tsering, don't you recognize me?

Pause.

Gaphel (*even more cautiously*) Do you recognize me?
I am Gaphel . . . you remember we were going to train together? You went and I did not?

Tsering Why didn't you train?

Gaphel (*silence*) I was afraid. I did not have the courage to join the fighters in the end.

Pause.

Tsering Why have I been arrested?

Gaphel Your daughter.

Tsering I heard she burnt herself?

Gaphel Yes.

Tsering So?

Gaphel For interrogation.

Tsering I have not seen her in years. Ever since she became a nun.

Gaphel We want to ask some basic questions.

Tsering Like?

Gaphel The truth.

Tsering The truth? (*Pause.*)

Gaphel About who made her do this?

Tsering You . . . or him. (*Pointing at a portrait of Mao Tse Tung.*)

Pause.

Tsering I do not know anything. Whatever your name is. May I go now? I have students waiting.

Gaphel What do you teach?

Tsering The truth.

Beat.

Gaphel I meant which subject?

Tsering Tibetan.

Gaphel Where?

Tsering In a school. I run from home.

Gaphel I tried to reach you. You weren't there

Tsering When?

Gaphel I came with the unit.

Tsering Now?

Gaphel For . . . re-education.

Tsering On the train, I presume?

Pause.

Gaphel Yes.

Tsering You burnt her.

Pause. **Tsering** *drinks water.*

Gaphel Your daughter's . . . burning . . . has caused protests in Lhasa. People are on the streets. And. (*Pause.*) And in one instance they have burnt a school.

Tsering I wouldn't know. I live in my province.

Gaphel In your province, five others have self-immolated in these years. She is the first of the nuns.

Tsering Is that the new name for it? Good. I wouldn't know, I don't go out much.

Gaphel You do realize, Commander, that she started it?

Tsering Oh . . . that's generous. I thought Mao Tse Tung did.

Gaphel Do you know if she received orders from anyone?

Tsering I don't.

Gaphel Didn't she meet you one last time . . . before /

Tsering I don't meet nuns and monks. No matter who they are.

Gaphel So, you are not a practicing Buddhist?

Tsering I am the only one.

Pause.

Gaphel Commander . . . do you realize that this is a big crime? Treason? They won't let you go easily. You must co operate.

Tsering They? Who's they? And why are you calling me Commander? What am I commanding?

Gaphel I am Gaphel, Commander. From your own village. Your childhood . . . You don't recognize me?

Tsering And you work for the parasites now? Brilliant.

Sorry . . . I do not recognize you. I do not recognize the Chinese state, the Chinese army, the Chinese government, Chinese products, Chinese flag, Chinese Olympics but most of all I do not recognize Tibetans who did not have the courage.

Long pause. **Tsering** *stares at* **Gaphel***.*

Gaphel This won't help.

Tsering What?

Gaphel You need to cooperate.

Tsering For what?

Gaphel   To be free.

Tsering   Free. If I cooperate, we will be free? Fine, I'll cooperate. Please let me know when is this freedom due though.

Gaphel   I meant leave the prison?

Tsering   Oh . . . that. You call that, walking around and shopping and visiting Nangma bars, freedom. That one.

Gaphel   Your daughter gave her life, Commander, for /

Tsering   I don't care about what monks and nuns do.

Gaphel   If you tell us what we need to know.

Tsering   I don't understand. What do you want me to tell you?

Gaphel   They want you to tell us if she received orders from . . .

Silence.

Tsering *looks at him.*

Gaphel *looks around. Takes out a picture of the Dalai Lama from an inner pocket in his coat and shows it to* **Tsering**.

Tsering (*laughs*)   You are afraid to say his name in your own office.

Gaphel   We turned non-violent when he ordered, Commander. The Party wants to know if this time he has ordered the violence.

Tsering   Violence. His Holiness. Is my god. I do not agree with him, but he is my god. I do not agree because there is no one more Marxist than His Holiness the Dalai Lama, who let his own troops die in the middle of nowhere. Even Chairman Mao loved his own. We had the Americans on our side. We could have been free by now. That was our best chance. Not this . . . not this BULL SHIT. (*Bangs the table in anger.*)

Gaphel   We were all wrong, Commander.
You are a Buddhist, and the Buddha proposed a middle path. And so does His Holiness. The middle path is your Dharma . . . your way of life /

Tsering   Middle path it is. Here I am, the ordinary Tibetan, bang in the middle of the god of compassion and the god of land rights . . . the Monk and the Marxist, (*looking at the picture of Dalai Lama and Mao*) bang in the middle of two absolutely genuine, well-meaning, peaceful people, wanting to liberate me!

Gaphel   You do not really believe, Commander Tsering, that the guerillas could have won over the Chinese in the guerilla war, do you? A few men trained in Colorado by the CIA, form an army of Khampas, a nomadic tribe for all practical purposes, and takes on the People's Liberation Army. What are the chances, that we would have won?

Tsering   And now . . . have we won? With our lamas leading our political thought, have we found what we were looking for?

Gaphel We have the Tibetan Government in Exile, commander. With the lamas leading from the front, or rather just one lama, His Holiness, you have the Tibetan culture intact.

Tsering Culture . . . of course. Of course, we have culture, because our children are brought up in other countries, watch Tibetan dance once in a while and sometime between drugs and sex even manage to turn that odd prayer wheel!

Gaphel I am talking about the government in /

Tsering And of course, we have the government in EXILE. What does that even mean, the government in exile.

Gaphel It means, when we get our land back, we will already have a democratic way of life in place. A foolproof plan for the future.

Tsering So, we have decided the colour of the walls of the imaginary house that we are going to build, on a patch of land that we do not own. The shape and size of the parliament, mind you, are all in place. Rejoice, Tibetans, your holiness has given you blueprints for science fiction. You have many lives, this time, placate yourself with the Nobel Prize, and after three lives, if you are still unfortunate enough to be Tibetan, come back for your democracy.

Gaphel His Holiness is doing the best he can.

Tsering *begins to laugh.*

Tsering I am really enjoying this. Now you, a bloody Chinese agent, is telling me that 'His Holiness' is doing the best he can . . . His Holiness called our movement off, you idiot. I was there in the room, in Mustang in Nepal, with the commanders. I heard the tape that His Holiness sent to order us to call of the movement. We are turning non-violent . . . Thank you. We are turning non-violent mind you . . . we were not . . . we were not convinced about non-violence earlier . . . but we took a little time, thank you very much, so drop your guns, walk back like little boys from the park and, oh yes, I will tell my elder brother, the one who started this, to just forget about it, and get back to teaching some more fluff in a university in some other country. You people can just shoot yourself.

In front of me, the two commanders shot themselves, you son of a bitch. They shot themselves because you do not start a guerilla war and turn non-violent on the men who are out there in the front! That . . . THAT is violence.
And cowards like you, Gaphel, will do anything, side with anyone to make a life.

Gaphel Commander Tsering! Stop judging me. Just look at what you have done to yourself.

Tsering I have not done this to myself . . . the two of you have. You and this lama.

Gaphel We have to stop these protests, Commander. If the army comes in there will be mass murder.

Tsering What's new? What else can the PLA do?

Gaphel I am for the middle path, Commander. His Holiness has asked for the middle path, I am with. (*Pause.*) Even I am for the revolution but /

Tsering You want a revolution, but you want chants to beat atomic bombs and automatic machine guns. The communists can only be defeated by the Americans, and that was our only real chance.

Gaphel There is no revolution, Commander. There is none. You swear by the Americans but everyone knows that we are nothing. Nothing on the face of the planet. The Americans are nobodies. They are loyal to none.

Tsering They were loyal to us, you bastard.

Gaphel You are wrong, Commander. Absolutely wrong.

If we had oil, the whole world would be fighting for us. You think the Americans care about our democracy and our Dalai Lama. They don't give a damn. Their film stars love our fluff, and they sell dumplings on the streets of New York with an imaginary snow lion flag on weekends, to relieve themselves of their moral burden. The Americans are imperialists Monday to Friday. On Saturday they want to save the world and on Sunday they go to church.

You want liberation . . . true liberation. Look for oil in Tibet. You will have American warships in our lakes. You want good music? . . . go ahead, fight for a free Tibet. Violently or non-violently.

Deng *walks in.* **Gaphel** *is startled. Quickly puts the picture away. Salutes.*

Deng *looks at* **Tsering**. *He remains seated.*

Deng (*to* **Gaphel**) Is there a problem, Constable?

Gaphel No . . . no, sir.

Deng Is he an old . . . friend or . . .

Gaphel No . . . no, sir.

Deng I am inspector Deng. Head. On deputation. Is that clear? What's with your daughter?

Tsering *remains quiet.*

Deng She didn't meet you before burning?

Pause.

No. I know you were a shit soldier from your files, are you a shit father as well?

Tsering *remains quiet.*

Deng I saw her.

Pause.

Deng Yes. And while she was being asked questions, she said Pah-la . . . Pah-la . . . that's why we got you.

Tsering You interrogated her?

Deng On life support. We want the truth.

Tsering You killed her!

Deng No.

Silence.

Tsering (*now almost in tears*)   Where is she?

Deng *takes out his phone. Shows him a picture.*

Deng Is this her?

Tsering *lets out a scream of horror. He is now in tears.*

Tsering Deshar . . .

Deng Now can we stop being smart and get on with what you know?

Tsering I want to see her . . . please . . . I want to.

Deng *shows him another picture.* **Tsering** *looks at it and looks at him.*

Deng That's my daughter. Liu. Eight years old. Missing for a week! I brought her up by myself like you brought yours up. And I want to see her, you asshole.

Silence.

Put him in the cell. Tomorrow morning, I want him in the room.

Goes close to **Tsering**.

Pray . . . pray that I find my daughter. Pray.

Scene Four

Late night.

Ling *is in the playground of the school. School bags, lunch boxes, water bottles are strewn around. Ribbons of little girls have fallen. Some of them are still tied to chunks of hair.*

A **Man** *with a stick is rummaging through it. He is picking up hair and putting it in a plastic bag.*

Man Police?

Ling *looks at her uniform. Takes off her batch and puts it in her pocket.*

Man Good. It's too late for the police. (*Pause.*) Your girl?

Ling

Man What?

110   Pah-La (Father)

Ling   No.

Man

Ling   Yes. Yes.

Man *looks at her curiously.*

Man   Some of them went there. Do you see that truck? It dropped them somewhere and came back.

Ling   Some?

Man   Yes. Some. Others . . . you can see can't you. (*Looking around.*)

Ling   My daughter runs quite fast.

Man   Faster than the others, I hope.

Ling   This? Here . . . this one . . .

Man   What is it?

Ling   It's her water bottle.

Man   Are you sure?

Ling   Yes. I think so. (*Looks at it curiously.*)

Man   Has a boy's name on it.

Ling   Where?

Man   Here, at the back.

Ling   Oh . . . yes.

Man   I hope you do not find any of her belongings here.

Ling   Why?

Man   Would mean she was not in danger, isn't it?

Ling   True.

(*Pause.*) Tell me where the /

Man   Take off your uniform.

Ling   What?

Man   I don't want to do any more favours on the police. Even if it is your child.

Ling   I don't have any /

Man (*loudly*)   Take off your uniform, I said!

Pause.

Ling   I am married.

Man   I don't want to marry you /

Ling Aren't you Buddhist?

Man Oh yes . . . here. (*Shows her beads.*)

Ling So, what about.

Man Listen . . . I don't want a moral lesson right now. There's enough of that in my life. My mind's buzzing with the moral theories of an ascetic. This . . . look. This is real life. You fuck with us, we fuck back with you.

Ling But.

Man You have a problem taking your clothes off in front of me. You have no problems stripping Tibetan nuns and inserting electric rods into them?

Silence.

You have no problem driving nails into people's heads? No problem in working with men who rape Tibetan women day in and out?
You have a problem in taking off your uniform in front of me, is it?

Ling I didn't do those things.

Man If three Tibetans who attacked a school are all the Tibetans, then I am afraid an army full of torturers cannot exclude you.

Pause.

Ling OK . . . so once I take my uniform off, you will give me the address?

Man Swear on the Buddha.

Ling *undresses.*

Ling I am ready.

Man Do you have . . . some . . . lipstick maybe?

Ling *looks a him in horror. Takes out her lipstick. Applies it. Throws it away.*

Man How will you go back?

Ling The way I came.

Man Is it quieter now?

Ling In some parts of the city.

Man I have never slept with a policewoman. That and the lipstick. It's something.

Ling Are you going to /

Man You tell me.

Ling What?

Man A violence that I am allowed. And I'll do that to you.

Ling *stands quietly.*

Man   And yet you are allowed everything?

Spread your legs.

Ling *does so.*

Man   Moan. Just a little, it turns me on. I am quite old you see. Becomes difficult.

Ling . . . *looks at him in disbelief.*

Ling   You want me to moan?

Man   Yes . . . yes . . . that would be nice. If you moan now, eventually it will be easier for you.

Ling   This is . . . This . . .

Man   I know. I know.

Ling   Can you keep your beads away at least.

Man   Oh why. How does it matter to you?

Ling   I am feeling more for them than you are, clearly.

Man   I am chanting. I am in. Not a moment when I do not remind myself to keep calm, love everyone, take responsibility for my actions and all that. Moan, come on.

Ling *moans.*

The **Man** *collects some more hair in his plastic bag. Walks down to* **Ling***. The* **Man** *falls and starts to cry.* **Ling** *looks at him.*

Man   Why are you doing this? Why are all of you doing this to us?

Ling *bends down. Holds him.*

Man   Give me a violence. Oh Buddha. Grant me one violence at least today grant me one /

Ling *suddenly spots something. Picks it up.*

Ling   This is . . . her diary. See . . . it has her name.

Man   Oh . . . let me see.

Ling   I know it . . . here . . . this is her . . .

Man   Oh . . . that's not good then.

Ling   What?

Man   If you get the diary.

Ling   Why?

Man   It means her bag was opened. As in there was time . . . I have to give you the other address now.

Ling   What other address?

Man Where those who were killed were dumped.

Ling What!

Man What else do you think everyone was running from?

Ling Why on earth would Buddhists kill children?

Man Those who killed were Buddhists? And those who are all over the city. Dying non-violently? Are they not Buddhists?

(*Pause.*) There were some people here trying to take their children out when the protests started. Your police . . . you . . . you attacked them and some of them locked the gates and retaliated. You know who saved the children?

Ling Who?

Man Us. Us other Buddhists. You are not making it easier to remain a Buddhist in this country!

Ling I cannot believe people attacked the school.

Man Your police attacked the people first. You have made violence normal. You are only surprised that it's against you.

Ling I have never hurt anyone.

Man I know. I know. I am saying you. I need a face to accuse. I have to live.

Pause.

Ling What's the address?

Man Sorry?

Ling The other address. Where those who were killed . . .

She sits down distraught with herself, holding on to the diary.

Man I came here two weeks ago. You are coming too late.

Ling Don't you work here?

Man No.

Ling Then?

Man My daughter was in this school too. My only daughter. She was all I had.

Ling Why did Tibetans attack Tibetan children?

Man Violence doesn't have a religion. It doesn't differentiate between children.

Pause.

Ling Your daughter?

Man I have found some of her hair. She had beautiful hair. It's in the bag.

They are quiet.

Man   Our children played together. See . . . maybe some of this belongs to your child. (*Shows her the bag and puts her hand in.*)

They embrace. Both of them cry holding each other.

Scene Five

Polygraph room. Dimly lit.

Deng *sits shocked in a chair.* **Ling** *is sitting holding his hand.*

Tsering *is brought in by* **Gaphel**. *He goes close to* **Deshar** *who is in a chair connected to a polygraph machine on the other side of the room.*

Deshar *has a butter lamp in her hands. Silence as* **Tsering** *looks at* **Deshar**.

Deshar *smiles.*

Tsering   Get alright and we will go home in three days. OK?

They laugh.

Tsering   OK . . . just get alright.

Deshar   How are you, Pah-la?

Tsering   Good. Healthy. Next door. Thank god for 'the system' else we could not have met.

Ling *walks up to them.*

Deshar   Meet Ling . . .

Pause.

She is a Buddha of the highest order. A revolutionary.

Deshar *smiles.*

Tsering *looks at* **Ling**. *Folds his hand in gratitude.* **Ling** *looks at him. Pause.*

Deshar   It was my decision to burn, Pah-la.

Tsering (*looking away*)   Yes.

Deshar   I burnt out of love, Pah-la. Not hatred.

Pause.

And if I feel so passionately, does it make me a lesser Buddhist, Pah-la?

Pause.

Tsering   I don't know, my dear . . . I don't know. To feel strongly is life. Is to be human. If a greater Buddhist is a lesser Human Being, then Buddhism must be thought out again. But you are not a lesser anything, my child . . . you are a giant. A giant from the roof of the world.

They smile.

Deshar Do you see why I did it, Pah-la?

Pause. **Tsering** *remains quiet and looks at her.*

Deshar I did not do it out of hatred, Pah-la.

Tsering *gets up from the chair annoyed. Walks away. Tries to calm himself, comes back and sits down.*

Deshar Hold this. (*Gives him the butter lamp.*)

Tsering *looks at her curiously and holds it.*

Tsering *looks at her.*

Deshar This is Amahla. Tell her you love her.

Tsering *keeps it back.*

Deshar Please, Pah-la.

Tsering *looks at* **Deshar***. Picks up the butter lamp.*

Pause.

Tsering (*looking at the lamp*) You . . . are my wife, and one day we will have a beautiful daughter together.

Deshar Tell her anything else you want to tell her. Look . . . she is dying, on a winter night, in the middle of snow. Right in front of the Buddha statue in our house, she is dying in your arms.

Pause.

Tsering Do you know what she said to me in the end?

Deshar No

Tsering I went to see His Holiness, not because I didn't believe in your revolution. But because I want to save Deshar from hatred.

Deshar And you?

Tsering (*still looking at the butter lamp*) Live. Please live. We saved her. Look. (*Pause.*) She bled to death on this arm. On the other arm, you slept. We had to save your life, Deshar.

Deshar I am sorry, Pah-la. My anger had blinded me.

Pause.

Tsering Will you please . . . please . . . please live, my child? Please . . . I have no one else.

Deshar You see this lamp, Pah-la . . . It will go on for a little longer . . . But when it extinguishes, the light of this moment goes off but it makes way for the light of the next.

Every moment this light is changing . . . it is new light every minute moment, the last light making way for the next.

If I die, Pah-la, something new will come by.

Tsering Then all of us should die my child . . . everyone should make way for the next. The old should die first, the young should live. Isn't that how the world is supposed to be?

Deshar The world is in our minds, Pah-la. It is a construction of our thoughts. It is neither meant to be one way or another. The world, Pah-la . . . is what it is . . .

Pause.

Do you know what were Rinpoche's last words?

Tsering

Deshar Leave Deshar and ask the Buddha to forgive me, my child. There was a moment when I almost hated Inspector Deng.

Silence.

Tsering (*goes up to her kneels on the floor and holds her hand*)   Live, my child . . . please . . . please live.

Deshar I am not brave enough to live with the burns, Pah-la . . . I am not enlightened.

Deng *comes closer. He looks at* **Ling**. *Signals her to leave. She bows in front of* **Deshar**, *kisses her hands. Looks at* **Deng**.

Ling For the motherland, comrade. For the motherland.

Deng I'm going to kill them. Kill both /

Ling It has to stop, Commander. This circle of violence. It has to /

Deng You can leave, Constable Ling. Your shift is over.

Ling Commander please . . . let me.

Deng It's an order. (*Says loudly.*)

Ling *softly holds his hand.*

Ling I am sorry for what happened, Commander. But remember everyone who did it was a father. Those who killed were fathers. Those who saved were fathers. The Chinese and the Tibetan fathers. Mao Tse Tung, a father. Dalai Lama, a father. Fathers of a people . . . fathers of a nation. Maybe that is the problem, Commander. There are too many fathers steering its future.

Deng *looks at* **Ling**.

Deng You may leave. They killed/

Ling No, Commander. The police attacked the school first.

Ling *takes out her badge. Hands it to him. Leaves.*

Harsh lights are switched on.

Deng   The Truth.

Pause.

Tonight. We . . .

Pause.

Deng (*goes to* **Deshar**)   My daughter Liu, is dead. Burnt by your people.

Deshar *shuts her eyes and prays.*

Deshar   I am sorry, Commander Deng. I am sorry for your loss. May that beautiful child not have suffered in the end.

Deng   You killed her.

Deshar   If taking my life, relieves you of your suffering, I am prepared.

Deng   Why did you burn yourself?

Deshar   To find a way of making my voice heard without hurting another sentient being.

Deng   My daughter isn't a sentient being?

Deshar   She is. We shouldn't turn violent.

Deng   You do not understand Liberation?

Deshar   Your way out of suffering is to liberate the outside. Mine, of liberating the inside. Our ways do not have to be at war with each other.

Deng   Can you bring my child back?

Deshar

Deng   If there is a god, can you do it?

Deshar   My god is a doctor of the mind.

Deng   Bring back my child. I will let you go.

Deshar

Deng   Pray for her to come back to life, I will stop the killings in interrogation room. Give her life and I will /

Deshar   If I could bring her to life, I wouldn't need you to do anything for it, Commander Deng, her death has made the world poorer.

Deng *sits on the floor. Next to* **Deshar***'s feet. Cries.* **Deshar** *holds him.*

His phone rings. He looks at it. Picks up the call.

Deng   Yes. Yes, comrade. Thank you, comrade. (*Pause.*) I have the prisoners here, comrade. Yes. (*Pause. Gets up.*) Where, comrade? Yes . . . (*Pause.*) Send them, comrade. All of them. For the motherland.

He looks at **Deshar**.

Deng   The party won't stop. Tibet will never be free.

Deshar   The evil in this world is ours. Yours and mine.

Deng   You are so full of empty wisdom. All of you should be shot dead.

Deng *picks out his gun. Points at* **Deshar**.

Tsering *is in shock.* **Gaphel** *immediately stops* **Deng**.

Gaphel   Commander . . . Commander, we cannot shoot her, Commander. We are in the polygraph room, we have orders to not do anything without the test. If she tells the truth, she can go, Commander. We cannot /

Deng   So, you are on their side now?

Gaphel   I am on the side of the people, Commander.

Deng   The People. Fine.

Pause.

Deng   Let's play a game. A Truth game. One of you sits on the chair . . . and we turn the polygraph on. Except that you play for the other.

I will ask you two simple questions. If it does not beep, it will be alright and the person you play for can go. It's a fair game. Not dependent on my judgement of you or your judgement of you. I am a Marxist, and I will keep my word. But if you are still lying, then the blood of a reactionary will be on your hands. So here you are, you can be free, unless you want not to be free. That's a different matter, if you ask for imprisonment, then we will have to kill you . . . because we need space.
Does that seem fair, Constable Gaphel?

Gaphel *remains quiet.*

Tsering   When I was a soldier, we fought like men. And here you are, sitting under the umbrella of the world's largest army and playing prison games. This is the fairness of the communists.

Tsering *gets up and sits on the chair.*

Deng   We'll have the nun first on the chair.

Gaphel *tentatively connects her to the controls.*

Deng   That measures the dilation of pupils, that your heart beat, and that one your sweat. Nothing . . . scientifically escapes this. This is why you need communism. Science.

Is there anything in Buddhism that can replace this nun Deshar?

Deshar   No. There isn't, Commander Deng. But, we are looking for different things.

Deng   I thought we are both looking for the truth.

Deshar   You are looking for the liar. We are looking for the intention of the lie.

Deng *looks at her sternly.*

Deng Two questions. One beep and you lose your father.

Deshar I am ready.

Deng Are you responsible for the death of my daughter, Liu?

Silence.

Are you responsi /

Gaphel This isn't a polygraph question, Commander.

Deng *gestures towards him to remain quiet.*

Deshar We are all responsible for every injustice that happens in this world. In this 'Samsara', the cycle of /

Deng I am asking you a yes or no question. I am not in your nunnery, you are in my prison.

Deshar *remains quiet.*

Deng Are you responsible for the death of my daughter Liu or not?

Deshar Every person in this room is responsible . . . yes, I am.

The green light on the polygraph glows. Does not beep.

Deng *looks at* **Tsering**.

Deng You are?

Deshar Everyone is. (*Pause.*) I am sorry. (*She looks at the green light.* **Deng** *looks at it.*)

Deng Did you receive orders from His Holiness the Dalai Lama from India to burn yourself? Directly or indirectly.

Deshar I did not.

The green light glows. No beep.

Deng You are free, Tsering. You may leave.

Tsering (*goes close to the interrogation chair*) Connect the wires to me. I am ready. (*Pause.* **Deng** *looks at him sternly.*)

Deng For what?

Tsering To play your game.

Deng The game is for prisoners. You are free.

Tsering It wasn't when you started.

Deng Yes, but now you are. We don't have anyone to play for the nun.

Silence.

Deng You should know what it means to lose your child.

Deshar (*with her eyes shut*) Don't hate him, Pah-la . . . don't hate him.

Pause.

Gaphel You cannot do this, Commander. The party does not allow you to change the rules!

Deng THE PARTY DID NOT ALLOW ME TO SAVE MY CHILD! THE PARTY CANNOT FORCE ME TO SAVE THEIR'S.

Gaphel You are a Marxist, Commander. You cannot /

Tsering *takes* **Gaphel***'s gun and points at* **Deng***, immediately* **Deng** *draws his gun and points back.*

Gaphel Commander. (*To* **Tsering**.) Keep your gun down, Commander. Commander please.

Tsering She hasn't lied, Deng. Not even once. You have no case. Let her go.

Deng Shoot.

Silence.

He lowers his gun slightly.

Shoot.

Deshar Pah-la, please put your gun /

Tsering I won't miss.

Deng I know. Shoot.

Gaphel Keep your gun down, Commander. (*To* **Deng**.) He won't.

Tsering I am sorry for the death of your child, Deng. If I were there, I would give up my life to protect her.

Deng You and I are violent men, Tsering

Tsering We have let our children down already. Now let her go.

Deng We are both bad fathers. In this world, fathers should not be ideological.

Tsering My daughter, is the last of her kind, Deng. A revolutionary who does not hate the oppressor. Without her, what world will you leave for your children?

Deng I don't have my child. I have no world to leave for anyone.

Tsering Revenge is not revolution, Deng.

Deng Revenge is not revolution. Write that on the epitaph of my daughter's murderers.

Tsering You cannot leave me out in the world and kill my daughter here, Deng. You cannot give me that freedom!

Tsering *moves forward to attack him without shooting.* **Deng** *holds him. A moment of silence.* **Deng** *shoots.* **Deshar** *screams.* **Gaphel** *closes his eyes.* **Tsering** *falls.*

Silence.

Gaphel (*takes out his badge, throws it on the floor in front of* **Deng***. Sits on the chair*)   I, I will play for the nun . . . Ask . . .

Pause.

Deng   I'll play for the nun Gaphel. You take your commander out of this hell.

Pause.

I'll play.

Gaphel *gets up, goes to* **Tsering***'s body, holds him tightly and cries sitting down.* **Deng** *sits at the chair.*

Deng   We cannot escape the system.

Deshar   We will all be free, Deng. What will become of you?

Deng   Help me . . . Bring back my . . .

Deshar   If my death gives you comfort. I am ready.

Deng   I'll play for you. Like your father would. (*Pause.*) You ask. I will tell the truth. I promise.

Deshar   The Truth.

She smiles.

Deng   Yes, the clear, objective, truth. (*Pause.*) Ask.

Deshar   The Blacksmith comes to the Buddha while he is in his death bed. He asks the Buddha to bring his dead child to life and says, if you are enlightened, bring my child back to life.

The Buddha realizes that the imposter is now, indeed a blacksmith and asks him to sit next to his bed. The Buddha has two seeds in his fist. One which can bring the child back to her recent life and give her the suffering of death all over again. Another which makes the Blacksmith realize that there is no magic in the first seed, and the child in fact continues to live in the way the Blacksmith lives with the other children in the kingdom. Which seed should the Blacksmith take?

Deng   Liu . . . (*Looks at her picture and cries.*)

Deshar   Deng. My voice has been heard. Relieve me.

Pause.

Deng   Ask.

Deshar   If you had to tell her the truth about how far can violence go, would you tell her the truth? Would you tell her the truth about violence?

Deng *looks at her . . . Silence.*

Deng   Yes, I would. I would tell her the truth about violence. (*The beeps come on, the red light switches on.*)

Silence.

Deshar   Relieve me, Inspector Deng. The truth has been recorded.

Deng *falls on the floor in exhaustion, next to* **Gaphel**. *Takes out his gun and points to* **Deshar**. *Gunshot. Blackout.*

On projection we see the list of all those who have self-immolated with the music. Actors arrive on stage and arrange butter lamps again.

End of play.

Djinns of Eidgah

Djinns of Eidgah opened at Rage Production's Writers' Bloc 3 Festival on 12 January, 2012 at the Prithvi Theatre, Mumbai. The Writers' Bloc 3 plays were mentored by Elyse Dodgson, Carl Miller and April de Angelis.

Original Cast and Crew

Director	Richard Twyman
Set Design	Payal Wadhwa
Production Design and Execution	Shama Shah
Light Design	Pushan Kripalani and Arghya Lahiri
On Lights	Yael Crishna
Music Producer	Taufiq Qureshi
Music Assistant	Gautam Sharma and Prathamesh Kandalkar
On Sound	Nadir Khan
Costume	Lovleen Bains
Make-up	Nandu Wadke
Production Team	Ayaz Ansari and Shazneen Acharia

The Cast Adhir Bhat, Ali Fazal, Ashwin Mushran, Divyang Thakkar, Faezeh Jalali Karan Pandit, Meher Acharia-Dar, Neil Bhoopalam, Rajit Kapur

The play was also presented at the Royal Court, London, between 18 October and 9 November, 2013 as part of International Playwrights: A Genesis Foundation Project, with additional support from the British Council.

Cast and Crew of Royal Court production

Director	Richard Twyman
Designer	Tom Scutt
Lighting Designer	Natasha Chivers
Composer	Benedict Taylor

The Cast Amit Chana, Ayesha Dharker, Aysha Kala, Danny Ashok, Jaz Deol, Nikesh Patel, Paul Bazley, Raj Bajaj, Vincent Ebrahim

Our grateful thanks to Bunty Walia and Mehraaj-ud-deen Wali.
A Rage Production, presented by JSW and The Bajaj Group in association with the British Council and the Royal Court Theatre.

Characters
Abbajan, *old Kashmiri man. Ashrafi and Bilal's father*
Ashrafi, *young Kashmiri girl. Bilal's sister*
Bilal, *Kashmiri man in his early twenties. Aspiring footballer. Ashrafi's elder brother*
Djinn, *an apparition of people killed, takes shape of various characters in the play*
Dr Baig, *experienced male doctor. Head of the local hospital*
Dr Wani, *young female doctor. Works with Dr Baig*
Khaled, *Kashmiri man in his early twenties. Aspiring footballer. Bilal's friend and teammate*
Mushtaq, *aspiring footballer, slightly older than Bilal and Khaled. Captain of their team*
Soldier 1, *Indian soldier from Central Reserve Police Force (CRPF), posted in Kashmir*
Soldier 2, *Indian soldier from CRPF, posted in Kashmir. Slightly younger than Soldier 1*

For Dr Mushtaq Margoob and his team of doctors in Kashmir.

For the Children of the Valley

In memory of Gautam Paul Bhattacharjee

'Gar firdaus bar roo-e zameen ast, Hameen ast-o hameen ast-o hameen ast.'
(If there is a paradise on earth, it is here, it is here, it is here)
Emperor Jahangir on Kashmir, quoting the Sufi poet Amir Khusro

Acknowledgements

Djinns of Eidgah has had a long journey and in this journey it has collected several debts. Many people have made the play possible and although it might not be possible to have everyone's name here as the playwright I am deeply indebted to all those voices who made this voice possible.

Thanks to Rajit Kapur for making this possible. Without him nothing would have happened.

To Shernaz Patel and Rahul da Cunha and everyone else at Rage Theatre. To all the other writers of Writers' Bloc at Vasind. This play is yours. Special thanks to Irawati Karnik for being a wonderful friend and a constant dramaturg.

Thanks to Anmol Vellani and Sunil Shanbagh for giving it direction that only they could have at an early stage.

Thanks to Syed Humayoun, Showkat Motta, Dr Ashraf, Dr Mushtaq Margoob, Dr Amit Sen, Dr Shalija Sen, Irfan Hasan, Ishfaq Hussain, Ashwath Bhat, Anand Vivek Taneja, Bilal, Khalid Wasim, Rizwaan Khan.

Thanks to Dr Hameedah Nayeem for being such an inspiration.

Special thanks to Rukmini Sen and Suvojit Bagchi.

Thanks to those three CRPF soldiers who cannot be named. No one can share their lives like you did.

Thanks to those countless freedom fighters who again cannot be named. No one can share their life like you did as well.

Thanks to Carl Miller for being the greatest friend a writer can have.

Thanks to Elyse Dodgson for believing in it much before I did. Thanks to Vicky Featherstone for being the dramaturg that she is. Special thanks to Richard Twynman for going through all the highs and lows of this play for two years.

Thanks Richard for your mind and for your friendship. Special thanks to Ayesha Dharker for all the love and thought she has given to this play over the years. Thanks to all the actors in London who have informed this play through the workshops and in the production at the Royal Court Theatre. This play could not have been written without your thoughts, ideas and embodiment of characters through the various stages of development.

Special thanks to the cast and crew of *Djinns of Eidgah* in Mumbai.

Special thanks to Mahmood Farooqui for reviving the Dastaan Goi. Special thanks to Sunil Khilnani for 'The Idea of India'.

Thanks to Joyeeta Bandyopadhyay, for being the first and most important storyteller in my life. To Pallavi Krishna for making the Dastaan worthwhile and for continuously nudging and guiding the play in several ways.

And finally, a very special thanks to Abbaji and Tabrez Alam. Without you, the world would not have revealed itself to us mortals. I hope wherever you are, you are resting in peace. Deeply indebted to you.

Note on the stage setting of the play: The settings of the rooms have been written keeping real rooms in mind. However, the play could be performed in an empty space with minimum and only the utmost essential of furniture.

Dr Baig's room could be done with just three chairs and a partition. **Ashrafi**'s house with only a mattress. The CRPF picket with only a picture of a god on a wall and barbed wire. The mortuary with many suggestions of bodies.

The playwright recommends maximum use of empty space and set-pieces that are almost transient in nature, as an essential ingredient of the play.

Scene One

A deep red Kashmiri carpet on stage. Another red carpet of exactly the same design but much larger suspended at an angle in the space. The carpets have floral designs on them. The carpet on the floor has **Abbajaan**, **Ashrafi** *and* **Bilal**, *sitting on their knees, looking at each other and smiling.* **Abbajaan** *is in his forties,* **Ashrafi** *is seven and* **Bilal** *is twelve. Their clothes are spotlessly white.*

There are two pillows on the carpet. One small and another slightly bigger. They are both green in colour with black lace-work around the borders of the pillows. The scene is lit in blue. The light must bounce off the clothes of the actors. The suspended carpet is lit to bring out the redness of the red.

Abbajaan *gestures to the children, suggesting that they should get their pillows. They get their pillows and put them on* **Abbajaan**'s *lap as he sits cross-legged. They lie down facing up, looking at him. He smiles.*

Abbajaan   Which one?

Ashrafi   The one in which . . . the one about Hamza and the flying lamps.

Bilal   No . . . no . . . no. (*Hits* **Ashrafi** *on the head.*) We just did that one yesterday. Abbu, the one in which Hamza tries to break the illusion . . .

Ashrafi (*hitting* **Bilal** *back*)   But Hamza tries to break the illusion in every dastaan!

Bilal   Yes, but he never succeeds, does he?

Abbajaan   OK . . . OK . . . OK . . . Shhh . . . Now both of you close your eyes . . . and we will see. If you sleep, we can have everything in our dastaan . . . The flying lamps and also Hamza trying to break the illusion of war . . . and if all goes well, insha'Allah, even succeeding at it.

Ashrafi (*smiling and excited*)   Really . . . Abbu . . . Can we have anything we want in our story?

Abbajaan: Yes anything. Anything that you want but only if you are good children . . . (*Like a proverb.*) If the children are good, the dastaan becomes the blanket.

Bilal *and* **Ashrafi** (*quickly shutting their eyes*)   And if the children are bad, the dastaan becomes the chilling wind . . .

Silence. **Abbajaan** *looks at them. The children pretend to shut their eyes but keep opening them to look at* **Abbajaan**. **Abbajaan** *looks at them and smiles. Looks up slowly.*

As he looks up, the children open their eyes as well and look at the ceiling.

Abbajaan   Dastaan . . . dastaan . . .

Bilal *and* **Ashrafi**   Dastaan . . . dastaan . . . (*They laugh out in excitement.*)

Abbajaan   Long, long ago . . . in a place that is much like today. In a place much like this, in the year of the Saturn . . . there lived the general of the prophet/

Bilal *and* **Ashrafi**   The king . . . the Prophet.

Beat.

Abbajaan   And there was his general.

Bilal   The gallant Amir Hamza.

Ashrafi (*pointing at* **Bilal**)
Hamzaaaaaaahhhh . . . (*She smiles.*)

Abbajaan   Shhh . . .

The children pretend to sleep again.

Abbajaan   . . . and Hamza, the general of the Army of the Prophet was fighting the army of the devil. . . . the evil Gulabuddin . . . a devil who claimed, that he . . . that he, may Allah forgive me . . . that he was Allah . . . And it was magicians battling magicians . . . and sorcerers fighting sorcerers, spells falling on spells and illusions creating more illusions . . . and the world was coming apart by the tricks and passions of the two armies . . . Hamza's and Gulabbudin's army of . . . (*He looks at the children, checking if they have slept.*)

Ashrafi   Of . . . Djinns . . . (*She smiles.*)

Abbajaan *softly taps her on the head.*

Abbajaan   Yes . . . of Djinns. Djinns . . . mighty creations of the Almighty . . . made of scorching smokeless fire . . . of pure passion and no reason . . . .

And the battle raged over red skies, fiery water, watery ice, green oceans, lavender mosques and a yellow . . . yellow . . . moon. And it was illusions fighting illusions, magicians battling magicians and Djinns ravaging Djinns.

And it is at this point in the battle that one night, Hamza's daughter, the little girl . . . the little girl Fatima came up to him, in his palace . . . and said, 'Abbajaan . . . my dear Abbajaan.' 'Fatima . . . my dear Fatima', replied Abbu.

'Abbu . . . my dear Abbu . . . my flying lamps have been stolen from the palace. I saw them move away last night, slowly, very slowly on their own . . . with no one visible . . . the lamps just went away one by one, over the ocean to some distant land and my room, Abbu, was plunged into darkness. So I ran to the window, Abbu, and looked at the ocean, which was the colour of moonlight. And slowly, very slowly, I saw the ocean recede, the ocean recede and the moon glide away. Glide away, away and far far away from the palace.
But just then two Djinns appeared, right in front of me.'

'Djinns,' said Amir Hamza.

'Yes, Djinns . . . Hafiz – Rafis. (**Abbu** *says this pointing at himself and* **Ashrafi**.) . . . Rafis – Hafiz. (*Pointing at* **Ashrafi** *and then himself.*)

Ashrafi (*repeating after* **Abba** *with the same gestures, pointing at herself and then him and vice versa*)   Rafis – Hafiz, Hafiz – Rafis . . .

Abba '... Gods, demons and angels all at once', she said in excitement. 'And they weren't your Djinns or Gulabbudin's, Abbu ... they were mine.' Fatima, who had not yet looked into Hamza's eyes, said, 'My Djinns appeared and told me that you will never win the war, Abbu, nor will Gulabuddin ...' 'What blasphemy', yelled Hamza. 'And where are these unscrupulous Djinns of yours?' said Hamza fuming. Fatima quietly looked up and said, 'The war is over, Abbu ... The war is over today. My Djinns have broken the illusion of war. They broke it the moment they remembered it is after all an illusion ... this war. When you fight you forget everything else, Abbu, and so does the evil Gulabbuddin. Both of you forget that this war isn't real, Abbu ... both of you fight as if it were. Look up at the skies, Abbu', she said, pulling Hamza. 'Those two stars up there, are ... are my eyes and they will forever be up there in the sky. The moment your eyes meet my eyes, you will break the illusion too. Abbu, whenever you look for my eyes in the sky, you shall find them and they shall remain there forever and ever.' Having said this she looked up at Hamza ... and Hamza looked at his daughter's face. There were two holes where her eyes should have been and up in the sky were her two stars. Hamza cried out aloud and held his daughter tightly.

'That evil Gulabuddin has taken my daughter's eyes', he said. 'I shall gouge out the eyes of every single child in his kingdom.' Saying which, Hamza got onto his magic horse and with his magic soldiers and his Djinns, went on war with Gulabuddin with a rage that the world had neither seen before nor has felt since then. The battles raged again and again ... but Fatima's eyes keep lurking in the sky.

And even tonight ... if you look up at the sky ... you will find Fatima's eyes waiting for her Abba to break the illusion ... to break the illusion by his eyes ... meeting her eyes ...

In the name of Allah the almighty ... may the queen of sleep bless you with pleasant and beautiful dreams ... Shabba-khair ...

He looks at the children. They are fast asleep. He bends and kisses both of them on the forehead. Places his head gently on **Bilal**'s *head.*

Scene Two

Bakshi Stadium. Day one. Morning.

Khaled *and* **Bilal** *are in the changing room. They are packing their clothes, shoes, etc. in the kit bag after training. It is a dirty, broken-down space. Has a window without a glass and from the window one can see soldiers' uniforms, drying on a clothesline.* **Bilal** *is standing and looking at the sole of his shoe.* **Khaled** *is wiping sweat off his body with a towel.*

Khaled   I have noticed this about you, Bilal ...

Bilal   What?

Khaled   Whenever we play in the campus of the girls' college, you tend to break your sole.

Bilal Bullshit.

Khaled I love that sudden burst of additional force in your kick and them going (*Imitating.*) Beeelaaal . . . Bilal . . . Beeelaaaal . . . Bilal.

Laughs.

Bilal Khaled, this is serious. They won't even consider me for the selections without boots. It's in the rules.

Khaled Heena . . . or was it Hamida . . . what was her name?

Bilal Khaled . . . I will kill you. What are you going on about?

Khaled That girl . . . what's her name? The one with the shrill voice.

Bilal Khaled, I AM SERIOUS!

Khaled About her?

Bilal *shakes his head.*

Khaled Her father is a Maulvi in the mosque, they will stuff your boots in your ass and play football with your balls!

He laughs, pretends to kick a really small ball.

Oh sorry, offside!!

He laughs out. **Bilal** *laughs as well.*

They sit down on the floor. **Khaled** *takes out a coloured energy drink. He takes a sip and gives it to* **Bilal**.

Bilal So your father's started smuggling gold biscuits to the Middle East. (*Laughs.*)

Khaled It is an energy drink, Bilal . . . it will help you run when that Heena or Hamida's father chases you.

Bilal Why does a goal keeper need an energy drink?

Khaled Why does an Argentina supporter want to go to Brazil?

Bilal Even if I do make it, Khaled, I maintain . . . Argentina is more heart.

Khaled And Brazil is more World Cups!

Bilal Shouldn't matter to you . . . In any case you are crazy about that robotic German club.

Khaled European football, Bilal . . . that's where my future is.

Bilal (*laughs*) You will make a terrific linesman in Europe. With a whistle in one hand and this coloured drink in another. Running up and down with complete dedication and ENERGY. (*Reading from the bottle, laughs.*)

Khaled European football is all TECHNIQUE . . . (*Mystifying the word.*)

Bilal Europeans play to not lose, South Americans play to win . . .

Khaled You should play for India . . . Indians play to run around the ball.

Both of them laugh out loud.

Bilal *looks at his shoe again.*

Khaled Won't last . . . not till day after.

Bilal Two days?

Khaled Unlikely.

Pause.

Bilal *pulls out a piece of paper from his bag.*

Bilal (*reading*) Ten kilometres . . . shot, dribble and pass drills and then the game . . . (**Bilal** *looks worried.*) and in the middle of all this, the stupid curfew. How will I get this fixed? Does anyone even remember what the curfew is for anymore?

Khaled Because the Indians want you to remember that you are not supposed to disturb the (*Sarcastically.*) '*peace talks*' with the sons of bitches while their soldiers breathe down your neck.

Bilal I am not talking about the Indian Army curfew . . . I am talking about (*Pause.*) yours . . .

Khaled 800,000 soldiers Bilal . . . do you even know how much that is? My Abbu says it's more than the number of American soldiers in Iraq and Afghanistan put together . . . can you imagine? And it's not my curfew, it's the people's curfew.

Bilal It's not the people's curfew, it is the Hurriyat Curfew. The Hurriyat might be a political party you worship but it is not the 'people'.

Khaled Really . . .? Then who is the people . . . you are the people? You?

Pause.

Bilal Do you know the timings for tomorrow?

Khaled All day except four to five in the evening. In the morning is the Army curfew and in the evening . . . ours.

Khaled Tomorrow afternoon/

Bilal (*sternly*) I won't be there.

Pause. **Bilal** *looks at* **Khaled**.

Bilal And neither should you.

Khaled Tomorrow is big, Bilal. Don't/

Bilal Day after is big.

Khaled Your father would be ashamed of you.

Bilal No. He would be proud.

Khaled People will spit on you.

Bilal I won't be around for people to spit on me.

Khaled So it's all about you now.

Bilal Yes.

Pause.

And it should be about you too.

Khaled Tomorrow/

Bilal Khaled, I don't care if people spit on me.

Khaled You don't care . . . about Kashmir?

Bilal I am Kashmir. And so are you. Play well day after.

Bilal *is about to leave. Pause.*

Khaled If you need shoes, you can borrow mine.

Bilal *turns around. Smiles at* **Khaled**.

Khaled We should ask them to keep our trials separate.

Bilal (*looks at his shoes*) I'll manage. My shoes will/

Khaled Won't last . . . and no one else will give it to you . . .

Silence.

The boys have been noticing you . . . you weren't even there yesterday after practice for the protest and the procession, so it hasn't gone down well with most of them.

Bilal I was there.

Khaled Yes . . . as long as it was naturally moving towards your house. I am not talking about getting caught in the procession, Bilal. I am talking about being in it.

Mushtaq *walks in.* **Mushtaq** *is slightly older than them. He is not the coach but he is a senior player who helps the team.*

Mushtaq Ohho . . . the bright lights of Kashmiri football in one room . . .

Khaled Mushtaq Bhai.

Shows him **Bilal**'s *shoes.* **Mushtaq** *takes one, looks at it.*

Mushtaq This won't last. Not another session.

Khaled Mushtaq Bhai, will our trials be together?

Mushtaq Depends on Coach Saheb and the foreign selector.

Khaled We just have one pair of shoes.

Mushtaq (*looks at the shoes*) OK. I will speak to Coach Saheb.

Takes out two slips from his pocket. Gives one each to both of them.

Here, these are your maps and timings. It will tell you when and where should you join the procession tomorrow. Memorize it and then chew the paper.

Khaled   Today?

Mushtaq   It's impossible today. We need to meet this evening to plan further. At the old school. I hope both of you will be there. (**Bilal** and **Khaled** *look at their slips. To* **Bilal**.) No excuses this time, Bilal. OK? It's right in front of your house.

Bilal *stands quietly.*

Mushtaq   Why did you disappear from the procession yesterday?

Bilal   The curfew/

Mushtaq   The curfew was only for you, in your backyard? I could stay and raise my voice, Khaled could stay and raise his voice . . . Youngsters are looking up at you. The team is now in international eye. And you are running away . . . just running away like a coward.

Bilal   I have a sister to take care of.

Mushtaq   And we don't have anyone. (*Pulls him over towards window.*) See. Look at that. This is your stadium. You play here. You practise here, look at them. What are they doing here? (*Showing him the soldiers' costumes.*) Don't you feel ashamed, Bilal, when you have to enter your own stadium like a thief, from the back gate, because some bastard in a green helmet can just stop you and threaten to shoot you for merely doing what you love doing the most? Don't you feel free, when you run, when you fall, when you scrape your shin, when you sweat, when your eyes water, when you win or when you lose? Look at them. It's not their game. This is yours.

Pause.

Play it . . .

Bilal *stands with his head hung low.*

Khaled   He will come, Mushtaq Bhai.

Mushtaq   This is Kashmir's hero! Who sits in his house, while a funeral procession gets shot at, right in front of his house. (*To* **Khaled**.) Does he know what happened yesterday in the afternoon . . . after he fled? (*To* **Bilal**.) Do you?

Silence.

Bilal   My sister Ashrafi collapsed when she heard the crowd passing by. When she heard bullets, I held her tightly for forty-five minutes, as she shook in my arms, with her head dug into my chest.

Perhaps she needs me more than your sister needs you, Mushtaq Bhai, or Khaled's sister needs him . . . because although she is fourteen her mental age is that of a nine- to ten-year-old. An age at which she travelled with our Abba's body on her lap, after he was shot dead in a bus. And all they were doing that day, Mushtaq Bhai, was that they were going for a wedding, dressed in new clothes . . . (*Pause.*) at an age when young girls love to wear new dresses, Mushtaq Bhai . . . my sister Ashrafi is afraid of them . . .

I am sorry, Mushtaq Bhai, Allah knows that if I get selected I can get her treated in a good hospital somewhere outside. My selection can go a long way to help us make something of our lives.

I can't take chances, Mushtaq Bhai, for her sake. And mine.

Mushtaq   Also, yesterday, in the afternoon, the soldiers in front of your house shot at the funeral procession you fled from . . . a funeral of a seven-year-old. In the shootout, they killed his brother, who was twelve. They killed his brother and imposed a curfew so that people could not gather and the child could not be buried. His mother will be sitting with his head on her lap for another twenty-four hours before her son can be buried.

Chances are, you will meet her soon in the same hospital. There is a lot that happens in Kashmir, every afternoon, Bilal . . . so before you bullshit with me, always remember, Bilal Naeem, jersey number six, Kashmir's star right out, right leg goal scoring machine . . . that special as you may be . . . Khaled's sister or my sister or anyone else's brother or sister, does not need us one bit less than your sister needs you.

Silence.

Are you meeting the doctor today?

Bilal (*tentatively*)   Yes. In the afternoon.

Mushtaq   Take this letter (*Gives him a letter.*) and give it to the doctor. Ask him to not go for the talks with the Indians. I can't believe he has agreed even after this. (**Bilal** *takes it tentatively.*)

Mushtaq   Look at me.

Bilal *does not.*

Mushtaq (*loudly*)   Look at me!

Pause.

Mushtaq *comes close to* **Bilal** *and holds him.*

Mushtaq   Insha'Allah, you will make it, Bilal. Insha'Allah you will be the star of Kashmiri football and reach where no one else did. And I am there with you, isn't it?

Bilal   Ji, Mushtaq Bhai.

Mushtaq   But for Mushtaq Bhai to be proud of his star Kashmiri players, there needs to be a Kashmir . . . no? A proud Kashmir. Give this letter, Bilal . . . please. Don't let that doctor humiliate us by going for the talk. One day you will be proud of yourself, believe me. Hmmm . . .?

Pause.

Bilal   I will give it, Mushtaq Bhai.

Bilal *and* **Khaled** *remain standing quietly.* **Mushtaq** *hugs* **Bilal**.

Mushtaq (*smiles at both of them*)   In the evening. Old school.

Bilal *and* **Khaled**   Ji.

Mushtaq   I will speak to Coach Saheb about not keeping your trials together. Give him your shoes, Khaled, but hide a nail inside.

Khaled *picks up his bag and is about to leave when he finds that* **Bilal** *is still looking at the soldiers' clothes on the clothesline.* **Khaled** *slaps him on the head, they stand together and keep looking at the military uniforms.*

Scene Three

Day one. Afternoon.

The government psychiatry hospital in Srinagar. **Dr Baig**'s *room.* **Dr Baig** *has placed his chair in front of his desk rather than behind it.*

There is a bench on another side of the room on which **Dr Wani** *sits with a notepad in her hands. She takes notes as the session proceeds. A partition separates this room from the outside. Outside on a bench is* **Bilal** *waiting for his sister with Mushtaq's letter in his hands.* **Ashrafi** *enters the clinic with her doll.*

Baig (*loudly*)   As-salamu alaykum, Ashrafi Begum /

Ashrafi (*coldly*)   Walekum asallam, Doctor Saheb.

Ashrafi *sits coldly in front of the doctor. She looks at her doll and mumbles to it.* **Baig** *smiles at her. Gestures towards the stool in front him.* **Ashrafi** *sits down.*

Wani (*in a voice that adults use to speak to children*)
As-salamu alaykum Ashrafi.

Ashrafi *takes her doll. Makes the doll look at* **Wani**.

Ashrafi (*to the doll*)   She is talking to you. Go on, speak to her. (*Imitates* **Wani**. *In the same adult-speaking-to-child voice.*) Walekum a saalam, Doctor Saheb.

Wani *smiles and opens a writing pad. She notes things as* **Baig** *and* **Ashrafi** *speak.*

Baig (*looks at his watch; making her comfortable*)   Yes, on time today.

Ashrafi *spreads her hand out.* **Baig** *takes out two small toffees from his drawer, places them next to each other.*

Baig   Éclair or sugar toffee?

Ashrafi *puts out the other hand as well.*

Baig   No, not both. One for getting here on time. And the other when we start playing. OK?

Ashrafi *nods.*

Baig   So, we were talking about a bus ride. The last time /

Ashrafi   Doctor Saheb. You did not give me the school bag you promised.

Baig   Oh. Is that why you are upset with me?

Ashrafi   Yes. (*Pause.*) No. The school bag. (*Looks around.*)

Baig   OK.

Silence.

Ashrafi, I will give you the school bag. But for that schools have to open/

Ashrafi   You. Why did you close the schools?

Baig   I did not.

Ashrafi   You did. I know.

Baig   No. Who told you that?

Ashrafi   I know. But if I tell you, you won't believe me, Doctor Saheb.

Baig   Why won't I believe you?

Ashrafi   Because you don't know. If you knew you would have known.

Baig   Ashrafi . . . OK. Look. I did not close the schools. I want the school to be open. For all of you to go out and play.

Silence. **Baig** *is looking at* **Ashrafi**.

Baig   Shall we start the bus ride?

Ashrafi   OK.
This is my bus, I am the driver.

She turns the chair around.

I am driving. Wooon . . . woon . . . (*Makes sounds.*) From their home in Mirpur to a wedding. . . (**Baig** *is looking at her intently as she play acts the bus ride.*) . . . yes. No no . . . this won't go there. Of course it will. Five rupees. You have. Good . . .

So, I am driving there . . . there comes Ashrafi and her father . . . the gallant Jamaal of Mirpur. They get in, they sit down and then I keep driving . . . I drive they are sitting . . . they are sitting over there . . .

Baig *gets up and just stands outside the make-believe bus, trying to get in. Waving his hand at the driver.* **Ashrafi** *looks at him but does not stop the make-believe bus.*

Ashrafi   The bus does not go where you want it to go.

Baig (*smiles*)   Why don't you try playing Abba, I will play Ashrafi.

Ashrafi (*gets up*)   OK but quickly. We need to get home. Bilal has to go for practice.

Baig   Where is Bilal?

Ashrafi (*taking another chair and making a place to sit in the bus*)   At home. He was not on the bus with us.

Baig OK. But where is he now?

Ashrafi Now, I am on the bus, and he is not on the bus.

Baig No, Ashrafi, see. Now we are in my room.

And we are *pretending* that you are in a bus. Right. So this is happening for real, (*Gesturing towards his room, desks, etc.*) and that is not happening now. (*Pointing at her make-believe bus.*) Right?

Ashrafi For you, because, Doctor Saheb, you are not in the bus. I am in the bus. This is happening for real. Come, come in to the bus. I really have to go early today . . .

Baig OK, so I will play Ashrafi /

Ashrafi No you can't play me. I am here in the bus.

Baig Then Abba.

Ashrafi (*agitated*) No, no, no, no . . . you can't . . . (*She seems really upset.*) Don't keep spoiling my game, Doctor Saheb. My bus. It's my bus! Play something else. This man or . . . this family of seven. Don't be part of my . . . I don't . . . Now I can't remember.

Baig But you remember more than this, Ashrafi.

Don't you? Just the other day we almost reached the wedding.

She sits down, starts crying. She is angry and weeping.

Ashrafi You are not in the bus, why can't you understand? Why can't you just stay where you need to be? Why can't you just watch my bus from outside? It's because of you, all because of you/

Baig *steps off the make-believe bus. Goes back to his chair.*

Baig (*calming her down*) OK. OK. Look, I am outside now. I am not in the bus. See . . .

Ashrafi *looks around. Still crying. Picks up her doll. Says something to the doll, looks at the doctor, talks to the doll again about the doctor and sits facing away from* **Dr Baig**.

Ashrafi The bus cannot go on, there is a curfew.

Baig Yes, there is a curfew.

Ashrafi I have to get home before the curfew starts.

Baig Yes.

Ashrafi *looks at* **Wani** *hoping that she understands what she is talking about. She looks back at* **Dr Baig**.

Ashrafi I have to get back home before the curfew starts, Baig Sahab. I heard the timings on the radio.

Baig You mean . . . NOW? As in today when you are here with me, Dr Baig?

Ashrafi *smiles and nods cheekily.*

Ashrafi   Yes. Yes of course.

(*Smiles.*) What? What did you think, Doctor Saheb?

Baig   I thought you were talking about the bus, Ashrafi.

Ashrafi   Which bus? This bus? (*She starts laughing.*) You are mad, Dr Baig. You are mad. I know, you are mad.

She keeps laughing.

Wani *and* **Baig** *look at each other.*

Baig   OK . . . Ashrafi. You can go home now. We will meet again tomorrow. OK?

Ashrafi *does not respond. She stretches her hand out again.* **Baig** *smiles, gives her the other toffee.*

Baig   Khuda Hafiz, Ashrafi Begum.

Ashrafi   Allah . . . (*Looks at her doll.*) Hafiz . . . (*Smiles and begins to move out.*)

Baig (*calling out*)   Bilal . . .

Bilal (*comes in urgently*)   Yes . . . yes, Doctor Saheb.

Ashrafi *holds* **Bilal**'s *hand and stands. In his other hand he has Mushtaq's letter.*

Bilal   Shefu . . . you go and sit there on the bench OK? I will meet Dr Sahib and come . . .

Ashrafi *does not leave him.*

Bilal   I can see you from here, Shefu . . . and see, if you bend like this you can also see me . . .

Ashrafi *shows him her teeth.*

Bilal   Very nice, Shefu . . . now go and /

She sticks her tongue out.

Yes . . . yes, Shefu . . . it's all neat and clean . . . you are a good girl . . . now sit there and I will be back . . . OK?

Ashrafi *nods and shows him her doll.*

Bilal   Yes . . . go and sit with Hafiz . . . OK?

Ashrafi *walks away.* **Bilal** *walks in. He stands in front of* **Baig**. **Baig** *looks at the letter in his hand for a moment.* **Bilal** *is about to speak when* **Baig** *pulls out a newspaper from his briefcase. Keeps it on the table.* **Bilal** *looks at it, hangs his head.*

Baig   Yes . . .

Bilal *does not say anything.*

Baig (*showing him the newspaper*)   Yes . . . Don't you have anything to say? When is your football trial?

Scene Three

Bilal   Day after, Baig Saheb.

Baig (*surprised*)   On Eid?

Bilal *nods.*

Wani *and* **Baig** *look at each other.*

Baig   Is this what you should be doing, Bilal? This?

Picks up the newspaper, reads:

'The pride of Kashmir, the football team was seen at the funeral procession last evening around Eidgah. Along with the protestors, the team joined in with stone pelting and sloganeering. And . . .' (*Mumbles.*) . . . and yes here you are. Pride of Kashmir. Here. On this page.

Is this what it's all about? Is this why you have left everything behind, and moved to Srinagar with your sister?

Bilal *puts the letter back in his pocket.*

Bilal (*looking down, tentatively*)   Dr Sahib, I was . . .

Baig   Bilal. You cannot afford to be stupid right now. If required, don't come back together with the other boys from practice. I was shocked to see you at that procession yesterday.

Wani (*looks up*)   Doctor Saheb . . . you were?

Baig   Yes, I was there. Returning from a patient's, when one of these . . . these (*Pointing at* **Bilal**.) boys threw a stone at my car . . .

Wani   Your car? Oh . . . Doctor Saheb . . . were you hurt?

Baig (*ignoring her, going up to* **Bilal**)   This valley needs heroes, Bilal. Fulfilled ones. Not the ones who were promising and did not finally get anywhere. (*Shakes his head.*)

You can be fulfilled. You can leave with your sister and give her a good life. You cannot afford to mess this up right now, Bilal. You understand, don't you?

Bilal *nods.*

Baig   Go . . . before the curfew starts again. I don't even remember which one is about to start now!

Pause. **Bilal** *is about to bring the letter out but stops.*

Bilal   Allah Hafiz, Doctor Saheb

Baig   Allah Hafiz, Bilal.

Bilal *leaves.* **Baig** *sits down.* **Wani** *is silent. Tense silence between them.*

Wani   Baig Saheb . . . the boys stoned your car?

Baig   Yes. They did. How did the whole city know about this, all of a sudden?

Wani It was on the television, Dr Baig. A news channel did a story on the people from the valley who have been selected for the talks with the Indians.

Pause.

The ones who have declined . . . and the ones who will be talking. People are already on the streets about the shooting of that seven-year-old boy and his twelve-year-old brother, and now this thing about the . . . the . . . peace talks . . . the list announced on the same evening as the killing of a child in cold blood . . . Dr Baig it has really made some people angry. And perhaps in their anger they . . .

Silence.

Baig Anger . . . Sometimes, I start believing the Indians. Maybe, we won't be able to handle this place, if it were given to us.

Wani *sits quietly.* **Baig** *looks at* **Wani**.

Baig Oh . . . of course, I forget.

Wani Doctor Saheb, the boys – (*Stops abruptly.*) They should not have stoned your car.

Baig No, no. Why not? Even you don't think I should talk to the Indians, isn't it?

Wani I never said that.

Baig Wani, I have known you long enough to be able to read your silence.

Pause.

You were the only person who did not come to my room, yesterday after I heard from the ministry. Which is why, Wani, you are the last one to know that my car was stoned by Kashmir's latest heroes. Kashmir's children.

Pause.

Wani Baig Saheb, forgive me but I am not sure if there is any point in talking to the Indians.

Pause.

Baig You are not sure, Wani? Sitting here, in this hospital, you are not sure if we should speak or not?

Look at this place. The only psychiatry hospital in the entire valley. With five doctors . . . just five, (*Laughs sarcastically.*) you and I have to be miracle workers in here. When I was stepping in today, Wani, I saw the number on the register . . . Forty-five thousand one hundred and seventy-eight . . . forty-five thousand . . . the sum total of the bravery and passions of our occupier and our revolutionaries . . . their report card on our register at the entrance.

That many people have walked in through that gate just this year and it's not even Eid . . . and five of us in here. Two are my students including you and two are yours . . . these are our chances. We are doctors, Wani . . . our job is to heal. People want revolution. Where will we keep it? We don't even have enough benches for our patients to sit on.

Pause.

Wani   When is it, Doctor Saheb?

Baig   Day after tomorrow.

Wani   Eid?

Baig (*smiles*)   Yes, they want to meet on Eid.

Wani (*laughs*)   These Indians. (*Pause.*) I can't tell what is more worrying, Dr Baig ... When they are openly hostile or when they are pretending to be friendly!

Scene Four

Dr Baig *stands outside the Eidgah at a slight distance. Suspended time. Between Life and Death.*

The **Djinn** *appears inside. He is painted green and golden. His face is not clearly visible but there is a disfiguration to his voice. It is like a hole, slightly larger than the size of a revolver bullet.*

There is a sound of the Islamic prayer for the dead, 'Fateha', behind but it seems unclear and muffled. The sound is layered with the sound of a father telling a young boy a story in Urdu. The child laughs and makes noises of wind, sword fights, rain, etc. in the soundtrack. The soundtrack layers these three sounds but the child sounds are clearer than others.

Dr Baig *takes very slow steps towards the gate. The* **Djinn** *walks to him as if mirroring his pace.* **Dr Baig** *goes really close and as the face of the* **Djinn** *becomes more visible, he stops. The* **Djinn**'s *stomach is visible and it seems to be burnt.*

As soon as **Dr Baig** *stops, the Djinn appears restless. He keeps looking at* **Dr Baig** *intently and tries to spread his arms open as* **Dr Baig** *recedes. The sounds reach a crescendo.*

Scene Five

Day one. Late afternoon.

Ashrafi *and* **Bilal**'s *house. A small room with an old television without the back so that its picture tube is visible. A mattress. A carpet.* **Ashrafi** *is doing 'make-up' on* **Bilal**. **Bilal** *is watching a football match. The window is open. Clock on the wall. A radio. Same day. Afternoon.*

Bilal (*looks at the clock. Irritably*)   How could you get it wrong, Shefu?

Ashrafi   You can get it fixed tomorrow, Bhaijaan.

Bilal   And what if it doesn't happen? How will I play?

Ashrafi Sit straight. (*Turns his neck.*)

Bilal (*checks a slip of paper*)   The curfew time has not changed. You heard it all wrong on the radio.

Ashrafi How do you know?

Bilal I asked Khaled. On the phone.

Ashrafi Then you should have asked Khaled Bhai in the first place, Bhaijaan, I am not him, I have things to do of my own. OK?

Bilal (*looks at* **Ashrafi**)   Shefu, you have to stop watching television.

Ashrafi *does not look at him, she keeps doing his make-up.*

Bilal Look at the way you speak. Even to Doctor Saheb. No one in the valley speaks to him like that. My god, Shefu! If Ammi were here, she would give you two tight ones . . .

Ashrafi If Ammi were here . . . (*She mumbles to* **Hafiz**.) she would let me go wherever I wanted . . . whenever I wanted . . . with Hafiz . . .

Bilal *looks at* **Ashrafi** *as she continues to apply make-up on his face.*

Bilal Your Hafiz!

Ashrafi Hafiz has also told me several other things, Bhaijaan . . . about that doctor.

Bilal Oh (*Laughs.*) really . . . like what?

Ashrafi That the doctor is mad . . . that he is a kafir, an infidel, which is why he never enters the gates of the Eidgah. He goes there every evening, and stands outside.

Silence.

Bilal Shefu . . . what do you know about the Eidgah?

Ashrafi That which everyone knows.

Bilal What?

Ashrafi That it is a graveyard of the martyrs. And in there are the Djinns. Living Djinns. And they are all living there, in that world.

Bilal You and your Hafiz . . . (*He looks at the clock.*)

. . . OK I have to go.

Ashrafi Bhaijaan.

Bilal No, no. Make-up after I come back from the team meeting, OK. Mushtaq Bhai will kill me if I don't go today. OK? (*As* **Bilal** *prepares to leave* **Ashrafi** *begins to panic.*)

Ashrafi But, Bhaijaan, how will you have the meeting.

The curfew is till eight.

Bilal There is no curfew that side.

Scene Five

Ashrafi   Tomorrow. Have the team meeting tomorrow, Bhaijaan.

Bilal   Shefu, the team needs to plan for the selections and everyone needs to meet OK? It's not in my hands.

Ashrafi   Bhaijaan . . . please don't go out in the curfew . . . please, Bhaijaan. I will . . .

Bilal *looks at her. Starts to wipe the make-up.*

Ashrafi   Bhaijaan no, no don't wipe the make-up please. You are my only model. Bhaijaan . . . Bhaijaan . . . (*Screams.*)

Pause.

Ashrafi *is flustered. She sits on the floor.* **Bilal** *stops. Looks at her, goes close to her and holds her.*

Bilal   Shefu . . . Shefu . . . see . . . I am here, for real . . . I am. You can feel my face with your hands . . . I am here. (*Puts* **Ashrafi***'s hands on his face. She seems to calm down with this gesture.*)

Ashrafi (*holds him tightly*)   You are my only . . . my only . . . model, Bhaijaan.

Bilal *laughs.*

Bilal   And you are also my only beautician, no?

Ashrafi *is still shaking.*

Bilal   OK . . . OK . . . Shefu, you know if I get through this football trial what will happen.

Ashrafi   You will go away.

Bilal   Yes, and you will also come with me to Brazil. We will be completely, completely . . . free. We can go wherever we want, whenever we want . . . you can go to school . . . everyday. And I will play the World Cup (*Laughs.*) and you . . . you will become a master beautician!

Ashrafi   Abba? Will he come with us? Where will he be?

Bilal   He will be . . . in his world.

Ashrafi   Which world?

Bilal   Abba is fine, Shefu. In his world. In the other world. OK?

Ashrafi *nods.*

Ashrafi   And Hafiz?

Bilal   We will take your Hafiz as well. Promise.

Ashrafi *looks around.*

Ashrafi   Bhaijaan, will you be gone for long?

Bilal   I will come back in no time.

Ashrafi   Bhaijaan . . . will you?

She pulls two pillows. A big one and a small one.

Bilal (*nods softly*)   Sleep and before you know I will be back.

She lies down. He sits next to her and begins to tell her a dastaan.

Dastaan . . . dastaaan . . . which one?

Ashrafi (*immediately*)   The one in which Hamza /

Bilal   Sends the flying lamps?

She nods and both of them laugh.

OK . . .

He strokes her head and she closes her eyes.

Long long ago, in a land much like ours, in the year of the Saturn, in the kingdom of Heaven, there was the general of the king . . .

Ashrafi   The king . . . the prophet . . . the king the prophet . . . Bhaijaan did a boy die yesterday?

Bilal   What?

Ashrafi   Didn't a boy die yesterday, Bhaijaan . . . right here . . . somewhere close by? Did he go to Allah Bhaijaan or has he now become a Djinn?

Bilal (*nervously*)   Shefu . . . what are you talking about . . . who told you that a boy died yesterday?

Ashrafi (*holding her doll*)   Hafiz . . . us Hafiz rafis . . . Rafiz Hafis . . . long long ago in the year of the?

Pause.

Bilal   Saturn . . . at a time much like this there lived /

Ashrafi   His mother (*Starts laughing.*) she thinks he is dead, Bhaijaan. She is sitting with his head on her lap.

Bilal   Shefu . . . Shefu . . . I don't know what you are talking about . . .

Ashrafi   It's in the dastaan, Bhaijaan . . . when Djinns die people think they are dead, the armies of Gulabbuddin and Hamza think that they are dead but . . . have you ever been to the funeral of a Djinn?

Bilal   No.

Ashrafi   And will you?

Bilal   No . . . don't know . . . Shefu, shefu . . . go to sleep.
What are you saying?

Ashrafi   Will you?

Bilal   Sometimes you sound like other people.

Ashrafi You're not telling me the dastaan, Bhaijaan.

Bilal I am Shefu . . . sleep. If the children are good the dastaan becomes the blanket and if the children are bad.

Ashrafi The dastaan becomes the chilling wind . . . Bhaijaan do you think that the boy, he felt cold when he died. Is death hot or cold, Bhaijaan?

Bilal Shefu, go to sleep, Shefu.

Ashrafi Will you go for his funeral or will you stay here, Bhaijaan . . . tomorrow . . . what will you do, Bhaijaan . . . are you with the Djinns or are you with the enemies of Hamza . . .

Bilal And as Hamza's eyes are to meet.

Ashrafi Fatima's eyes.

Bilal (*rapidly*) Fatima's eyes hanging in the air, if Hamza's eyes meet Fatima's eyes . . . that day /

Ashrafi They will never meet, they will . . . will you get me your shoes, magicians battling magicians battling magicians.

Bilal *holds her tight and embraces her. Silence.*

Bilal Sleep, Shefu . . . sleep . . . shhhh . . . shh . . .

Kisses her on the forehead.

May the queen of sleep bless you with good dreams. In the name of Allah the merciful . . . Shabba Khair.

He puts **Ashrafi** *to bed. She is fast asleep. He sits next to her. One one side of her is* **Ashrafi** *and on the other his football boots. He looks outside but holds her and keeps sitting.*

Scene Six

Day one. Night.

The bunker of the Central Reserved Police Force (CRPF) close to the Eidgah. Same night. The gate of the Eidgah is visible. This is the complete form of the gate that is visible between the **Djinn** *and* **Dr Baig**. *It's not very brightly lit.* **Soldier 2 (S2)** (*early twenties*) *is ringing a small bell and praying to pictures of Hindu gods on the walls.* **Soldier 1 (S1)** (*early forties*) *comes running in, looks at him in shock. Keeps his gun aside, and slaps him on his head.* **S2** *stops and salutes.*

S2 Sir!

S1 *slaps him again on his head.*

S1 Don't 'sir' me, I am the same post as you.

S2 Still, sir, you are older.

S1 (*takes his bell*)   What is this?

S2   Sir, today is Tuesday.

S1   So?

S2   Good day for Lord Hanuman.

S1   Here. Next to the Eidgah, when everyone is breaking their fast for Ramzan, you are thinking of Lord Hanuman!

S2   Sir, this is our country, we can . . . /

S1 *slaps him on his head again*

S1   This is not our country. We are sitting here, OK? And this has got nothing to do with Lord Hanuman anyway. Just stand guard and watch out for movement.

S2 *stands guard, unhappily. On the way to the window of the bunker he apologizes to Lord Hanuman quietly.*

S1   They are not there.

S2   In the school?

S1   No.

S2   Behind the mosque?

S1   No . . . no.

S2   Then they must be home.

Pause.

S1   All of them? All the boys?

S2   Yes, sir, they must be tired of planning for tomorrow. (*Laughs.*)

S1   These boys from the mountain; they don't tire that easily.

S2   You really think they will come till here tomorrow.

S1   I am sure. In hordes. They would have, yesterday itself but the procession got shot at Lal Chowk itself. Tomorrow not only will they get here, they will get here with stones in their hands and blood on their hands.

S2   Saheb, when will our shift change?

S1   Not till this things gets over I'm sure.

S2   But will we have back up by tomorrow?

S1   Hopefully.

S2   If they come here . . . I will . . . I will shoot.

S1   They will skin us alive. Don't do anything stupid.

S2   By the grace of Lord /

S1 Shut up! Will you shut up and look.

Pause.

S2 Sir, don't mind me asking, but you are not Hindu?

S1 Yes, I am.

S2 So . . .

S1 What?

S2 If you are Hindu, you don't pray to /

S1 I am Hindu but I am not stupid . . .

S2 A true Hindu cannot get hurt by stones, sir.

S1 *looks at* **S2** *in disbelief.*

S1 Good. Stand in front of the bunker tomorrow morning then.

Pause.

S2 Sir, how long have you been here?

S1 Three years in Srinagar. This picket is new though. About six months old.

S2 Why, sir . . . here? (*Looking around.*) Where are the militants here? It's just houses all around . . . isn't it? What can possibly happen /

S1 Stay here for two more days and you will realize what can happen over here.

S2 What, sir . . . you are making me a little nervous, I must say.

S1 You see that gate? . . .

S2 Yes . . . sir.

S1 What does it say? Read it?

S2 (*tries to read*) It's in Urdu . . .

S1 Underneath that . . . look at the gate . . . that's in English.

S2 (*reads*) LEST YOU FORGET, WE GAVE OUR TODAY FOR YOUR TOMORROW . . . Who has given . . . this is a martyr's graveyard, Saheb?

S1 Yes . . . good. You are not as dumb as I thought you were.

S2 *quickly goes close to the photo of the god, rings the bell, puts a red 'tika' (a mark) on his forehead and comes back and stands.*

S1 You are . . . not very smart after all. Erase it . . . are you stupid?

S2 *looks at* **S1** *in disbelief that being a Hindu* (**S1**) *is asking him to erase his 'tika'.*

S1 You want to stand guard next to the Eidgah, surrounded by God knows how many of these bloodthirsty boys with a red tika on your forehead! What are you . . . Lord Hanuman's disciple or Lord Hanuman himself!

S2   This will ward off the evil, sir. Mine will work for both of us, but I suggest you also apply some. It will be more foolproof!
These graveyards are full of ghosts, sir . . . I am telling you . . . all kinds of ghosts are /

S1   Shut up . . . you idiot. They have posted us here so that there is no trouble. Things do not go out of hand. So that even if they get provoked or heated up in some funeral procession, with all those slogans pumping their blood onto their foreheads, we can control the population . . . the 'awaam'. Do you know what that means . . . to control them . . . not to provoke them further by standing here with a red tika on your head. God . . . why do I get posted with idiots . . . always!

Ashrafi *appears in front of the gates of Eidgah. Just her silhouette is seen. She sits down outside the gate and appears to be speaking to someone who is inside. She seems to be talking, mumbling, laughing.*

S2 *notices her. Abruptly takes aim and loads his gun.*

S1   What . . . what are you doing?

S2   She is meeting someone, Saheb . . . I was right . . . Saheb . . .

S1   Who? Can you see anyone?

S2   She is laughing, Saheb. I am sure she is, you don't know these people, Saheb, they are . . .

S1   Shhh . . . shh . . . what's wrong with you?

S2   I know these people, Saheb. Saheb you shoot her.

S1   What?

S2   Yes, Saheb.

S2 *picks up a gun and gives it to* **S1**.

S1   What . . . are you /

S1 *pushes* **S2** *and he falls.*

S2   Saheb, I will forget who you are . . . you are just same post as me . . . don't.

He picks up the gun and tries to go towards the window himself.

S1 *hits him again.*

S1   What's wrong with you?

S2   It's a curfew, she can't /

S1   It's OK. You can't shoot her for /

S2   I know these people, Saheb, I have seen . . . even their children . . .

He gets up again to shoot. **S1** *hits him even harder and snatches his gun.* **S2** *is bleeding.*

S2 (*loudly. In panic*)   What are you doing, Saheb . . . she will blow up. She will blow up on our faces and we will be in shreds, like cloth, lying around . . . you don't understand . . . These people are mad . . . she is . . . is . . .

S1 *holds him by the collar.*

S1 I don't know about her but you are mad. Completely mad. Tomorrow morning, the first thing I do is to report you to the commandant.

S2 I will report you. You are standing here and fighting with a man of your own post to defend a girl who has broken the law. You have broken orders, we can shoot. We must shoot. We can shoot anyone we like. Anyone we suspect. You are mad, all you old soldiers are mad . . . you deserve it . . . deserve this . . . this hell . . . not us . . .

S1 *comes charging at* **S2***, slaps him hard on the back of his head.* **S2** *falls on the floor.* **S1** *loads his gun and points at* **S2***.*

S2 (*closes his eyes. Loudly*) My god . . . oh my god . . . what are you doing? Will you kill me . . . why . . . but what did I do?

S1 SHUT UP!!

Silence.

I will kill you if you are stupid. I can afford insanity, OK? But stupidity, no. Not here. I will not be lynched by a mob of boys because of an idiot like you.

S1 *goes to the window of the bunker and keeps observing* **Ashrafi** *closely.* **Ashrafi** *comes out of the bunker with her wooden doll, she faces the soldier.* **S1** *smiles at* **Ashrafi***.* **Ashrafi** *smiles at the soldier.* **Ashrafi** *leaves.*

Scene Seven

Day two. Morning

Bakshi Stadium. None of the equipment that was there in the previous scene is present. Outside the room, on the other side, where all the military uniforms can be seen hanging on a clothesline; footballs, kit bags, a pair of goalkeeping gloves and a huge pile of jerseys are kept.

Khaled, **Bilal** *and* **Mushtaq** *are present in the room.* **Mushtaq** *is sitting in one corner looking out. An eerie stillness.* **Khaled** *and* **Bilal** *do not have their jerseys on.* **Mushtaq** *gets up, takes a steel mug that is lying around and throws it in the direction of the military camp. He comes back and stands next to* **Bilal** *and* **Khaled***.*

Mushtaq We'll practise. Come.

Khaled *and* **Bilal** *look at him.*

He removes his shoes and makes a goal post.

Bilal Coach Saheb?

Mushtaq He cannot come today. I heard from him this morning.

Khaled Why?

Mushtaq   They are looking for his son.

Pause.

Come (*To* **Bilal** *and* **Khaled**.) We will play.

Bilal (*tentatively*)   Just the two of us?

Mushtaq   You and Khaled are the only real chance we have of sending someone to a decent club abroad . . . out of this . . . this prison of a stadium. (*Pause.*) You don't turn up for meetings I ask you to come for, Bilal, but I still need to make sure you do justice to your game. Isn't it?

You boys are wimps. Two of you are sitting here without your shirts in shame and the others are hiding on being asked to surrender their equipment. In my team we would have torn at those Indians.

Khaled (*goes towards* **Mushtaq**)   We will play, Mushtaq Bhai . . . for our team and yours.

Mushtaq   Yes you must and you must come for the procession, later in the day today. For that twelve-year-old martyr, may Allah be with him. It is going to be a huge protest.

Khaled   Is that why . . .

Mushtaq   Yes. The bastards want to show us who is in charge.

Khaled (*to* **Bilal**)   It's going to be massive . . . Three battalions are covering just ways from Lal Chowk to the Eidgah. Apparently, even women and young girls are coming out of their houses.

Mushtaq   Kashmir has pledged that it will bury its son where it wants today.

Pause. **Mushtaq** *looks out towards the soldiers.*

Bilal   Our practice . . .

Mushtaq (*turns to* **Khaled** *and* **Bilal**)   You will practice . . . the more they try to stop you the more I want you to practise. This isn't a game . . . you know that don't you? I have stood here, year after year recalling that day when the Indians locked the stadium and took two of our best boys in custody. Rizwaan and Rasool. The best. We never saw them again.

And you know what the real story is . . . it has nothing to do with militancy. None of the boys of our team crossed the border to Pakistan or trained in weapons. It was a protest, here in Bakshi Stadium by a bunch of sportsmen, merely demanding that the military camps should be moved out of the stadium. And guess what did the Indians do? The peaceful, peace loving Gandhian sons of bitches . . . they came in and beat Rasool and Rizwaan, our two star players, to a pulp a few days before the Asian Games trial. Locked the stadium and. . . .

Man is a beast, and that over there . . . is the worst beast of them all. A kind of man who was ruled by others for over 300 years and is here now to rule someone else. There is nothing . . . nothing more dangerous, believe me, than a ruler who has been a slave before. And there it is, staring at you . . . with your equipment under the nozzle of its gun. (*Pause.*) And our boys, a bunch of wimps . . . have gone away after turning in their jerseys; jerseys which have made them who they are today. (*Pause.*)

Bilal   They haven't gone anywhere, Mushtaq Bhai . . . see (*He takes him to the window and stands.*) there . . . behind the gate . . . can you see the boys? They are just not allowing anyone else in anymore.

Mushtaq   So, what are they waiting for?

Bilal   For practice . . .

Khaled   And then to go for the procession. (*Looks at* **Bilal**.) They are waiting outside, so that even if the practice does not happen, the procession against the army curfew can /

Bilal   But right now, it's the practice that matters.

Silence.

Mushtaq   We will practise. Now . . . (*Looks into his bag.*) here, Bilal . . . you're number six. (**Mushtaq** *throws a brush dipped in green paint to him.*)

Bilal   Ji, Mushtaq Bhai . . . (**Bilal** *paints it on his body gladly.*)

Mushtaq   And here, Khaled . . . take seven . . . idiot . . . the only goalie in the whole planet who wears number seven.

Khaled   It's my lucky number, Mushtaq Bhai.

Mushtaq *paints seven on* **Khaled**.

Mushtaq   Sure . . . Lucky number . . . that's why you are sitting here without a jersey in the middle of a stadium with one more player and the captain of a disbanded football team.

Bilal   Mushtaq Bhai . . . we don't have a ball!

Silence.

Mushtaq   You have your brain . . . and your feet . . . you two have played enough football in your life to imagine the ball if it's taken away. Haven't you?

Pause.

Close your eyes.

Khaled . . . walk to the goal post. If this was the field, where would the goal post be?

Khaled *closes his eyes and walks to a place that he thinks is the goal post.*

Mushtaq   Now take position. Bilal . . . you start charging from the left flank . . . and I will keep calling out names . . .

Khaled   Ji.

Mushtaq   Pass . . . Bilal to Basher . . . Basher to Majid . . . Majid to Bilal . . . back pass . . . Bilal . . . run down flank . . . cross to Basher, Basher heads . . .

Khaled *jumps up and mimes catching the ball.*

They smile. **Khaled** *and* **Bilal** *still have their eyes shut.*

Mushtaq   Once more . . . Basher runs down right . . . back passes to Majid . . . Majid makes ball for Bilal . . . Bilal shoots . . .

Khaled *dives exactly in the direction in which* **Bilal** *shoots.*

Khaled *opens his eyes,* **Bilal** *opens his eyes and they laugh out loud.*

Mushtaq   Good . . . Now play with your eyes open . . . I will call and you just play all the moves we have practised . . . let's practise all the moves that we have done . . .

Music plays and the boys practise. Needs to be a complete sequence.

Mushtaq   Bilal . . . I have asked Coach Saheb to keep your trial separately from Khaled's.

Bilal   Shukriya, Mushtaq Bhai.

Mushtaq *nods at him and smiles.*

Khaled *walks up to* **Bilal** *as* **Mushtaq** *goes to talk to other boys.*

Khaled   I hope you are staying back, Bilal.

Bilal   No, Khaled, I am not. I have to go home. Shefu is alone.

Khaled *slaps him hard.* **Bilal** *falls on the ground.*

Mushtaq   Let him go, Khaled.

Khaled   You don't even care about football, do you? They take everything away from you and still . . . still it doesn't make you angry enough.

Pause.

Your session will be before mine. I will get the shoes early don't worry. You can play and become whatever you want to become, Bilal . . . just don't come in front of me.

Pause.

Bilal   I don't want to imagine my equipment and my team all my life, Khaled. Do you get it? Is it too unreasonable a desire?

Khaled   No, Bilal . . . it's too reasonable. A bit too reasonable for us. Don't you think?

Pause.

Go, Bilal. Go away before I start despising you. You are my friend and insha'Allah you will be the star of Kashmiri football one day. I don't want to look down upon you, the way I so want to . . . at this moment. Get out of the stadium before I genuinely start hating you.

Bilal *leaves.* **Khaled** *and* **Mushtaq** *Bhai remain standing, looking at him leave.*

Scene Eight

Day two. Morning.

An hour after the previous scene.

Dr Wani *and* **Dr Baig** *in* **Dr Baig**'s *office.* **Wani** *is injured. Her white coat is soiled with blood and her head is bleeding.* **Dr Baig** *is trying to stop the bleeding with cotton.*

Wani It's OK, Doctor Saheb.

Baig I don't believe this.

Wani It's OK, Dr Baig.

Baig Sit still, Wani.

He ties a bandage. And sits in front of **Wani**. *He is shaken.* **Baig** *looks at* **Wani**. *Smiles. Goes close to her. Touches her forehead with affection and sits at the table holding her lightly.*

Wani It was also my fault.

Baig No it wasn't. I should have asked everyone to stay at home. Till this meeting with the Indians gets over. I am sorry, Wani. You are like my own . . . my daughter if I had one. I am /

Wani It's my duty, Doctor Saheb . . .

Baig This place has made me stubborn. (*Pause.*)
You are young, Wani. A young woman. Don't be like me. Stay at home on such days.

Wani Doctor Saheb, I have stayed at home a little too long.

Dr Baig *looks at* **Wani**.

Wani (*smiles*) I even took my son out, today. (*Proudly.*) The processions, the barricades. He enjoyed it.

Baig I hope you are not telling him . . .

Wani No, Baig Sahib . . . I am telling you.

Baig What?

Wani That I don't want to be here anymore.

Baig What?

Wani Yes, Baig Sahib . . . forgive me but what is going on outside the compound of this hospital right now is so . . . so brutal that I don't understand my role inside the safety of these walls anymore.

Baig Don't be stupid, Wani. You are one of the only qualified doctors here. One of five psychiatrists. What are you talking about?

Wani   Maybe I will practise psychiatry, Doctor Baig, but outside. Outside where I can see what is really going on . . . and also show the world to my son.

Baig   Wonderful . . . not only have you lost your senses now you are also taking your son out to processions and protests . . . telling him all of kinds of half-baked, ill-thought, ill-informed /

Wani (*smiles*)   Doctor Saheb, you will be surprised.

I haven't told him anything, but my eight-year-old son stuck his head out of the window of the car today. Around Lal Chowk.

And the moment I was about to pull him in, he looked at a soldier straight in his eyes and screamed, 'Azaadi'. And I, I did not pull my son back in. I let him keep his head out. He kept it high, he looked people in the eye. He felt the wind on his face. On his own.

Without his mother.

Silence.

Baig   Mother . . . is this what you want to raise? Is this your idea of a child, Wani?

Wani   I am a mother, Baig Saheb. A child is not an idea for me. It is a real thing.

Baig   You must be teaching him all this nonsense.

Wani   No. I am not. Perhaps he has his own reasons. His own reasons to be angry.

Pause.

Baig   If we have no reason to be angry, we will go insane, for that is our only memory of ourselves. (*Pause.*) Grow up, Wani. This thing needs to end somewhere. We can't keep teaching our children the same thing over and over again. We have to look ahead.

Wani   But I am not teaching him anything.

Baig   Then how does he know. How does he know all this at this age. What does a child know about politics. What does a child care? You people are ruining Kashmir, not ruining, killing it, with your need to be heroes in front of your own children.

Wani   You're right, Baig Saheb, my son knows nothing about politics, but sometimes when I see him, I wonder if this whole thing is not about knowing at all. It's human instinct.

To be free. Even birth, Dr Baig, is an act of freedom. A child cries out loud, and wails and fears that she will die, and only very, very slowly, learns to breathe. But a child still wants to be born. To be free. Freedom, Baig Saheb, is perhaps larger than reason. Larger than reason, religion, the mind or medicine. Perhaps it is just pure human instinct.

Silence.

And . . . and . . . your family, Dr Baig. May Allah be with them. Forgive me for speaking out of turn, if we were free, they would have lived. Perhaps.

Silence. **Dr Baig** *looks at her in anger.*

Baig How is that? How is it, that of all people, you know if my family would have lived or died, Wani? What do you want to say . . . no really. What is it?

Your son takes his head out of the car and like a complete idiot you allow it, and I am supposed to learn what from it?

Wani Doctor Saheb, I didn't mean to say anything like that . . .

Baig No . . . Wani . . . you think I can't see it in your eyes. You think I can't see it in the eyes of every single person who has been looking at me with contempt or disgust for the last fifteen years. My son Junaid . . . loses his way. Goes across the borders, trains in some godforsaken camp and comes back with a changed name . . . 'Pareen . . . Pareen the star of the east.' A glorified murderer. Is it my mistake that he turned out to be a militant?

Wani Doctor Saheb . . .

Baig A freedom fighter! Oh I forget, a freedom fighter! A boy who does not care about his mother and father and . . . (*Breathlessly*.) becomes a freedom fighter. Who teaches our children this idea of freedom? Their parents?

I did not even know, Wani, at which point did he chose to give up his name, at which point did he decide to go and train in a camp full of Afghan and Syrian mujahideen . . . and now people look at me as if I killed him. Their hero! Everyone wants a hero in their neighbour's house isn't it?

Every leader . . . every single separatist leader of this godforsaken movement has sent their children away to study in England or America, and here you are . . .

THE PEOPLE . . . population . . . the bloody 'awaam' . . . the common bloody man and now the woman: a bunch of fools, killing your children over this ill-thought, ill-motivated celebration of murder!

You, Wani . . . have your son by your side . . . I have held my son's burnt dead body . . . burnt in molten plastic in my hands . . . his organs stuck to my hand . . . and even now when I rub my palms together to wash my hands . . . I can only feel his bile . . . soft . . . green but burnt . . .

And he wasn't killed by any army or police. You know, Wani . . . that burnt bile of his which still haunts me was burnt by his own boys.

His own Mujahideen.

So don't you dare tell me, that if we were free, my family . . . would have lived. Did you?

Silence.

Wani Yes, Baig Saheb. I could not resist it.

Baig You . . .

Wani Yes. My son was holding on to my left hand, and with my right hand I threw a stone.

Baig Do you know, Wani, what effect it can /

Wani I know what effect it will have on his mind, if he grows up thinking that his mother never raised her voice. He is a child of today, Doctor Saheb. He won't let history pass him by.

Baig Don't you dare talk like an illiterate, Wani. Being my student, don't talk like a bloody villager, an illiterate, violent, godforsaken kafir, an infidel who quotes the Quran like an idiot, who knows nothing, neither about science nor about religion, a bloody villager . . .

Silence.

Wani It's relieving, Dr Baig . . . to see that even you have your prejudice. Even the Almighty does not treat everyone equally, from what I know.

I am glad that, considering you look down upon our anger so much, there are things that still make you angry, Baig Saheb.

Silence.

Baig Saheb . . . I just don't want my son to be hiding in the outskirts of Srinagar, in some medical college when the whole city is in flames.

Baig You have lived. That's why you take it lightly. When you were in college, Wani, sitting in medical college, safely in the outskirts of Srinagar, don't forget that thousands of boys were killing each other in the name of jehad. Thousands were killed not by any armed forces but by each other. For guns, for money . . .

Wani Doctor Saheb, I am your student. I always will be. But if I have an opportunity, I will throw a stone again. I loved it.

Baig I know what this is, Wani . . . glorification. A common human error-prone habit. The habit of glorifying other people's sorrows and making them public events.

You people are not allowing that mother to bury her son for two days now . . . do you realize that? For two days she is watching his body rot . . . smelling him as his corpse decays. Two whole days.

It took me seven to bury Junaid. Seven days after he was floating in the river Jhelum and that . . . that was three days after he was burnt to death. My last memory of my son is not a glorified warrior . . . no . . . that is yours and the rest of Kashmir's, of everyone who is buried there at the Eidgah.

My last memory is the smell of him rotting, the shit, the bile and urine inside his body smelling through his pores. Or was it his soul that was smelling so bad those seven days, Wani? Desperate to get out of the limitations of his biology and the politics of his people.

This is what you are giving that mother. You people, the public . . . are no less violent than the army.

You can leave.

Silence.

Wani   Thank you, Dr Baig . . . I have learnt a lot from you.

Baig   No, Wani . . . I am not living with that guilt. There must be some other imperfection in me, otherwise how is it possible that all my children become so unrecognizable one day. (*Looks at her*.) My students have all turned out to be just fine.

Wani   You know what your problem is, Baig Sahib. You are a great doctor but a poor storyteller. You have one story about everything . . . about the hospital, Junaid, Pareen, Wani and Kashmir. Even if someone tells you another story you can destroy it with reason. I really wish we had another Dr Baig in the valley. Someone who could read your mind and heal you. Show you more than one possibilities to your dastaan. Something you do very well with others.

Silence. They look at each other.

Baig (*preparing to leave*)   I am not your father. You don't have to be with me forever. Go . . .

Wani   Baig Sahib, the city is in flames . . . and since your name is on the list, I think you should stay indoors.

Baig   Thank you for your concern, Wani . . . but I just have to get to Ashrafi's place . . . I am sure that in these conditions she won't be able to make it here.
Fifteen years ago I thought I was shaping young minds. Clearly I need to start younger.

Scene Nine

Day two. Afternoon.

Ashrafi *is sitting in her room. She is mumbling to her doll.* **Dr Baig** *enters. He notices her from a distance as she mumbles.*

Baig   As-salamu alaykum, Ashrafi Begum.

Ashrafi (*tentatively*)   Walekum a saalam, Doctor Sahab.

Baig   Where is Bilal?

Ashrafi   He has gone for practice. He has his selections tomorrow and then we are going to Brazil

Baig (*smiles*)   OK . . . good. That is really good. Has he told you when is he going to get back?

Ashrafi   He will come back after playing.

Baig   OK . . . should we play as well?

Ashrafi   Us? What can we play?

Baig   Let's see . . . what have we got here? (*Gives her a bag.*)

Ashrafi *looks into the bag and pulls out little toy figures, like GI Joes. There are soldiers, people, guns, aircrafts etc.*

Ashrafi (*looks at the doctor in anger*)   Is this my age to play with toys?

Baig   No, no, we are not playing with toys. We are playing Djinns.

Ashrafi   Djinns?

Baig   Yes, you and I can be like Hafiz.

Ashrafi *looks pleased with the proposition.*

Ashrafi   Us Hafiz (*Pointing at herself.*) . . . . and . . . (*Thinks.*) Rafiz (*Pointing at the doctor.*) Hafiz – Rafis . . . Rafis – Hafiz . . .

Baig   OK . . . Hafiz (*Pointing at her.*) and Rafis (*Pointing at himself.*) . . .

Ashrafi   This, (*Pointing at a carpet which she spreads on the floor.*) is Kashmir and that is Amir Hamza. Looking out at the world. (*She looks far.*)

Baig   Where?

Ashrafi   There . . . over there . . . you can't see him because you are a Kafir.

Baig   I thought I was a Djinn . . . a Djinn in the army of Amir Hamza . . . the general in the army of /

Ashrafi   Yes, the general of the army of the Prophet, the king . . .

Baig (*excited*)   OK . . . good.

Ashrafi   But how do we play Djinns?

Baig   Both of us take out things from the bag . . . and call it whatever we want.

Ashrafi   And when we call it something, we make it that?

Baig   Yes

Ashrafi   We call something, something and we build the world around it . . . we create the world in our calling.

Baig   Yes.

Ashrafi   Just like the Djinns . . .

She is excited, her body is shaking with excitement.

Baig   Yes . . .

Ashrafi *picks the first one out.*

Ashrafi   My flying lamp.

Baig   The magician Amar Ayyar.

Ashrafi *laughs.*

Ashrafi   My receding ocean.

Baig   The moonlit moon.

Ashrafi   My bridge of smoke.

Baig   The . . . the . . . you have to tell me more of the story.

Ashrafi   How can I tell you more of your story, Rafis . . . your story, you make as your dastaan moves along.

Baig   My story or the Djinn's story?

Ashrafi   Your story of the Djinns or the Djinns' story of you . . . who is telling whose story? (*She laughs.*) My blue mosque in the middle of a . . .

Baig   My . . .

Ashrafi   My paradise.

Baig   My . . .

Ashrafi   My magic mirror for fallen magicians.

Baig   My . . . scooter.

Ashrafi   My hair.

Baig   My briefcase.

Ashrafi   My nails.

Baig   My hen.

They laugh.

Ashrafi   My absolute power.

Baig   My wife, my child.

Ashrafi   My complete night.

Baig   My potato field.

Ashrafi   My sunflower's guide to staying awake.

The sound of the procession gets louder outside the house.

Baig   My watch.

Baig   My glasses.

Ashrafi   My water's book of staying wet.

Baig   My house full of flies.

Ashrafi   Sky full of vultures.

Baig   My bus to the hospital.

Ashrafi   My light.

Baig My third grandchild.

Ashrafi My grandfather.

My father's bicycle.

Baig My . . .

Ashrafi *gets more involved and picks out objects in quick succession.*

Ashrafi My father's back.

My father's /

Baig My father's?

Ashrafi My /

Baig My son's watch.

Ashrafi A clock my father looked at every morning.

Baig A clock my son /

Ashrafi A fly in my father's cup of tea.

Baig My son's back.

Ashrafi My father's plate full of food.

Baig My son's last meal.

Ashrafi My father's /

Baig My father's?

Ashrafi I wipe.

Baig I erase.

Ashrafi I wake up. I check my book. My sunflower's guide to staying awake.

Baig My father's?

Ashrafi The last curfew. My father's bus.

Baig The last curfew, your father's bus.

Ashrafi The Djinns outside, on both sides of the road . . .

Baig The Djinns outside . . .

Ashrafi And in-between, my father . . .

Silence.

Abbajaan . . .

She stops.

The **Djinn** *appears in the room visible only to* **Baig**.

Scene Ten

Baig *and the* **Djinn** *in the same space as* **Ashrafi**.

Time suspended. Between Life and Death.

Baig You . . . you are a ghost.

Djinn You . . . you are the ghost, Abbajaan. Blind, burnt, battered and now betrayed.

Baig You are the one who was betrayed, Junaid.

Betrayed by your own boys /

Djinn You are right, Abbu, I was. The Junaid in me was betrayed, but by you. The Pareen never was!

Baig Don't make up lies for yourself. For you to go on and on . . . at least in death, be truthful. If not to me, to yourself at least.

Djinn You should not have traded me.

Pause.

Baig No one can watch their son go there.

Djinn There were many boys. We were all prepared.

Baig Who prepares for being beaten up naked and being dipped in a pool of oil, who prepares for electric shocks in the penis . . . (*Closes his eyes.*)

Djinn I was, Abbu. We all were.

Baig I can't be speaking to you. You are dead.

This is insane.

Djinn Just . . . Just like the others. The moment it's your fault, we are insane. The moment it isn't simple, it's just madness. (*Pause. Looks around.*) These boys /

Baig These boys are fighting, out of anger. Anger at themselves /

Djinn No, Abbu. No. (*Pause.*) They are fighting for their Djinns. For hundreds of thousands of Djinns, who are still around . . .

It's not a war of right and wrong. For cars and jobs. Of books and blankets. It's a war of the living and the dead. Between those who are fighting for tomorrow and those who are laying down their lives for eternity. These boys, Abbu, will keep coming back, again and again.

Pause.

Baig They wrapped you in plastic, and burnt you alive. And still you /

Djinn They were our boys too. It hurt, but you know what my last words were.

Baig Yes I heard. (*Pause.*) Shoot me, I have gone too far. (*Pause.*) You were scared. It's completely normal to be scared. I was just trying to save my son /

Djinn   You tried to save Junaid, Abbu. In doing so you killed Pareen.

Baig   Pareen . . . that's who you are? Not my son . . . not my son Junaid.

Djinn   (*proudly*)   Pareen, the star of the east. A maker of men. A leader of boys/

Baig   Pareen, a misled boy. A mujahideen . . . the day you joined them /

Djinn   Why, Abbu . . . why do you find it so difficult to believe that there was a boy, deep deep inside your son who was more than just your son. Who was not a coward like you? Who could stand up and fight even then for what was right . . . what was just . . . what was . . . (*Pause.*)

Do you know, Abbu, why we change our names when we take up our arms?

Baig   So that you can cheat yourself . . .

Djinn   No, Abbu . . . so that we always remember we are more than our father's sons. So that at the time of justice our hands do not tremble under the weight of the names our fathers have given us . . . we have only one father . . . that father . . . the one and only . . . in the name of the merciful . . . in the name of Allah . . . !

Baig   Don't you dare, don't you dare make Allah your shield. I know the likes of you.

Pause.

What do you want from me?

Pause.

Djinn   Don't speak to the Indians, Abbu . . . humiliate them, insult them, blow up on their faces.

Baig   You cannot be saying these things to me . . . No son asks their father to blow up on people's faces . . . I am not your Abbu . . . you mean nothing to me.

Djinn   I am your son.

Baig   Junaid, my son. Pareen . . . a . . . a violent mind.

Djinn   Every evening you come here, Abbu, with prayers on your lips . . . prayers that you never recite . . . and every evening you stop outside. Everyone's Abbu has come and gone and it's only you who does not set me free.

Baig   I don't come here every evening to say my prayers . . . for you.

Djinn   Then why do you come here every evening, Abba Jaan?

Baig   To see, if my Junaid is here. But every evening I find Pareen.

Djinn   It was you, Abbu, you who gave me my name. Junaid . . . a warrior . . . a warrior of /

Baig   Of peace. The day they changed your name, they changed your soul and left you here.

Here. In-between, as nothing, as dust, as . . .

Djinn   All of us are . . . All of us are in-between.

Baig   Mad, you are mad, even in your undoing you are mad . . . insane . . .

Djinn   It surprises me. A doctor of the mind, you know so little about insanity, my Abbajaan.

Silence.

Baig *shuts his eyes.*

Baig   I can't be speaking to you . . . you are dead . . .

Djinn   You are not speaking to the dead, Abbu . . . you are speaking to the living . . . you are the one who is dead. You are speaking to your own desire, Abbu . . . you are speaking to your Djinns . . . Pure passion, made from smokeless fire, Allah made the Djinn first, Abbu . . . you are talking to the first creation of the Quran.

Baig   Don't you dare teach me the Quran . . . you cannot be the Djinn of someone . . . if you are a Djinn, you cannot be a soul, if you are a soul, you cannot be a Djinn . . . there are no Djinns of the dead . . . souls are souls and Djinns are Djinns . . . and boys are boys and sons are . . .

Djinn   How can you want everything so neatly, Abbu . . . in this madness, in this chaos, in this churning ocean of violence, not only have our lives got mixed . . . so have our deaths. Our stories, our gods and demons and angels . . . have all collided in this infinite churning of passion. Don't expect reason from a world gone wrong, Abbu . . . don't wish the universe into an understandable falsehood . . . this is real, Abbu . . . and reality cannot be that simple.

Pause.

You wanted to save Junaid . . . But you don't realize that when you killed Pareen, there was no Junaid left in me. No Junaid left, in your house.

Baig   Then I made a mistake, a huge mistake. (*Pause.*) Now I don't even know whose Djinn you are. But whoever you are, it was a mistake. A huge mistake. You should have rather died by an army bullet, than being burnt by your own boys. Burnt in molten plastic, with your insides clinging on . . .

Djinn   For Allah /

Baig   Don't take his name with your infidel 'kafir' soul . . . The Quran forbids the burning of even a rabid dog. You know nothing about God. And there is no god that you can call your own. You are right it's not a war for books and blankets. It's a war of the godless. The godless fighting the godless.

Pause.

Ashrafi *is seen sitting on the floor of her house. Her eyes closed as she feels her doll. As she recites the following verse like a prayer,* **Dr Baig** *and the* **Djinn** *recede.*

Ashrafi

>   The threadbare setting of the sun
>   The last dwindling rays,

The final scream of the boys of snow
The way they die,
On tables and mats.
The last song of their lungs
The need to breathe
The urge to open one's eyes
Everyone wants to live in the end
Everyone wishes another breath.

Scene Eleven

Day two. Evening.

An evening before Eid.

Ashrafi and **Bilal** *are at a mortuary of a government hospital in Srinagar. The mortuary is on the first floor of the hospital. The room is dark.* **Bilal** *and* **Ashrafi** *are just outside the door of the mortuary.* **Bilal** *switches on the torch of his cellphone.*

Bilal   Yes.

Ashrafi   Is this it?

Bilal   Go home Shefu. I am telling you.

Ashrafi   No, Bhaijaan. You are not coming out alone in the curfew.

Pause.

Bilal *looks around.*

Bilal   Shefu, there will be bodies inside.

Ashrafi   I know, Bhaijaan. (*Pause.*) But you will also be there.

Bilal   Shefu . . .

Ashrafi   Hmmm . . .

Bilal   I am scared.

Pause.

Ashrafi   You must say your prayers for Khaled . . .

Bilal   Yes.

Bilal *slowly opens the door of the mortuary. They go in and slowly start walking around the mortuary trying to find* **Khaled***'s body.*

Ashrafi (*smells something. She finds it repulsive*)   . . . This

Bilal   Shhh . . .

He gives her his handkerchief. She covers her nose.

Ashrafi   Why is it smelling?

Bilal *bumps into something.*

Bilal   Stale.

Ashrafi   What?

Bilal   The bodies.

Pause.

Ashrafi *covers her nose even more strongly with the handkerchief. Turns around and is about to leave.* **Bilal** *grabs her from the back.*

Bilal   What!

Ashrafi   I can't bear the /

Bilal   You'll get used to it. (*Pulls her back. Sternly.*) I have been here before. I know it.

Ashrafi *suspiciously looks at* **Bilal***. They continue to look at the bodies. Hopping over the ones on the ground. Uncovering their faces.* **Bilal** *is more definite in his search than* **Ashrafi***.*

Ashrafi   We should go back.

Bilal   No.

Ashrafi   What if he isn't here?

Bilal   He has to be. I know.

Ashrafi   How do you know?

Bilal   Shit.

Ashrafi   What?

Bilal   Women. (*Pause. Looks around.*) All of them.

Ashrafi *looks around at the uncovered faces. She is about to throw up.* **Bilal** *covers her face.*

Bilal   Swallow it.

Ashrafi   What!

Bilal   Swallow it, we can't leave anything behind.

Bilal *covers her face strongly.*

Bilal (*still holding the handkerchief*)   I did it. (*Pause.*) I came with Khaled when his brother was killed. Swallow it once, it won't come back.

Bilal *holds her strongly as she swallows it.* **Bilal** *is relieved.*

Bilal   No sweat, no saliva, no blood, no vomit. Nothing.

Ashrafi *nods.*

Bilal The men . . .

Ashrafi This.

She is looking at a body whose face she has uncovered. **Bilal** *uncovers some more.*

Bilal Here on.

He frantically begins to look. Both of them look. **Bilal** *trips on a body on the floor and falls. His light falls on the ground, throwing light on another dead body.*

Ashrafi Bhaijaan . . . Bhaijaan . . .

She is scampering on bodies nervously. She looks through them slowly. She can't hear any sound or see anything.

Pause.

A moment of silence. They just look at the bodies. **Bilal***'s voice)* Shh . . . shh . . .

Ashrafi Bhaijaan. (*In sobs, out of fear.*) . . . .

Silence.

Suddenly **Bilal** *turns and picks up the light and points at her face from nowhere.*

Bilal Shh . . .

Ashrafi *hugs him. Breaks down with her face dug into his chest.*

Bilal Let's finish this quickly and leave.

Ashrafi (*shaking her head*)   Let's go, Bhaijaan. Let's go . . .

Bilal Look . . . (*Makes her feel his face.*) . . . I am here.

Ashrafi Bhaijaan, please let's . . .

Bilal Khaled is my friend. I have to. Don't I?

Ashrafi It's too late, Bhaijaan. He is dead.

Bilal *holds her tightly.*

Bilal (*softly*)   Shefu . . . I need his shoes.

Ashrafi What . . .

Bilal Yes . . . I need his shoes, don't I?

Ashrafi We are here for his shoes!

Bilal Shh . . . I need them, Shefu. You know. More than anyone else.

Ashrafi *looks at him in disbelief.* **Bilal** *continues to search.*

Ashrafi *follows him. Shaken.*

Bilal The boys.

Bilal *uncovers one. Uncovers another.*

Bilal   Majid, Rafiq, Riyaaz . . . One, two, three . . . oh God.

Ashrafi   What?

Bilal *sits down on his haunches.*

Ashrafi   What, Bhaijaan . . . ?

Bilal   Majid, Rafiq, Riyaz, Basher . . . one two, three, four . . . they lined them up and . . . (*Pause. Gathers himself.*) Khaled, seven . . . (*He counts.*) five, six . . . six? This must be him.

Ashrafi   Seven . . .

Bilal   This is him. (*Pause.*) I am six.

Bilal *and* **Ashrafi** *look at each other.*

Ashrafi   Let's leave, Bhaijaan . . .

Goes towards the body. Uncovers the face. **Bilal** *looks at it, holds the face.*

Ashrafi   Is it . . .

Bilal *nods. He covers the face. Suddenly some noises are heard from outside.*

Bilal   Go . . . go . . . check the door.

He shows the light. **Ashrafi** *goes and looks down the window.*

Ashrafi   Downstairs . . . come, Bhaijaan . . . we must /

Suddenly we hear **Bilal** *gasp. He has removed the sheet from the other side of* **Khaled**'s *body. He breathes heavily and continuously gasps.*

Ashrafi   What . . . Bhaijaan . . .

Bilal   He has no . . . no . . . feet.

Ashrafi   What?

She runs towards him. **Bilal** *has uncovered two other bodies.*

Bilal   Basher, Riyaaz . . . no . . . no feet . . .

Bilal *begins to throw up.* **Ashrafi** *forces the handkerchief on his face.*

Ashrafi (*dragging him*)   Come, Bhaijaan . . . come . . . leave it . . . we will find other /

Bilal   No feet, Shefu . . . no feet . . . They have no feet.

The light of his cell phone goes off. They exit the room gasping.

The **Djinn** *appears in front of* **Ashrafi**. **Bilal** *remains on stage looking at the dead bodies.* **Bilal** *is between the* **Djinn** *and* **Ashrafi**.

Djinn   Your highness . . . (*Smiles.*) Your Bhaijaan . . . our general.

Ashrafi   What?

Djinn   It is time, Your Highness. For Hamza to return. To return as your beloved Bhaijaan.

Ashrafi *looks at him doubtfully.*

Ashrafi   Let someone else be Hamza . . . Let someone else . . . not my Bhaijaan.

Djinn   I am not doing a thing, Your Highness, you are making this up. It's your story . . . I am not even here, Your Highness. Your brother Bilal, is leading from the front, because that is the way you want it to be.

Ashrafi   No, I don't want Bilal to go anywhere. And I don't want you to become him or him to become you.

Djinn   That is what you say, Your Highness, not what you feel deep down inside. I am everything you feel deep down inside. Your Djinn appears as your deepest desire . . . your darkest secret, your strongest wish. You have made Bilal from me. You have made me from Bilal.

Hafiz *ties the black cloth around his face. He is about to leave.*

Ashrafi   But what if my deepest desire is wrong, Hafiz.

If my desire is not my deepest desire. If I want something simpler. Something, more basic, more easy. What if it is not about freedom, not about war, my deepest desire, Hafiz, is to cut out magazines and show my Bhaijaan, and his to be able to tie my hair! We don't want our deepest desires. Our deep desires are not our own . . .

The **Djinn***, who has his face covered turns around and looks at* **Ashrafi***. He comes close to her, takes off the cloth from his face. Kisses her on the forehead. He picks up a stone and begins to recede.*

Ashrafi (*speaking to empty space*)   No, Hafiz . . . no . . . don't do that . . . please Hafiz.

Bilal *gets up with a stone in his hand.*

Ashrafi   Bhaijaan . . . no, Bhaijaan

Bilal *comes closer. Pulls her to a corner and they hide.*

Bilal   Shefu.

Ashrafi   Bhaijaan.

Bilal (*screaming*)   Shefu . . . who are you talking to . . . there's no one there . . . there's no one there, just stop talking all the time . . . just stop it, Shefu.

Ashrafi *looks at him as he leaves her hand.* **Bilal** *looks down, picks up some stones and comes out of the hiding.* **Ashrafi** *remains hidden in a corner. He throws stones, one after another at the window of the mortuary in rage. Whistles are heard.* **Ashrafi** *begins to pull him. The sound of soldiers, running towards them. Their boots, guns and sticks. As the sound gets closer,* **Bilal** *stands and waits for them even more* *decisively.* **Ashrafi** *pulls him with all her might. He throws a stone at the soldiers.* **Ashrafi** *pulls him back into the corner.*

Ashrafi   Come, Bhaijaan . . . let's go . . . run, Bhaijaan . . . they will take us in, Bhaijaan . . . what are you doing, Bhaijaan . . . this isn't you, this is the Djinn. This isn't you, Bhaijaan . . . what are you / (*Screaming.*)

Bilal   Run, Shefu . . . just run away and go straight to the clinic . . . go, Shefu . . .

Ashrafi   What are you /

Bilal   They shouldn't get you, Shefu . . . just go . . . go . . .

Bilal *pushes* **Ashrafi**. *She refuses to move.* **Bilal** *slaps her hard. She stands shocked.*

Bilal   Do it, Shefu. Just go. Listen to me alright. I can't be with you forever. I am tired of you. You are insane. Do you get it? Just get lost!!

Ashrafi   Bhaijaan . . . Bhaijaan . . . this isn't you speaking . . . it's the Djinn . . . Bhaijaan, he is making you /

Bilal *holds her by her hair and pushes her away. She falls. They are both panting.*

Silence.

Bilal   This isn't the Djinn, Shefu. There are no Djinns. All those boys, you saw up there, they are real boys. Real boys cut into pieces. This is me . . . for real. And I need to do this . . . Go, Shefu . . . Go . . .

Bilal *is in absolute rage and* **Ashrafi** *begins to slowly move away in fear.*

He tries to come closer and lift her but she gets scared of him and quickly gets up and runs away. **Bilal** *remains standing in the corner. Watches her go away. He then comes out and stands facing the soldiers who are running towards him. He screams and picks up stone after stone to throw at them. Sounds of bullets.*

Flashes of light. Blackout.

Scene Twelve

Day two. Late evening.

The CRPF bunker next to the Eidgah. **S2** *sits in front of an electrical heater, stirring instant noodles.* **S1** *is trying to catch a frequency on his wireless.*

S2   When is our next supply coming, Saheb?

S1   Shh . . .

He is trying to listen to the messages on the wireless which are unclear.

S2   We will starve like this, Saheb. What is this thing? (*Picks up the packet.*) Did I join the force and risk my life to eat instant noodles? In my village, Saheb, we had so much /

S1 Shut up . . . shut up . . . I know what's there in your village and what's not . . . so just shut up. (*Pause.*) I don't know. I can't pick up a single frequency. What about you?

S2 No, Saheb.

S1 I have never seen you use your wireless? Where is it?

S2 It's in my bag, Saheb. Safe.

S1 Idiot. What is it doing in your bag? What do you think it is . . . your wife's photograph, that you have saved it for a lonely day? Bring it out.

S2 (*feeling shy*)   I am not married, Saheb. I will get married, this time when I go home.

S1 Good. Very good. Now can we please try catching a frequency on your wireless? If no one comes with supplies, we will starve in two days.

Loud sounds of procession are heard. Deafening. They take their guns quickly and stand guard. They are unable to see anyone but the procession sounds are clearly heard.

S1 *and* **S2** *stand tense.*

S1 Don't shoot. OK?

S2 We should just kill some of these assholes and put an end to these funerals!

S1 (*looks at* **S2** *in disbelief*)   They are not here.

S2 Then?

S1 They are in the other lane, behind the houses. They are going around right now, from house to house.

Pause . . . the sounds continue.

S1 Oh . . .

S2 What, Saheb?

S1 They haven't buried that boy as yet.

S2 But I thought /

S1 They haven't . . . they won't do it till they get here.

S2 You shoot, Saheb . . . you shoot, then they won't come here.

S1 If we shoot they'll come here immediately.

S2 Crazy . . . crazy assholes. Motherfuckers, sons of bitches . . . bastards.

S1 Shut up . . . just shut up and /

Suddenly the sounds fade away. As it fades they stand quiet. **S1** *is relieved when it goes away completely.* **S2** *falls on the ground shivering.* **S1** *comes and stands next to* him. *Gives him a glass of water.* **S2** *takes it abruptly and splashes the water on his face. He is sweating.*

S1 It's OK. What? . . . what is it?

S2 *is still in a state of shock.*

S1 Which sector were you in before this?

S2 Rajouri.

S1 Rajouri! You . . . you were in Rajouri? (*Laughs.*) Isn't there an operation every night in Rajouri.

S2 Ji . . . ji, Saheb.

S1 Then . . .

S2 These children are insane, Saheb. I am telling you. I have seen them. Those militants are at least people. But these are all ghosts. They don't have eyes. They have something else. Something else, that no one can see through . . . even when they die their eyes don't shut, Saheb. No matter what you do /

S1 (*suspiciously*) Have you seen them die?

Pause.

S2 Yes . . . yes, Saheb . . . I have.

S1 Where?

S2 I have buried some of them with my own hands, Saheb. And one of them, a little girl . . . of seven I think, her eyes just wouldn't shut. (*Pause.*) I shot her thrice after she died. (*Pause.*) Twice on her eyeballs . . . finally . . . just to get away from that ugly . . . ugly stare . . .

Silence. **S1** *keeps looking at* **S2**. *He goes and sits next to* **S1**. *Just pats him on his back in a placating manner.*

S1 Isn't Rajouri the place, where. . . where it happened. The . . . commandant who . . .

Silence.

S2 Yes Saheb. (*Pause.*) I saw him do it. That night he went insane. He was so angry at everyone. His child had died back home, and he did not get leave to go back.

He went into the village and shot three children, and then in one of the houses, he . . . he raped a mother . . . in front of her daughter.

S1 Were you there with him?

S2 Not when he left the barrack . . . But by the time our next senior officer took some of us into the village to look for the commandant, he had already shot this woman's elder son and he was making the younger daughter sit and watch . . . the . . .

S1 And did you try to /

S2   No, Saheb. It was an order. My father has served the force, my grandfather has served the force . . . he asked me to keep watch outside, I stayed at the door.

S1   And the girl?

S2   Three days later, Saheb . . . I was standing at my post and I saw two men and a young girl walk towards the camp . . . they were not Kashmiris, these men.

The girl was wearing a hijab . . . they came close to the camp and the men left. The girl just walked closer and closer towards the gate . . . towards my post and I thought she wanted something. Water or food . . . I stepped out with my water bottle . . . went close to her and suddenly she took her hijab off, and I saw, Saheb . . . it was this girl . . . she had mad eyes, insane . . . she was looking at me like she would burn me with her eyes . . . and I started running back to the post and she . . . she started to run behind me . . . this little girl . . . Saheb . . . was chasing me to my own post, to an entire barrack and then she made it to the sand bags and just . . . just . . . (*Closes his eyes.*)

S1   What?

S2   She blew up, Saheb . . . right in front of me . . . into pieces . . . and a part of her head fell right in front of me. (*Pause.*) That night I was asked to bury her, and I saw her eyes . . . they just wouldn't close . . . I prayed, and prayed to extinguish her ghost but she would not go away . . . she was dead but her eyes were alive . . . she kept staring at me, Saheb . . . I shot her eyes . . . and her head . . . but her eyes just would not shut . . . and as I was burying her, I just kept hearing sounds from their mosques. Their god was keeping her head alive . . . just her head . . . they are demons . . . these . . .

S1   Just pray to Lord Hanuman that either they bury that child elsewhere or the force gets us out of here.

Silence.

S2   How did they get this close, Saheb?

S1   The patrol is receding. Two battalions have already been called back.

S1 *goes to the pan and starts stirring it.* **S2** *is nervous.*

S1   Come, it's ready . . .

S1 *takes two aluminum plates and serves the instant noodles.* **S2** *keeps sitting still.* **S1** *places* **S2**'*s plate in front of him.* **S2** *keeps sitting quietly.*

S2   The strange thing is you know what, Saheb?

S1   What?

S2   My unit sent me to a doctor. He made me tell him everything. And then he made a report that said, I was imagining everything. I hated his voice . . . the sound of him . . . he was pretending to be my father but calling me insane . . .

S1   What does the report say?

S2   That I am overworked and I need to go home . . .

S1 Then you should.

S2 But I was not imagining it, Saheb, I saw it.

S1 *begins to laugh. Not hysterically but trying to conceal his laughter.*

S2 *looks at him.*

S1 You saw it . . . (*Laughs.*)

S2 *hits* **S1**'s *plate of food and it falls on the ground.*

S2 What are you laughing about?

S1 Are you crazy . . . what are you doing?

S1 *tries pick the food up and put it back up on the plate.* **S2** *kicks his plate away again.*

S2 No tell me first what the fuck are you laughing about? Is this a joke to you . . . my imagination!

S1 Listen I understand you, now don't test me.
Don't waste food or I will kill you.

S2 *kicks* **S1**'s *plate again.*

S1 *gets up and hits* **S2** *hard.* **S2** *falls on the ground.* **S1** *hits* **S2** *again with the back of his gun. He is shocked and badly hurt.*

Silence.

S2 *slowly gets up and sits.*

S1 Now eat . . . if you waste food, I will kill you myself. I don't pray but I don't waste food and water. These are your gods right now. These instant noodles, this bottle of water, your automatic and me. And if your other god . . . your wireless . . . does not tell you anything soon . . . you are short of a god . . . and then it's really bad news. There are several ways in which we could die in the next few hours. Starving each other doesn't need to be one of them.

S1 *starts eating.* **S2** *looks on. He quietly joins in. Both of them eat in silence.*

Scene Thirteen

Day two. Night.

A bench inside the Police Station in Badgaum, on the outskirts of Srinagar.

On one corner **Ashrafi** *sits, looking away and mumbling. Her doll is in her left hand. Her right hand is lightly held by* **Dr Wani**.

Dr Baig *enters after meeting the police officer. He looks at* **Wani**. *A moment of silence. Comes and sits down next to her. He appears flustered and breathes heavily.*

Silence.

Baig We can meet him now. He's in a solitary cell.

Silence.

Wani Is he . . .? Have they hurt him?

Baig (*rhetorically*) What do you think, Wani?

Silence.

Wani You do not need to do this, Dr Baig. I can meet him and /

Baig I need to, Wani. This time I need to. (*Pause.*) I should have done this a long time ago. Back then, I did not have the courage to see my son in prison, but this time . . .

Wani We should not have brought her along, perhaps.

Baig Without her they won't let us see him.

Wani And what are they saying?

Baig They'll keep him here till the end of the talks. He is apparently a 'high-risk' prisoner!

Tense silence. **Wani** *looks at* **Dr Baig** *in horror.*

Wani Dr Baig, we have to get him out. You have been called from the ministry, you can get him out.

Baig He is here on the orders of the ministry.
They showed me a letter.

Wani Saying?

Baig Saying Bilal Naeem is a high-risk prisoner. He needs to be arrested for precaution and kept in prison till the talks are over. It is an official letter. Signed, government of Jammu and Kashmir . . .

Pause.

All the cells are full of boys who have been taken in on precautionary grounds, before the . . . the talks.

Wani He has been kept in a solitary cell . . . Do they suspect that he is . . . I mean do they really think he is a high-risk prisoner? Baig Saheb, we have to do something. If they have a letter from a ministry, they won't take chances would they, they will . . . they . . . will just . . . Dr Baig.

Baig They have kept him there, separately . . . because of me, Wani.

Wani *looks at* **Dr Baig**, *comes closer to him and sits, holding his hand.*

Wani Or maybe because youngsters look up to him? You cannot blame yourself for this, Dr Baig.

Baig Can't you see, Wani . . . they are trying to put pressure on me before the talks. The inspector . . . that bastard in there is showing me a list and asking me to identify potential antisocial elements. (*Sarcastically.*) I have a reputation after all . . . (*Pause.*) and this boy is paying for it.

Looks at **Wani**.

They will kill him?

Ashrafi *looks at* **Dr Baig**. *Silence. She keeps looking at him intently, as* **Dr Baig** *completely unaware of the stare, looks flustered and keeps looking into thin air in the direction of the prison.* **Dr Baig** *is seen to be mumbling things to himself. He is almost an adult mirror of* **Ashrafi**.

She slowly walks towards **Dr Baig**. *Stands in front of him. Gently gives him her doll. He holds it, looking at her. She embraces him. For the first time* **Dr Baig** *holds her.*

Ashrafi Doctor Saheb, I will do whatever you want. Play every game and come on time. Will you take me to my Bhaijaan? Just once . . .

Silence.

Baig I will . . . I will, Ashrafi . . .

Ashrafi You can have my Hafiz, Doctor Saheb . . . you can have him too. He told me you play Djinns every night, every night at the Eidgah. Here he is, Dr Baig, you keep him. You can take him along and play with him. We can go together. You and I.

Baig I will, Ashrafi . . . I will get your Bhaijaan home.

Ashrafi Can you take me to him . . . please, Doctor Saheb /

Baig I will, Ashrafi . . . I will . . . I promise.

Dr Baig *gestures towards* **Wani**, *for her to sit with* **Ashrafi**. **Wani** *gently holds* **Ashrafi**, *sits down with her on the bench.* **Dr Baig** *gets up. Looks inside. Waits. Walks in purposefully.*

Inside, is a prison cell. On one corner which is dimly lit, lies **Bilal**. *Naked. He can be seen in partial light. There is a bulb in one corner of the room which lights his face and his body partly. He does not come into light in the beginning.* **Dr Baig** *stops and tries to look at him.*

Baig (*hesitantly*) Bilal . . .

Bilal *does not reply.* **Dr Baig** *bends over to see. He goes and sits next to the cell on his knees.*

Baig Bilal . . .

Bilal *recoils fast and disappears into darkness.*

Baig Bilal, it is me . . . it is me . . . Dr Baig . . .

Bilal *slowly brings his face into light. He is badly bruised. His lips are swollen and one of his eyes is completely busted.*

Baig Bilal . . .

Bilal Doctor Saheb . . . Shefu reached you . . . didn't she?

Baig *nods.*

Bilal I had to let her go, Baig Saheb, otherwise . . . otherwise they would get her too . . . and then . . .

Baig I understand, Bilal . . . I understand. Don't worry, she is fine.

Bilal *seems to want to stand up and come closer but struggles.*

Baig Bilal are you /

Bilal They did that to me, Baig Saheb . . .

Baig (*in horror*) They . . .

Bilal They inserted a wire into my . . . my penis, Baig Saheb. And gave me . . . shocks in my . . . I cannot . . . I am bleeding, Baig Saheb . . . from . . . I am scared, Baig Saheb.

Baig (*unable to hold his voice*) Bilal . . . Bilal . . . my . . . my son . . . you are /

Bilal Everyone's been killed, Baig Saheb . . . Basher, Majid, Riaz . . . Khaled. And they chopped their feet . . . Khaled has no feet, Baig Saheb . . .

Baig Oh . . . did Ashrafi see it too?

Silence.

Bilal She did, Baig Saheb. I did not know . . .

Baig I understand, Bilal. I understand.

Silence.

Bilal Are you still going to speak to them, Baig Saheb?

Pause.

Baig I will get you out, Bilal.

Bilal Three boys were killed here, right in front of me. They won't let me go.

Baig I will speak to the people in the ministry . . . OK . . . don't worry, I will /

Bilal Baig Saheb . . . will you take care of Ashrafi?

Baig Yes, Bilal, I will. But I will also get you out . . . I promise . . .

Bilal Baig Saheb . . .

Baig Yes, Bilal.

Bilal Just promise me one thing, Baig Saheb.

Baig Yes . . . yes tell me, Bilal . . .

Bilal You won't trade me for someone else . . . (*Silence.*) . . . and get someone else in . . .

Pause.

Baig I won't. I won't . . . my son . . . I won't trade you for anyone.

Pause.

Bilal I am sorry, Dr Baig, I had to ask you.

Everyone in the station was talking about it. About, how you traded your son for another boy when he was caught.

Pause.

Baig Are you hurting?

Bilal I want to see Shefu, Baig Saheb . . .

Baig (*flustered*) Yes . . . yes of course . . . but don't worry I will get you out . . . whatever it is.

Bilal Baig Saheb, I know it. They will kill me before dawn. (*Pause.*) I heard what the inspector told you. My cell is right behind his desk. See. But you shouldn't /

Baig I won't tell them about anyone else, Bilal. They do this all the time. Catch someone and then get someone else. I know, that the boy they are asking for is . . . (*Unconvincingly.*) innocent.

Bilal (*sternly*) I know him, Baig Saheb. He is Coach Saheb's son. I know where he is. They asked me about him but I did not tell them anything. Which is why they've let you come in.

Baig You . . . Know him! What are you saying, Bilal, you know where he is . . . I can't believe you have started keeping track of the whereabouts of mujahideens nowadays! . . . it's a disgrace, if you know people like . . . like . . . (**Baig** *appears flustered and undecided.*)

Silence.

Bilal (*sternly*) He crossed over last week . . . To a training camp in Muzaffarabad but you don't know why or how? You know nothing about him because he hasn't come to your clinic, Baig Sahib. But isn't it possible that he is also worthy of as much understanding as your patients. Don't trade him. They won't find him but will kill one of his brothers and set me free. Set me free and then kill me on another day. I don't want my freedom at someone else's cost.

Pause.

Baig *looks at* **Bilal** *in disbelief. In anger. Gets up slowly, begins to go. He takes off his phiran and throws it to* **Bilal**.

Baig I don't want Ashrafi to see you like this. She has to live . . . and live with better images. You are wrong, Bilal. Once again you are wrong.

Your great sacrifice (*Mocking him.*) your act of bravery is still at someone's expense. If not for yourself, for her you could have /

Bilal For her, I should have stopped myself from throwing a stone? I should have come back from the mortuary, unaffected, unmoved, stoic, like a rock as if nothing has happened?

Pause.

You are blind, Baig Saheb. Absolutely blind. You are treating our minds . . . I wish I could treat your soul. Even now, you are just angry with me, since I know about a boy who has gone to a training camp in Muzaffarabad. A boy you know nothing about. Even now, I am absolutely sure, your instinct is to treat his mind but not stand up against the mind that creates him.

Why are you curing our anger, Baig Saheb . . . why? Cure our children, Baig Saheb, but not their anger . . . please!

Silence.

Dr Baig *keeps looking at* **Bilal** *in disbelief.*

Forgive me, Baig Saheb, for speaking to you like this . . . you will take care of Shefu won't you . . .

Baig I will . . . you know I will . . .

Dr Baig *turns around and walks away. He comes out where* **Wani** *and* **Ashrafi** *are sitting. He gestures to* **Wani** *to send* **Ashrafi** *in.* **Wani** *gets up to go with her.* **Dr Baig** *stops her and gestures to send her alone. He sits down distraught but stern. Visibly disturbed.*

Ashrafi *walks in.* **Wani** *stands between* **Dr Baig** *and* **Ashrafi**.

Ashrafi *comes and stands in front of the cell with her doll.* **Bilal** *sits under the bulb in his room, wearing* **Dr Baig**'s *phiran, smiling.*

Ashrafi Bhaijaan . . .

Bilal (*in a storyteller tone*) Shefu . . . Welcome to your Bhaijaan's cave . . . hahahahahaha!!!

Ashrafi Bhaijaan . . . what happened to your face?

Bilal The lions of Hamza have been fighting with the lions of /

Ashrafi Bhaijaan . . . are you hurt?

Bilal (*trying to get her back to the story mode*) The gallant warriors of the gallant horses, rose up from their cavalries and flew up and up in the sky till the lightning from the stars /

She comes close to the cell to see and then extends her right hand.

Ashrafi Are you hurt, Bhaijaan?

Bilal *stops the story and comes close to* **Ashrafi**. **Ashrafi** *touches his face. He writhes in pain. She withdraws. He looks at her and brings her hand closer again.*

Ashrafi Did they beat you up, Bhaijaan?

Bilal Yes Shefu. They did . . . are you alright?

Ashrafi Yes . . . (*Pause.*) why did you do it, Bhaijaan?

Bilal I am sorry, Shefu . . . I just had to.

Ashrafi You should not have, Bhaijaan . . . we would have been free in two days . . .

Bilal We wouldn't have been, Shefu. We might have been able to get away from here but we wouldn't have been free.

Pause.

Shefu, I am sorry . . . I . . . hit you /

Ashrafi If you hadn't I wouldn't have gone away, Bhaijaan . . . you saved me. I ran to the clinic and that doctor . . . he was still there, he took me home. (*Looks at the doll.*) Bhaijaan . . . you know what Hafiz told me? Just now, as I was waiting outside . . .

Bilal What did Hafiz tell you, Shefu?

Ashrafi That you will become the moon.

Bilal This Eid?

Ashrafi Yes . . . will you?

Bilal *comes closer and looks into* **Ashrafi***'s eyes and now feels her face.*

Bilal A half-moon . . .

Ashrafi Half-moon – half-man . . .

Bilal Half and half.

Ashrafi Half-man-half-Djinn . . . half and half.

Bilal Half-light and half-darkness. (*Laughs.*)

Ashrafi Half-Bilal and Half-Shefu. (*She laughs.*)

Bilal Half-football player.

Ashrafi And half-Ashrafi Naeem's model. (*She laughs.*)

Bilal Half . . . the moon circle . . . in the sky.

Ashrafi I had a dream last night, Bhaijaan.

Bilal Hmmm . . .

Ashrafi Abba came to meet me. That doctor, he made me see him today.

Bilal He did? (*He smiles.*) And then?

By now they sit holding each other across the bars and appear comfortable.

Ashrafi Abbajaan, came to me today . . . the first time after he died, Bhaijaan, and you know what he said?

Bilal What?

Ashrafi I will never go away, Shefu . . . never. I am a star and your Bhaijaan will become the moon this Eid. And forever we will be there, and appear on every single Eid. (*Smiles.*)

Bilal Yes, Shefu. (*Laughs.*)

Ashrafi You will die, Bhaijaan?

Bilal (*smiling*) Yes. Yes, Shefu. I will.

Ashrafi You know what happens when we die?

Bilal We go to Heaven . . . 'Jannat' . . . or Hell. 'Dozakh' . . .

Ashrafi No, Bhaijaan . . . Abbu told me the other day what happens.

Bilal Really?

Ashrafi In the last moments of one's life, one gets a dream, he said. This is the dream we have always wanted to see. 'Actually, we are dreaming people', he said. We live in-between dreams and not dream in-between life.

Bilal Shefu, you are talking like a Pir Saheb . . . like a saint. (*Laughs.*)

Ashrafi Abbu says, our entire life is about this dream. This one that we want to see. Everything we live takes us closer to it . . . and in the end if we see this dream, it is Jannat. (*Pointing up.*) If we don't it is Dozakh. (*Pointing down.*) . . . We don't go to Heaven or Hell, Bhaijaan . . . this dream itself is it. Death, is the dream at the end of life and life, the dream at the end of death . . . it's just that.

Bilal So did Abbu get to Jannat or Dozakh?

Ashrafi Abbu . . . he died so quickly, he did not see a dream he said. He is with us, Bhaijaan, always. But I know you will see your dream . . . you will die in peace. And then become . . . the half moon.

Ashrafi pulls Bilal closer, kisses his eyes. Gives him her doll.

Ashrafi Keep my Hafiz with you, Bhaijaan . . . he will make the pain lesser.

Bilal It seems like you are older to me, Shefu. (*Smiles.*)

Ashrafi I am, Bhaijaan . . . I am very old. I am as old as this land itself. If they get the land, I will become the moon, if they get the moon, I will become the sun . . . they will never get me, Bhaijaan . . . they will never get us. We will all becomes Djinns . . . Djinns . . . at the Eidgah.

Bilal (*in storyteller mode again*) Made of fire, dust and smoke.

Ashrafi (*in the same storyteller mode*) Allah made Djinns before he made Men.

Bilal And set them free to be pure passion . . .

Ashrafi Pure passion . . . no reason, no thought . . . everything that man wants to be.

They laugh.

Bilal   Our Abba told us wonderful stories, Shefu . . . didn't he?

Ashrafi   Our Abbu told us the truth . . . the truth of in-between . . .

Silence.

She gets up.

Don't be afraid, Bhaijaan . . . you won't die, you will just change. From man to moon.

Bilal   I know. (*Smiles.*) Shefu they won't even give you my body. . .you will never see me again.

Ashrafi   As this . . . (*Touching him. She smiles.*) You always insisted, Bhaijaan . . . this is you . . . for real. (*Imitating him.*) In real . . . you are something else. Something much larger . . .

I won't miss this, Bhaijaan . . . I will say your prayers at the Eidgah. I will say your prayers to the sky . . .

Bilal *pulls her closer and kisses her hands.*

Ashrafi   Allah Hafiz, Bhaijaan.

Bilal   Allah Hafiz, Shefu . . . Allah Hafiz.

Scene Fourteen

Day two. Late night.

S1 *and* **S2** *at the CRPF barrack. In the background there is a sound of a young girl reciting the 'Fateha', the prayer for the dead.* **S2** *has an injury on his head from the attack by* **S1**. **S1** *is sitting on the chair trying to listen to something on his wireless on which some distorted sounds are heard.* **S1** *listens to it. Looks irritated and angry.*

S2 (*trying to look out*)   Saheb, if commandant Saheb comes please don't make a complaint against me . . . please, Saheb.

S1   Wasn't he supposed to come today?

S2   Yes . . . Yes, Saheb. Perhaps he will. Later at night . . .

Pause.

S1   Switch on your walkie-talkie . . . now.

S2 *switches it on. He tries turning it on but there is no signal. He tries desperately. Says 'hello hello'.*

S1   We are off.

S2   What?

S1   Yes that's it. What did they tell you about this posting? Why were you sent here?

S2   Saheb (*Nervous.*) this is my punishment posting, Saheb. After the doctor's report, they sent me here on punishment, saying there is no 'action'.

S1 No action! Of course.

S1 *is looking around.*

S2 What, Saheb? I am feeling /

S1 This is where all the action will be. Everything. Can't you see?

S2 *also starts looking around.*

S2 What, Saheb.

S1 We are on our own. And the only picket in the middle of a completely residential area. And that too right next to the Eidgah.

S2 So . . .

S1 They didn't come, because they want us to shoot at the boys. And then the boys will stone us, and before tomorrow, before Eid, before the talks begin it will be clear, that Kashmiri boys are killing Indian soldiers.

S2 *nervously paces inside the picket. Keeps looking out. Picks up his gun.*

S2 Why should they stone us, what did we do to them?

S1 Why should we kill them, what did they do to us?

S2 We are bloody standing here in this cold, away from home to save these . . .

S1 *picks up his gun and shoots the two walkie-talkies. Loud sound. A still silence.*

S2 *completely panics at the sound of the gunshot . . . he coils to one corner of the picket.* **S1** *looks at him in surprise.* **S2** *gets up suddenly and in one move comes and hits* **S1** *hard with the butt of his gun.* **S1** *falls.* **S2** *snatches his gun and vehemently starts kicking his face and body.* **S1** *bleeds as he tries to fight back but* **S2** *beats him up in rage.*

Dr Baig *appears outside. At the gate . . .* **S2** *notices him and rushes out.*

S1 What are you doing? Are you crazy, where are you going?

S2 *hits him again, very hard.* **S1** *lies bleeding.* **S2** *comes out in the open, screams out at* **Dr Baig**. **Dr Baig** *stands unperturbed outside the gate of the Eidgah, looking inside.*

S2 Oi . . . ei . . .

Dr Baig *turns around. Looks at* **S2** *in the eye.*

Silence.

S2 *points his gun at* **Dr Baig**.

S2 Oi . . . hands . . . hands!

Dr Baig *looks puzzled.*

S2 Hands . . . behind your head. Walk.

Dr Baig *does not place his hands behind his head. He remains sitting unmoved.*

S2   Oi . . . ei . . . hands . . . hands. (*Loads his gun.*) . . .

S2 *walks up to* **Dr Baig** *and pushes him hard.* **Dr Baig** *falls on the ground.*

S1 *comes out, struggling to stand.*

Baig   What is the matter with you?

S2   Can't you hear me? Should I kill you? You bastard, bloody . . . how did you get here?

Dr Baig *looks at* **S1** *as he struggles to come closer. He is bleeding all over.*

Baig   What are you /

S2 *places his gun on* **Dr Baig**'s *head.*

Baig   If you could shoot, you would have . . . long back.

S2 *slaps* **Dr Baig**. *Hard.*

Dr Baig *is stunned.*

S2   Don't be smug with me alright. I am here to guard you, you asshole . . . just tell me how did you get here?

Baig   I got here walking . . . like you saw. There is no curfew at this hour and I am not a teenager to be kept away on precautionary grounds!

S1   Oi . . . what are you (*To* **Baig**.) Are . . . Doctor Saheb. Sorry, Doctor Saheb. (*To* **S2**.) Listen, everyone here knows him, OK. He comes here every evening, his family is /

S2 (*points the gun again at* **S1**)   Shut up . . .

Dr Baig *gets up and starts walking towards* **S2**.

S2   Where are you coming? Go . . . go /

Baig   Listen . . . son, it's OK. Just keep your gun down.

S2   Don't come towards me . . . I am telling you, I will shoot you.

S1   Shit.

S2   What?

S1   Now we have to kill him, you idiot. If you let him go out, he will tell everyone what's going on here. And in no time /

Baig   Don't worry, I have nothing to tell anyone.

S2   Oh . . . so now you are scared for your life, you bastard.

Baig   I am scared for yours, son. I am speaking to your people tomorrow.

S2 *slaps him again. Holds him by his collar. Makes him kneel right in front of the gate of the Eidgah.*

S2 Sit here. Just fucking sit here, OK. I can't stand it. When you assholes get smart with us. What do you think, we are enjoying this. This is my idea of a life. You bastard, you are talking to my people. Well talk to them. Talk to them if you /

Baig Shoot me. Go on

S2 *points his gun. Again.*

Baig Yes, go on . . .

S2 *tries hard. His face goes red. His eyes water. He sweats. He sits down on the floor. Holds his rifle.* **S1** *watches in amazement.*

Baig I know. You can't. You are scared, of the sound of bullets.

S1 *laughs at* **S2**.

S1 He's scared of the sounds of bullets . . . really . . . you are. (*Laughs.*) No wonder . . . punishment posting.

Baig It's a common disorder, in soldiers.
Especially like you. It's alright.

S1 Great. Now we are surely dead. I don't have a gun and you are scared of the sound of bullets. Excellent. (*Starts laughing.*)

S2 *walks up to* **S1** *and hits him again. Really hard. A few blows with the back of his gun.* **S1** *screams and falls bleeding badly.*

Baig What are you doing? (*Screaming.*) Why are you . . .! (*Breathes heavily.*) Let him go . . . listen . . . I can get you out of here. If you leave with me, no one will touch you around Eidgah. You will be safe.

S1 (*struggling*) We have to kill him now. Doctor Saheb, I am sorry, I have nothing against you personally, but we can't trust you.

Baig We, who is we? You and I are at gunpoint here. He is not.

S2 Shut up. Just shut up. Both of you.

Baig You are making a huge mistake, son . . .

S2 *charges at* **Dr Baig** *again. Is about to hit him.*

S2 Listen, don't make me hit you again and again. OK. I am not your son. Don't call me that.

Baig I am trying to help you . . . you are disturbed . . . you need some rest . . . some time away . . . listen . . .

S2 *grabs* **Dr Baig** *by the collar.*

S2 Listen, asshole, don't play this trick on me. I know your type. Don't pretend to be large. I can't stand saints in such places. I maybe scared of the sound of bullets, but I could stab you or strangle you or burn you to death. I am the one being large here. So stop feeling good about yourself at my expense.

Loud speeches from the mosque.

(*To* **Dr Baig**.) What are they saying?

Pause.

Baig   They are saying, the child will be buried on Eid and as of now the Imam has not spotted the moon.

S2   But the moon is surely there.

Baig   It is. But if the Imam does not see it, we have to wait another night for Eid.

S2 (*to* **S1**)   So, if there is no Eid, they will keep circling us another day with that corpse?

They won't have the meeting and no one will come.

Baig   Maybe not.

Silence.

S2 *sits down on the floor dejected and not knowing what he should do. He desperately gets up and walks around to find a way out of the place.*

Baig   You Indians want to meet on Eid.

S2 (*snaps*)   What do you mean Indian, you asshole? What are you?

Dr Baig *remains quiet.*

S2   You are not Indian? Then why am I protecting you . . . your children . . . your mother. Why am I protecting you?

Baig   I am not Indian. And you are not protecting my mother.

S2 *goes up to* **Dr Baig** *and hits him hard. Takes out a small book from his jacket, holds it in one hand and in the other hand holds his knife.*

S2   OK . . . come here. (*Pushes him down to the floor.* **Baig**'s *face is covered in mud.*) Can you read this? This?

Baig   No.

S2   You can't, because this is in Marathi. Not in Hindi. I am Maharashtrian. But I am also Indian. OK? You asshole. Get your facts right.

Baig   I am Kashmiri. But I am not Indian. If I were Maharashtrian, I would be.

S2 *slaps him hard again.* **Dr Baig** *falls on the ground.*

S2   He is mad. This asshole. And he calls me a lunatic. Look at him.

S1   Don't start this fight now. Kill him or let him go. But don't get into this /

S2   You. Maybe I should kill you first. I had my doubts. Right from the beginning. Maybe you are also one of them. Maybe you are not Hindu. Maybe . . . (*Takes a knife.*)

S2 *goes towards* **S1**. *Places his knife on* **S1**'s *stomach.*

With his other hand **S2** *unzips* **S1**'s *pants. Pulls his underwear.*

S1 *and* **S2** *are sweating.* **Dr Baig** *is lying in one part of the picket. Everyone is breathing heavily.* **S1** *is in a state of shock.*

Baig   You are sick. Totally sick. (**S2** *looks at* **Dr Baig** *enraged.*) You don't understand, this war is not about gods at all. It has nothing to do with /

S2 *gets up grabs* **Dr Baig** *again. Drags him to gate of the Eidgah. Pulls out a small prayer bell from his pocket and places a knife on* **Baig**'s *neck. Keeps the guns on the ground.*

The speeches from the mosques are distant but charged up.

S2   Fold your hands. Go on, asshole. Fold your hands. Yes, even if they are tied. Fold your hands, close your eyes and repeat after me . . . start . . . fold your hands (**Dr Baig** *hesitates.*) no . . . why this war is not about gods isn't it . . . then . . . what's the problem?

Baig   You are making it about gods but it's not. I am not forcing you to pray to my god . . . /

S2 (*places the knife on his neck*)   What did I tell you. Don't do this shit with me. You are not forcing me to pray to your god? Will you let me stay here, if I pray to mine. Will you allow it?

I still have your neck on the blade of my knife, and if I did not, who knows you might have had my neck on your blade. And you know what, whenever someone chops someone's head off . . . both of them, take their own god's names at the end. Those are everyone's last words.

Baig   Both of them just scream. Everyone just screams at the end. The name of the god, yours or mine, is just an excuse.

S2 *holds* **Dr Baig** *by the hair. Pushes him down on the floor. Makes him kneel down in front of the picture.*

S2   OK, please me. Your Imam has not spotted the moon, so your god is not coming out for you tonight.

So go ahead and pray to mine. Mine is always there you know. Moon or no moon. Go on.

S2 *presses the knife on* **Baig**'s *neck. It starts to bleed.*

S2 *begins to ring the bell. Loudly. He begins to chant, when all the mosques together, do the evening 'azaan'. The sound is deafening.* **S2** *closes his eyes. Presses the knife and tries to ring the bell even louder and faster, as loud as he can. The azaan gets louder.*

Dr Baig *does not say the prayer even though his neck bleeds.* **S2** *keeps looking at* **Dr Baig** *in rage, till* **S2** *collapses, sits next to* **Dr Baig** *and starts to cry. He wails loudly. Lets out a scream.* **Dr Baig** *immediately comes closer. Embraces him.*

They sit still.

Silence.

S2 *opens his eyes. He can see* **Ashrafi** *approaching from the Eidgah. He is silent and stunned.* **Ashrafi** *is wearing a hijab.*

Baig (*facing the other way, holding him*)   You will be fine . . . you will be . . . my son . . . you will be. (*He shuts his eyes.*) You don't need to kill anyone, my son . . . remember the story your Abbu told you . . . in the sky one night there will be Fatima's eyes . . . forever and ever . . . and after that the moon will come out . . .

Ashrafi *keeps walking towards the* **S2** *from within the Eidgah.*

Baig   And as long as Fatima's eyes are there . . . she will keep watching you . . . forever and ever . . . and . . . (*He holds him.*)

S2 *pushes* **Dr Baig**, *picks up his gun and shoots him.*

Silence.

Ashrafi *is unfazed. She removes her veil. Her eyes are visible. She looks at the soldier straight into his eyes.*

S2   Go . . . go away or I will kill you. I promise you. You . . . (*To* **Dr Baig**'s *dead body.*) Tell her . . . tell her to go away or /

S2 *panics on realizing that he is speaking to a dead body.*

Ashrafi *stares coldly at* **S2**.

S2   Just close your eyes . . . I am telling you . . . you just close your eyes or . . .

He points his gun at her.

Ashrafi *bends down, picks up a stone.*

Ashrafi   Shoot me . . . and I will come back again . . . and again . . . and again . . . (*Slowly but decisively like a chant.*) And again and again and again . . . shoot me . . . and I will return . . . again and again . . .

S2 *points the gun at* **Ashrafi**. *The morning azaan is called loudly from the mosque. As the azaan plays,* **Ashrafi** *just keeps looking at him and says 'again and again . . . and again' . . . under her breath as if it were a chant.* **S2** *puts the nozzle of the gun in his mouth. A loud gunshot.*

Blackout.

Epilogue

Suspended time. Between Life and Death.

S1 *and* **Ashrafi** *are on either sides of the gate.*

Dr Baig *is now inside the Eidgah. The* **Djinn** *is in the same clothes as* **Dr Baig**. *But painted.*

A big red carpet between **Dr Baig** *and the* **Djinn**.

Djinn Abbajaan . . .

Baig Not you . . . Not now.

Djinn It's time.

Baig Not yet . . .

Djinn Yes.

Baig Pareen. Not with you . . .

Djinn Abbajaan . . .

Baig Don't call me that, Pareen. For me you are a Kafir.

Djinn How blind can you be? At least now, at the end, at the very end stop hating me. I am here, as I was meant to be. Perhaps I can say my prayers for you, as you never said yours for me. Perhaps then, Abbajaan, we won't be Djinns anymore. Perhaps then, we really will be free. Neither ghosts, nor Djinns, nor souls trapped in this madness . . . but free . . .

Pause.

Baig (*somehow turns his head towards* **Djinn**) Do you know why you are here, my son? Why are you still a Djinn . . .

Pause.

Djinn Because I chose to be.

Baig You didn't choose, my son. No one can choose this in-between.

Djinn You chose, Abbu. You are the Djinn . . .

Baig On the day of judgement, if Allah asks me, am I right or wrong . . . I will ask him in-turn (*Pause.*) . . . . why didn't you say anything about us in your book? We, the people of in-between . . . what do we choose, where do we go? Am I a Kafir or am I not . . . where do I begin my faith, my maker . . . by healing my children or by fighting their war?

What if, Oh Merciful . . . your book was for simpler times . . . on Judgement Day, what if I am prepared but you don't find the chapter for my world?

Pause.

Junaid . . . my son . . . I just want you to know . . . Since . . . these are my last words . . . your Abbu loves you.

The **Djinn** *recedes slowly as he recites the 'Fateha', the prayer for the dead.*

Silence.

End.

Muktidham: The Abode of Salvation

Translated from Hindi by Sakshi Agarwal

This play was supported by India Foundation for the Arts, under its
Arts Practice programme

Muktidham first premiered on 27 January, 2017 at Ranga Shankara, Bangalore, India.

Original Cast and Crew

Scenography	Mohit Takalkar
Lighting Design	Anmol Vellani
Music	M. D. Pallavi and Abhijeet Tambe
Movement Director	Anannya Tripathyi
Production Manager	Vivek Madan
Agnivesh	Sandeep Shikhar
Ahilya	Ipshita Chakraborty
Angad	Irawati Karnik
Ghasidas	Ashwini Kumar Chakre
Guru ma/Sugriv	Kumud Mishra
Bhikhuni	M. D. Pallavi
Nikunth	Neel Sengupta
Srihari	Ajeet Singh Palawat
The Nath (Mathadheesh)	Shubhrajyoti Barat
Yuyutsu/ Hanuman	Pratyush Singh
Chorus	Abhijit Pakrashi, Abhitej Gupta, Abubakar Siddiq, Kafeel Jafri, Poorvi Sardar and Shambhavi Yadav

Characters

Agnivesh, *middle-aged male, a teacher in the Birpur math and contender against Yuyutsu for the position of the head of the math, Mathadheesh*

Ahilya, *middle-aged female, a motherly figure employed by the math, who looks after the disciples and teachers of the math, and wife of the Nath and lover of Agnivesh*

Angad, *young male, a Nat employed by the math, son of Sugriv*

Ghasidas, *middle-aged male, a former actor owing to his caste – he was born a Nat – who works as a porter at present*

Guru Ma, *old female, a fellow disciple of the Nath, who at present looks after the disciples and teachers of the math*

Hanuman, *old male, a Nat employed by the math*

Bhikhuni, *old female, formerly of the Nat caste and converted to Buddhism, now a monk and Birpur's religious chief*

Nikunth, *young male, a disciple of the Bhikhuni at the Buddhist monastery*

Shrihari, *young male, a disciple at the math*

Sugriv, *old male, a Nat employed by the math, father of Angad*

The Nath (Mathadheesh), *also known as the Nath Nand, old male, the present head of the math, the Mathadheesh, and husband of Ahilya*

Yuyutsu, *middle-aged male, a teacher in the Birpur math and contender against Agnivesh for the position of the head of the math, Mathadheesh*

Scene One

It is late into the night. **Shrihari** *and* **Agnivesh** *are on the rooftop. Buddhist chants and people's voices are audible in the distance.* **Agnivesh** *is gazing at the positions of the stars in the sky.*

Agnivesh   What are you looking at?

Shrihari   Acharya? No, Acharya . . . nothing. (*Looks up.*)

Agnivesh   Look . . . here, it tells you the time of the solar eclipse . . . and right near it . . .

Shrihari   Are you listening to this, Acharya?

Agnivesh   Yes.

Shrihari   It is all happening outside, right outside the main entrance of the town.

Agnivesh   How many are they?

Shrihari   I saw them from afar. Without a doubt, there are at least thirty or thirty-five . . . there could be more.

Agnivesh   It's a good thing, religious conversions should happen beyond the doors of the town only . . . All these lower castes, Chura (*sweepers*), Chamar (*tanners*), Mahar (*disposers of animal carcasses*), whatever these Shudras do, they should do it outside.
Are you looking at the positions of the stars in the sky? A marvellous constellation has appeared today . . .

Shrihari   How, Acharya?

Agnivesh   Look. Here's the sun, here's the moon. And along this path, here it points to one direction . . . and here, another. And both changed their direction, twice in one evening.

Shrihari   Only you, my teacher, Acharya, can comprehend whatever you are saying /

Agnivesh   Mathematics . . . (*Laughs.*) mathematics is not about figures, but reasoning.

Shrihari   Only a teacher like you, who has been embraced by the high philosophy of mathematics, and that too with open arms, can say such things, Acharya. (*Laughs.*)

Agnivesh   All right, come, let us see. (*Pulling* **Shrihari** *closer to the side of the terrace from where the conversion ritual can be seen clearly and they can also be seen clearly.*)

Shrihari   Oh no . . . not at such a late hour, Acharya. I was just (afraid of Agnivesh) /

Agnivesh   There are two scholars on the rooftop. The first's mind is occupied with what the second is worrying about . . . the second is ironically contemplating whether the first is attempting to read his mind . . . if this goes on and they never develop any thought at all, will either of the two remain worthy of being called scholars by the end?

Ask me.

Shrihari *looks on.*

Shrihari Forgive me, Acharya, but the sounds, the Buddhist chants, the religious conversions, they all trouble me greatly.

Look, more people have arrived! All the residents . . . of the town of Birpur shall be down there in some time. Acharya Nath is still in Muktidham and these people don't even feel shameful enough to do all this in their own village . . . right at the entrance of the town of Birpur /

Agnivesh Ask, ask me the questions racing through your mind.

Shrihari I am enquiring, with all due respect, don't you think we should do something?

Agnivesh Tomorrow is the debate, after which Acharya Nath shall appoint either Yuyutsu or me as the Mathadheesh. Just let that happen. If I become the head priest of this mammoth Hindu monastery, the Buddhists are done. Enough with all this Buddham Sharanam no one shall take refuge in the Buddha any longer. (*Laughs.*)

Shrihari (*tentatively*) Yuyutsu is the son of the Buddhist king's own head priest. He is learned too. Not more than you . . . but he belongs to the Brahmin caste. Your victory is uncertain. Tomorrow, Acharya Nath shall declare your caste to the whole town . . . after the debate.

Agnivesh *does not say a word.*

I have no doubt that you belong to the Brahminic caste, otherwise why would Acharya Nath provide you with an education, and why would he nominate you for the position of Mathadheesh . . . but . . . there is fear in Birpur that if Yuyutsu becomes the head of the math, our religion, our temple, our principles, they shall all be under threat.

The moment Yuyutsu assumes power, he shall remove the sangh. Then who shall protect Hinduism against the forces of these Buddhists, this Buddhist king?

Agnivesh The people of Birpur have expressed no such worry till now.

Shrihari Forgive me, Acharya. You are highly knowledgeable when it comes to constellations. Era, time, history, mathematics, religion, debate, they are all well within your grasp. But I spend my life among the people of Birpur. They just need one sign . . . that you are with them.

Agnivesh The decision rests with Acharya Nath, Shrihari, not the people of Birpur.

Shrihari May I ask you a question, Acharya . . . from 'mathematics'. A question of reason?

Pause.

There are two individuals. One is about to face death, after acting as the Mathadheesh for forty years. And even in his last days, Hindus are being converted into Buddhists at the entrance of the town.

The other has one direction . . . towards the protection of this religion. There is a sangh, which is strong. Which has been waiting for this moment for years.

The people of this town . . . what expectations would they hold, in their hearts? That their new Mathadheesh is akin to his predecessor or a new era is initiated, an era wherein they do not have to murder their own manhood?

Agnivesh Nevertheless, the decision rests with Acharya Nath.

Shrihari If it is his decision to make, then Acharya Yuyustu is the preacher of the path of peace. And peace? You can see what it has done for Birpur in the events unfolding at the entrance.

Agnivesh *does not say anything.*

One sign, Acharya . . . if it becomes clear that the people of Birpur believe you to be their Mathadheesh, then Acharya Nath will not make the choice in accordance with only his own thoughts, this is what I have inferred.

Agnivesh (*laughs*) you have grown up.

Shrihari It is only with your blessings, Acharya.

Agnivesh *begins gazing at the positions once again.* **Shrihari** *is watching him.*

Agnivesh Your father received the death sentence, didn't he?

Shrihari Yes, Acharya.

Agnivesh He had gone to destroy the Buddhist monastery?

Shrihari Yes, Acharya . . . (*Pauses.*) but ten years earlier, we /

Agnivesh And you feel that by leaving his people at the mercy of the Buddhist king, Acharya Nath wronged them . . . isn't it?

Shrihari *remains silent.*

If he hadn't done so at that point in time, would the Buddhist king have allowed the monastery, our math to remain here? In the past decade, whatever work we have done has empowered the sangh to fend for us . . . it can at least fight the war for us until the kings of other Hindu kingdoms send their armies. It can close down the entrance. Was it capable of all this ten years ago?

Pauses.

Shrihari Do you think of me as your own son?

Agnivesh *turns his gaze to him.*

Shrihari Forgive me . . .

Agnivesh *is watching the positions.*

Agnivesh These positions are not the sky, Shrihari, but we can't see the complete sky . . .

Shrihari Yes, Acharya.

Agnivesh I can never replace your father . . . but if you consider me to be even his planetary shadow, it shall be my good fate.

Shrihari *smiles.*

Shrihari Acharya Agnivesh – our consciousness . . . the great text of laws, Manusmriti – our guide . . . this is the slogan.

Agnivesh Friendship, love, affection, it is all mere coincidence, Shrihari. Only the relationship between a teacher and his student is transcendental. Everything else is temporary.

Pause.

Alright, you go. Acharya Yuyutsu must be expecting us. I'll come.

Shrihari I shall stay, Acharya.

Agnivesh I have to pray.

Shrihari Yes, Acharya.

Pause.

May I leave?

Agnivesh Do not take the path by the door.

Shrihari Acharya?

Agnivesh There are two Churas who are sacrificing their religion to become Buddhists. Even now, they hold the knife of animosity in one hand, and the urn of non-violence in the other. They are still a few seconds away from becoming wholly Buddhist . . . if in such a condition, a Brahmin walks by in proximity, which hand will they use? Mathematics. (*Laughs.*)

Shrihari Yes, Acharya . . . Pranam.

Scene Two

Ahilya *and* **Agnivesh** *are in* **Ahilya**'s *room. They are having sex. End of climax, Agnivesh gets up and starts to chant.*

Ahilya Acharya, the moment you are done, you begin to spout the Manusmriti. (*Laughs.*)

Agnivesh Blood?

Ahilya It is a human's, not a wolf's. Look at your excitement, it's as if you have never seen blood before (*Shows her shoulder.*) you have bitten my entire breast. Now will you eat my shoulder too? (*Laughs.*)

Agnivesh Devi Ahilya . . . it is you?

Ahilya (*laughing*) Devi Ahilya . . .! Goddess Ahilya . . .! Yes, yes . . . tell me, Acharya . . . now I am a goddess. Just a few moments ago you were saying that 'I am a casteless animal. And you are my food.' (*Laughs loudly.*)

Agnivesh   Words spoken in desire carry depth, Devi Ahilya. They must not be spoken of after.

Ahilya   How long should I wait?

Agnivesh   Oh, it is just now that . . . are you a demon?

Ahilya   You have a lot of experience with demons, is it, swami ji? (*Laughs.*) Come, come . . . do not take too long. Tomorrow if you become the Mathadheesh and put a stop to our sexual life, I shall die after having been only called the mother of the monastery.

Agnivesh   Oh, no, no . . . what will we do with such honour to your name? (*Looks out the window.*) Acharya Nath, is he still awake?

Ahilya (*looking in the opposite direction*)   Are the lamps burning?

Agnivesh   Yes . . . look?

Ahilya   I cannot look in that direction . . . (*Pause.* **Agnivesh** *looks in her direction.*) before leaving for Muktidham, he had given me the order . . . I /

Agnivesh *laughs loudly.*

Agnivesh   But he said instead, Ahilya, after I take up residence in Muktidham, you must continue your work with my students /

Ahilya   You are talking as if we did not have any relations before his passage to Muktidham. As if I share the same relationship with every student as the one I have with you. For you, desire may be the science of life, for me, it is the soul.

Agnivesh   It is the soul for me too, but you are so noble . . . that it feels sinful. (*Laughs.*) Enough, this is the last time. After this, never. It is my vow.

Ahilya   Take your vow in darkness, it shall be far more convenient to break.

Agnivesh   How did you come to be so sarcastic at such a young age?

Ahilya   When you receive my caresses and my food, you call me a goddess. But the moment you take off your dhoti, the realisation of my age hits you, is it, swami ji?

Agnivesh   Oh, I'll tell you all about the realisation of age . . . please do come here.

Ahilya   Listen, don't do anything that'll make me shout.

Agnivesh   Shout, for all I care.

Ahilya   All this bravery without the dhoti . . . and the second you put it on, the most dignified among men!

Agnivesh   Did I ask you to agree to child marriage?

Ahilya   Acharya Nath has been very kind to me.

Agnivesh   And I have been very kind to him . . . if I wasn't there, in his endeavour to assuage your thirst, he would have achieved salvation . . . all of the Sanatan Dharma would have cascaded off your body.

Ahilya   You . . . what all do you spout . . . move, move . . .

Agnivesh   Na . . . na . . . you have been my lover for years . . . I can say anything. I shall not move, na.

Agnivesh *begins kissing* **Ahilya** *again.*

Ahilya   Why did you go blank in the assembly?

Agnivesh *suddenly stops. He sits up. Pauses.*

Agnivesh   He did not say anything inappropriate in my introduction. In fact, he was praising me /

Ahilya   It was just a day before the debate, Acharya Agnivesh, nobody is all praise for anyone. Yuyutsu is no less clever. If during his introduction, it was not required that someone announce his caste to be Brahmin, then why was it necessary to mention in your introduction that Acharya Nath shall proclaim your caste tomorrow, before the debate?

Pause.

Agnivesh   Because he shall proclaim it.

Ahilya   He shall tell you. He is not going to proclaim it to the whole town of Birpur. And what can be so shocking about the revelation of your caste?
After all, Acharya Nath himself has nominated you for the position of the Mathadheesh.

Agnivesh   It is natural for Yuyutsu to be here, Ahilya, but not me.

Ahilya   You have been brought here by virtue of Nath Nand's dreams. I don't see anything more natural than that.

Agnivesh   Yuyutsu's father was the lone priest in the worship of Vishnu in the Buddhist kingdom. For me /

Ahilya   Faith in Ram in a Buddhist kingdom? I don't understand how you consider it to be natural.

Agnivesh   Are you insulting me?

Ahilya *forces back* **Agnivesh** *to lie on his back and perches herself on him.*

Ahilya (*laughs*)   No, no, Acharya Agnivesh. The soon-to-be Nath of the math of Birpur . . . absolutely not. I couldn't even think of doing such a thing.

Ahilya *kisses* **Agnivesh***'s body.* **Agnivesh** *completely relaxes his body. In the next few lines,* **Agnivesh** *begins to unwrap* **Ahilya***'s sari.*

Ahilya   I don't have a child. After the Nath's death . . . if you become the Nath, you could marry me.

Pause. **Agnivesh** *looks towards* **Ahilya***.*

What is your opinion?

Agnivesh   Do you know what you are saying?

Ahilya   Yes. I am not saying anything, it's just that . . . it is stated in the laws of the math. It is written in the treatises.

Agnivesh   Is that what you want?

Ahilya   Is it not what you want?

Agnivesh   Nothing could give me greater happiness, Ahilya, than calling someone completely mine . . .

Ahilya   But you want to wager this future on a debate?

Agnivesh   It is the norm, Ahilya.

Ahilya   And what happened today, at the assembly, was it not against the norm?

Agnivesh   What do you mean?

Ahilya   I mean that Yuyutsu is aware that the residents of Birpur are on your side. And in mere conversation, in a full assembly, he sowed a seed of doubt in everyone's mind about you.

Agnivesh   What are you saying?

Ahilya   He is the son of the royalty's head priest. And you, the scholar who has always trusted him. If you want that /

Agnivesh   I do want you to be mine, Ahilya. If you can be mine after I become the Nath – that I desire even more. Who do I have with whom my relationship could even be an image of what this relationship means to me?

Ahilya   Then give this town the news that Acharya Agnivesh stands by them. They have become adept at staying silent . . . but there is a storm raging within. These Buddhist chants aren't taking place every night in front of that door for no reason. They are giving us a warning. You must do the same . . .

Agnivesh   This is the revolution of the learned. I do not want to commit a foolery. Right now, the Nath is at Muktidham, and in his final moments /

Ahilya   Mukti? What is salvation? Acharya Agnivesh, when a mortal becomes one with God . . . when his form is that of God, when his energy is God's, when his nothingness is God's, it is said that, that is when he achieves salvation. In his final days, if the Nath can forget the ghosts of his religion and understand its present, it shall only aid his salvation, not hinder it.

Agnivesh   I want to have a complete life with you, Ahilya.

Both of them sit in each other's embrace.

Ahilya   Then there would be no obscurity.

Agnivesh   None.

Ahilya   And then . . .

Agnivesh   I shall not hesitate to light a lamp. (*He laughs.*)

Ahilya   And then . . .

Agnivesh   I shall make my home in your flesh.

Ahilya   Just my flesh?

Agnivesh   Everything from your flesh to your dreams, I shall keep them to myself. Whenever my heart desires, I shall dive into them like a child . . .

Ahilya   When you are like a child, you become a better lover.

Agnivesh   I can smell your scent even when I am in prayer.

Ahilya   When you leave at the break of dawn, the birds do not return to the courtyard.

Agnivesh   When you are near, I am not aware of any other being in the cosmos.

Ahilya   You do not belong to any caste . . . you are only capable of love.

Agnivesh   I . . .

Ahilya *covers* **Agnivesh**'*s mouth.*

Agnivesh   I /

Ahilya   Quiet . . . (*Kisses his eyes.*) shhhhh . . .

Both lie together in silence.

Agnivesh   When you are silent, it feels like the cosmos is being built, at this very moment . . .

Ahilya *smiles.*

Ahilya   Whatever happens tomorrow, come straight here.

Agnivesh   Where else will I go, Ahilya?

Ahilya *kisses him.*

Ahilya   What does the Manusmriti say about kissing, Acharya? (*Teasing* **Agnivesh**.)

Agnivesh (*rises and begins wearing his dhoti*)   It says . . . kiss wantonly.

Ahilya   Are you leaving?

Agnivesh   Yes . . . To meet my enemy from childhood.

Pause. **Ahilya** *looks at him with anger.*

Ahilya   Leave your dhoti here . . . I will wrap myself. And sleep in it.

Agnivesh *smiles. He extinguishes the lamp and leaves.*

Scene Three

Yuyutsu *and* **Agnivesh** *are climbing a hill. They are children.* **Yuyutsu** *is sitting on* **Agnivesh***'s back.*

Yuyutsu   Be careful . . .

Agnivesh   I'll let you fall from here only.

Yuyutsu   First off, I have been given a punishment because of you. Otherwise, have I lost my mind that I would climb on your back?

Agnivesh   If I hadn't taken the blame on my head, I would be on your back. You waste of air . . .

Yuyutsu   How many times did I tell you to keep the ganjika hidden? But no . . . I shouldn't get anything for you from home.

Agnivesh   Did I ask you to get it?

Yuyutsu   You never go anywhere during the vacations. You just plop here in the math, all alone. And then when I get you something, I am the one who is to be caught? Be thankful that Acharya Nath did not throw us out.

Agnivesh   When there is no one at my house, where will I go? And as if you achieved great feats by going home . . . after getting beaten up by your father, you have got a handful of ganjika.

Yuyutsu   Carefully . . . carefully . . . Acharya Nath is watching us from below.

Agnivesh   I'll make you fall as soon as we reach the top.

Yuyutsu   Acharya Nath will incinerate us from down below. You'll be enveloped by the fire.

Agnivesh   If I'm enveloped, I'll light my final ganjika.

Yuyutsu   Two scholars were terminated in a day. One fell off the cliff, the other was incinerated. (*Laughs.*)

Agnivesh   I don't want to become a scholar . . . there is cave on that cliff. I'll hide there.

Yuyutsu   Ganjika is not suitable for children.

Agnivesh   Then why did you get it?

Yuyutsu   It is what the people say . . . it's not written in the treatises. (*Laughs.*)

Agnivesh   I saved you today . . . otherwise, there would have been a portion added to the law books on ganjika.

Yuyutsu   If I ever become Nath Nand someday . . . I shall distribute ganjika.

Agnivesh   If you ever become Nath Nand, I'll incinerate myself.

They both reach the top. Now they are in the present. **Agnivesh** *walks offstage. On the hill, behind a rock,* **Yuyutsu** *begins rolling a joint and looks up at the map of the sky. From within the hill, the sound of breaking stone emerges. There is a fire burning in the front.*

Behind them stand **Shrihari***, and* **Ghasidas***, a man of the Nat caste who now works as a porter and not an entertainer. When they are far from the cave, they talk in high volumes. In proximity of the cave, their voices drop.*

Ghasidas   Acharya, I shall not give it to you with my own hands, but light this ganjika and try it . . .

Shrihari   Where did you get it from?

Ghasidas   Far from home, Acharya . . . if I lie, may my tongue be cut off.

Shrihari   Swamiji did not hear you.

Ghasidas   If I turn towards him and speak, the ganjika will get polluted, Chhote Acharya. If I say it in this direction, I'm gone. If I say it facing upwards, the gods shall curse me. If I say it facing down, what can I say about my own people now . . .

Shrihari   Just because you are an actor by caste, you will try to act at every turn?

Ghasidas   Acharya, actually, the /

Shrihari   Stop, stop . . . I have heard enough. Garrulous . . . I am asking you, who has sent this?

Ghasidas   The few remaining Brahmins down there in the village . . . they asked me to give it to Acharya. My shadow should not fall on it. So, keeping my feet in the opposite direction of the moon and my hands facing it, I came. My waist is all twisted. My spinal cord has become like a snake.

Shrihari   So?

Ghasidas   My apologies.

Yuyutsu   What is he saying?

Shrihari   Acharya, he has brought some more ganjika.

Yuyutsu   Tell him Yuyutsu already has ganjika.

Ghasidas   You are on the verge of opening the math gates for the lower castes, Acharya. This is a mere present.

Pause.

All right then. I shall go then and tell them that the ganjika of the lower caste will not /

Yuyutsu (*gesturing to* **Shrihari**)   Come, Ghasidas . . . come closer.

Ghasidas   Pranam, Acharya.

Yuyutsu   Pranam, now tell me . . . have you come only to bring this ganjika to Yuyutsu or is there something else?

Shrihari (*pointing towards the cave*)   Have you come to learn the arts from this Buddhist?

Ghasidas   The arts? No, no, my lord. Not under any circumstances. Not on any occasion /

Yuyutsu   Speak coherently . . . have no fear . . .

Ghasidas *smiles.*

Ghasidas   Am I insane, my lord, that I shall learn another art? I am already in regret from being born into one art. I have left that too now. Have some faith in me, I have only come to give you this.

Yuyutsu   Look inside, how many do you see?

Ghasidas   Yes, my lord. (**Ghasidas** *peeks into the cave.*)

Shrihari   Inside? He will glance inside the cave, Acharya? Will their art not be polluted?

Yuyutsu   They do not believe so.

Shrihari   Ram . . . Ram . . .

Ghasidas   There is only one. Alone.

Yuyutsu (*to* **Shrihari**)   Those who do not get along with anyone become Buddhists. (*Laughs.*)

Shrihari   Look carefully. Are there any weapons?

Ghasidas   He is holding a hammer with spikes. He is making the painting of a blue lady.

Shrihari   Blue lady?

Yuyutsu   Blue-Krishna, blue of the sky, blue of the honey-minded Neelkanth . . .

Shrihari   But, what is the blue lady, Acharya?

Yuyutsu *gestures to* **Shrihari**. **Shrihari** *runs to the cave.* **Ghasidas** *steps aside.* **Shrihari** *peeks in.*

Shrihari (*with arrogance*)   Bheegu . . . it is Bheegu, isn't it? Look.

Ghasidas *looks in.*

Ghasidas   Yes, my lord. It is Bheegu. The dawn of Acharya Nath's departure to Muktidham was also the dawn of Bheegu's conversion to Buddhism.

Yuyutsu   He became a Buddhist. How?

Ghasidas   In the same manner that the entire village became Buddhist.

Yuyutsu   What has to be done, in order to become a Buddhist?

Ghasidas   They sprinkle a few drops of water on their forehead. There is one chant that everyone does. That's it, it's done!

Yuyutsu   Budhh did not even say all this. You are Buddhist simply if your thoughts are Buddhist . . .

Shrihari   Human beings are lazy by nature. Just make any task easy enough . . . and you will never fall short of followers.

Ghasidas   Forgive me, my liege . . . how is it easy? He has come in the night to break the stones . . . alone.

They all laugh.

Shrihari   He is also an actor by caste, isn't he?

Ghasidas   He was, my lord . . . no more. You are well aware of this . . . Buddhists do not uphold the caste system.

Shrihari   I do not know what is there in upholding or refusing to uphold the rules of one's dharma.

Yuyutsu   The ganjika is adequate . . . Shrihari, you too?

Pause.

Shrihari   Acharya, if I have your permission?

Yuyutsu   Yes, of course . . . why not? You are no longer a child. (*To* **Ghasidas**.) how did this Bheegu become a stone sculptor from a Nat?

Ghasidas   Artists are artists, my lord . . . since the temple stopped hosting Nats, they no longer had work. By becoming Buddhists, he has received the opportunity to perform an art form once again. And this time, not for others, but for his own peace of mind.

Yuyutsu   If it is such an invaluable opportunity, why don't you convert to Buddhism? Has anyone stopped you . . . Sanatan Dharma does not stop or stagnate anyone.

Ghasidas   At this age, what is the point in becoming Buddhist, Acharya? The Buddhists say there is no God. I have spent my entire life in fear of God. Now, just when I am approaching death, I can't do it.

Agnivesh's *entrance.*

Agnivesh   Buddhists . . . are atheists . . . neither dualists, nor monistic, nor specifically monistic, not worshippers of Shiv, not followers of Mimansa, not pre-presumed. Not gluttonous, not materialistic . . . nothing . . . Buddhists . . . only atheists. Give an atheist language and he shall be a Buddhist. You are intelligent, Nat, that you are not committing this sin in your old age.

Shrihari   Pranam, Acharya.

Yuyutsu *stands up and embraces* **Agnivesh**.

Yuyutsu   Come, my friend, let us smoke ganjika . . .

Agnivesh   I have not come here to smoke ganjika.

Yuyutsu (*smiles*)   That is the sole reason we were anticipating your presence. Who knows what you were off doing?

Pause.

Agnivesh   Whatever I may have been doing . . . at least I wasn't sitting here on the hill, there, right across from Muktidham, enjoying myself in the company of Churas, Chamars and Nats.

Yuyutsu   Acharya, why are you getting so agitated? Sit . . . let's smoke ganjika to our heart's satisfaction. After tomorrow, whoever becomes the Nath, his relationship with ganjika shall end here in this life. (**Yuyutsu** and **Shrihari** *laugh*.)

Agnivesh   How easy it was for you, today, in the assembly, to taint my status!

Yuyutsu   How, Acharya? I am your friend . . . I was praising you.

Agnivesh   Do not teach me, Acharya Yuyutsu . . . you are a childhood friend of mine, I know you inside out. There has always been a chasm between what you say and what you do.

Yuyutsu   You are angry at the Buddhists. We are all well aware of what your sangh will do to the Buddhists if you become the Mathadheesh . . . but such rage at your own friends?

Agnivesh   We have always been friends, Yuyutsu. But I have never said a word about what may be unknown about your caste or knowledge . . . or anything about you at all.

Yuyutsu   Are these your words or is it coming from the consciousness derived from the mothers these days?

Pause.

Agnivesh *slaps* **Yuyutsu** *hard.* **Yuyutsu** *is about to fall down but* **Shrihari** *saves him.* **Ghasidas**, *who was standing right in front of them, steps away from their path.*

Pause.

Yuyutsu   Ghasidas, you go from here.

Ghasidas   Yes . . . yes, Acharya . . . immediately . . .

Agnivesh   Wait.

Pause.

Yuyutsu   This is between us friends. Ghasidas, leave.

Agnivesh   I said wait.

Ghasidas   Acharya . . .

Agnivesh   What is it that you wanted? That Acharya Yuyutsu falls from the hill and loses his life?

Ghasidas   No . . . no, Acharya . . .

Agnivesh   Then why did you move away?

Ghasidas   How could I touch him, Acharya?

Agnivesh   You can bring ganjika with your own hands. You can render the Acharyas of Hinduism unconscious. But you can't help them in a crisis?

Ghasidas   Crisis? Acharya, you were the one who?

Yuyutsu   Acharya Agnivesh . . . you can let him go please . . . he only /

Agnivesh   You shall be punished.

Ghasidas   A punishment, my lord? What did I do?

Agnivesh   A Brahmin could have died because of you . . .

Yuyutsu   What are you doing . . . Agnivesh?

Agnivesh   Why not? You are a Brahmin for certain . . . is your life not valuable?

Ghasidas   My lord, what can I . . . what did I . . .

Agnivesh   There is only one path to repentance, Ghasidas.

Ghasidas   Yes, Acharya . . . yes . . . anything . . . just my life . . .

Agnivesh   Shrihari . . . step aside . . .

Shrihari *moves from where he was standing.*

Agnivesh   Block the entrance to this cave, Ghasidas.

Yuyutsu   He cannot do that, Agnivesh.

Agnivesh   Why?

Yuyutsu   I shall not let this happen. It is violence . . .

Agnivesh   And this . . . for a Nat, you are raising your voice against an Acharya from your own math . . . is this what the future holds for Birpur?

Yuyutsu   The actions you are taking, they are not worthy of a math's Acharya. There can be a debate on this . . .

Agnivesh   Debate . . . you will debate on every topic?

Shrihari, step aside. Ghasidas, block the entrance. Otherwise, you do know what will happen to you after tomorrow.

Yuyutsu   Nothing will happen to you, Ghasidas . . . don't do it.

Agnivesh   All right. The decision is yours, Ghasidas. Do as you deem fit, however you may see the future of Birpur.

Agnivesh *sits down and lights the joint. Everyone is watching* **Ghasidas**. *Frozen to his spot, he begins to cry. He folds his hands.* **Agnivesh** *faces the opposite direction and smokes.*

Ghasidas *turns and begins blocking the entrance to the cave, but he is unable to do it alone.*

Agnivesh *joins him.* **Shrihari** *also gives them a hand.* **Yuyutsu** *just stands there.*

Agnivesh   You will not support your own people in the protection of a Buddhist, Yuyutsu?

Yuyutsu *watches wordlessly. Then, he also lends a hand. The sound of people struggling emerges from within the cave. The sound of breaking stone has ceased.*

Everyone sits down and smokes together. They are all panting.

Scene Four

The next morning. At the cliff of Muktidham.

*Below, in the village of Birpur, the preparations for the evening debate are underway. Acharya Nath (***Nand***), seated within Muktidham, is looking down at the village.*

Ahilya *is standing at the door, holding a pot of water. She is watching the Acharya.*

Inside, near Acharya **Nand***, three old men are sitting, dressed as monkeys –* **Angad***,* **Sugriv** *and* **Hanuman***. They are continuously looking up and chanting Ram-Ram.*

Down below, in Birpur, there is a commotion. The monkeys step outside.

Sugriv   Pranam, Devi.

Ahilya   Pranam . . . what is it today?

Hanuman   Acharya has instructed us to recite a portion of the legend of Ram.

Ahilya   Why are you dressed like this?

Sugriv   I am Sugriv, he is Angad, and he is Hanuman.

Ahilya   It is a very unique solution to employ the Nats.

Hanuman   It has been like this for years, Devi. The math has banned the theatre of Nats. If we perform the legend of Ram there, we have to face the rage of the Buddhist king. This is all that is left . . .

Ahilya   Where is your tail?

Angad   We had only two tails in our store, Devi. So, we had to cut back on Angad a little.

Ahilya   Miserliness even when it comes to salvation?

Sugriv   Devi, we did all we could manage . . . it is not as if we have separate finances for salvation, that we take some money from the box.

Ahilya (*smiling*)   Did you see Ram?

Angad   Ram graces us with his presence every week . . . twice.

Ahilya Is that so?

Hanuman Yes, in person.

Ahilya Where . . .

Hanuman Here . . . in Muktidham. He comes here . . . and takes them.

Ahilya Who?

Sugriv The souls who are pure.

Ahilya Have you seen it for yourself?

Sugriv Certainly . . . without a doubt!

Ahilya I had the knowledge that this task had been given to Yamraj by Ram? (*Pause.*)

Hanuman Yes, you have heard right.

Ahilya So?

Hanuman So?

Ahilya I am asking you . . . that /

Angad Yes, yes . . . I, I shall explain it to you.

Sugriv Yes, you explain it to her.

Hanuman He shall explain. He is young . . . he explains well.

Angad Is Shri Ram in everyone?

Ahilya *eyes* **Angad** *with suspicion.*

Hanuman *and* **Sugriv** Yes. Yes . . . he is in everyone . . . he is . . . in everyone . . .

Angad So, he is in Yamraj as well then?

Hanuman *and* **Sugriv** Yes . . . yes . . . absolutely. Shri Ram is in Yamraj too.

Angad Therefore . . . (*Laughing.*)

Hanuman Those who are going, he is in them also?

Angad *and* **Sugriv** Yes . . . yes . . . certainly.

Hanuman Where . . . they are going. He is there . . . and where they are going from . . . he is there too.

Everyone On all sides, there is just Ram Ram Ram.

Ahilya Well done . . . eat some almonds . . .

Hanuman Thank you, Devi (*Taking the almonds.*) in the end, Shri Ram . . . is coming to take himself . . . and he is coming himself . . . from his own nest to his own nest.

Sugriv *and* **Angad**   Yes . . . yes . . .

Nand (*the voice comes from inside*)   Ahilya.

Ahilya *fumbles and heads inside.*

Ahilya   Yes . . . yes . . . pranam, Acharya.

Ahilya *enters inside. She is about to move forward when Acharya* **Nand** *stops her, showing her the palm of his hand.*

Nand   Sugriv.

Sugriv   Yes . . . yes . . . my lord.

Nand   Step inside.

Sugriv   Yes . . . yes, my lord.

Nand (*to* **Sugriv**)   Recite, recite the name of Ram.

Sugriv   Yes, Acharya.

Sugriv *goes to a corner and begins chanting the name of Ram.* **Ahilya** *had stepped inside, just past the doorway and come to a stop. Acharya* **Nand** *is looking down.*

Ahilya   Water?

Nand   There is ample . . . (*Shows her his pot.*)

Ahilya   Food?

Nand   Ample . . .

Ahilya *stands, silent.* **Sugriv***'s chants of Ram-Ram are becoming more and more anxious.*

Nand   What is all this noise, Ahilya?

Pause.

What I have heard, is it true? Do you have any knowledge of this?

Ahilya   A Buddhist artisan was found dead.

Nand   Or murdered?

Ahilya *does not say a word.*

Do you know who did it?

Ahilya   No.

Nand   And people are going around the town beating drums? Has everyone lost their mind? Anytime now, the Buddhist king shall arrive. At this time . . . in this manner . . . where is Agnivesh?

Ahilya   Acharya?

Nand   You must know?

Ahilya   Acharya, no.

Nand Could it be the work of his *sangh*?

Ahilya The sangh . . . works for the welfare of the people, Acharya. Last year, they had saved countless lives when the town was flooded. And before that /

Nand They had saved the lives of only Brahmins, no?

Pause.

This occurrence may escalate catastrophically, Ahilya. And my gut is telling me that you know something about this . . .

Ahilya You take rest. You are now free from these concerns. Your work is only the next Nath's /

Nand When I was down there in the temple, there was so much to do. The religious, the societal, the mundane, but now, all I have is my focus in Ram and the legend of Ram . . . and yet, my focus is unable to pull me away from the temptations of life . . . shockingly, I find myself closer to them . . . and now this . . . this violence!

Will Ram accept me?

Ahilya Acharya . . . you should take rest. You (**Ahilya** *walks into proximity with him, so she can seat him on the cot.*) /

Nand There is one subject that I have focussed on immensely . . . and that is love? Pure, mighty, grand, the all-consuming emotion that makes you indifferent to everything else every quarter of the day.

Sugriv . . . what is your opinion? Is love virtuous or a crime? Is it freedom or attachment?

Sugriv I . . . how would I know, my lord? I am a monkey.

Nand (*to* **Ahilya**) after murdering his own brother, Bali, he had married his wife, Tara. He believed Tara to be his mother and he was in love with her as well . . . his /

Ahilya After Bali's death, had he achieved salvation or not, Acharya?

Nand Pardon?

Ahilya Acharya, did Bali achieve salvation after his death?

Nand Yes . . . Bali was an incarnation of Vishnu . . . he achieved sal /

Ahilya (*with a touch of irony*) That is why the legend of Ram is so popular. Everyone achieves everything . . . Bali achieved salvation . . . Sugriv, Tara . . . Tara, love . . . Jai Shri Ram. (*Shuts her eyes to praise God.*)

Sugriv May I take your leave, my lord?

Nand No, no . . . monkey. Why will you go? It is my journey.

Ahilya Drink some water, my lord. In a short while, your disciples shall come to you for their final lesson and the debate . . . (*Forcing the water down his throat.*) by no means should you give your successor his lesson with a parched throat.

Nand Yes, and I have to declare his caste as well.

Nand *takes the water from* **Ahilya**. *Pause.*

Ahilya Drag your cot and place it by the window. You shall be able to see the preparations underway from there.

Nand The moment I look down . . . all I can hear is this new pandemonium. This glorification . . . in a single night, this town . . . what has happened after a single death? Were they always like this, and I just never understood them?

Ahilya You are a scholar, Swami.

Nand Ram was a Kshatriya . . . Buddh was a Kshatriya . . . priests, Brahmins, scholars hold no significance.

Ahilya If you begin to cast doubt on the faith you have held on to steadfast, what will happen to Birpur?

Nand I always believed that in the end, humans approach their pyres free from suspicions. Love, suffering, anger . . . after emerging triumphant against all these. But, in the end, there is only suspicion left, Ahilya. Love and suspicion. Nothingness is nowhere to be found!

He closes his eyes. **Ahilya** *pulls his cot to the window.*

The love of religion, the love of salvation, the love of . . . oh god, the love of the body . . . (*He touches* **Ahilya**, *and then suddenly lets go. He chants Ram-Ram along with* **Sugriv**. **Ahilya** *stands before* **Sugriv**, *unprepared.*)

I have spent years in the pursuit of knowledge and they have taught me that love is not an elemental entity. It is by no means so in the case of a husband and wife. The love that is pure is one where there is the possibility . . . of the nurturing of many varieties of love. Where every kind of love finds its foundation.

In his love for Ma Sita, Shri Ram broke the bow, then loving her as his own sibling, he went to the forest with Lakshman, then he loved her like a father, then a friend, then like a warrior loves his people, he loved her . . . in the fear of that love, he declared war, and in the end, he coerced Sita ma into yielding herself to the test of fire . . . marriage is the union of many different kinds of love, in the past few days, I have come to this knowledge.

Ahilya Forgive me, Acharya, but may I say something?

Nand Certainly . . . put forth your own thoughts.

Ahilya Ma Sita may feel the opposite in her love for Shri Ram.

Sugriv Acharya, may I leave?

Acharya **Nand** *gestures with his hand and he sits down again.*

Ahilya First, she was presented as a gift in the ceremony to fix her marriage, then she was sent off with scorn, she went and stayed in the jungle with Shri Ram's brother, a demon like Raavan was able to abduct her owing to Lakshman's foolishness, and in the end, when, after fourteen years of waiting, she met Shri Ram, she was tormented into performing the test of fire. What possibilities are thriving here, my lord? Are these not solely instances of injustice?

Pause.

Lie down, the cot is ready.

Acharya **Nand** *lies down on the cot.*

Nand Method . . . the method cannot possibly be the same, can it? The differences between men and women, the differences depending on caste . . . they can be as endless as the difference between the ocean and the desert.

Ahilya But what is the difference in the water of the oceans, my lord? Or the difference between two grains of sand? The question is whether we are the two grains of sand in the desert, or are we distinct as the ocean and desert . . . and even if we are distinct, it is not as if the ocean is superior and the desert lesser? Before the Manusmriti, there would have been a time when within this religion, everyone would have been equal, Swami?

Nand The topic is love and you are debating about Sanatan Dharma. If there is similarity, is love adamant, Devi? Is there no sameness between you and I?

Pause.

Ahilya Are you talking about the legend of Ram, Acharya, or us?

Nand Whatever you understood.

Ahilya Love is not adamant, Acharya. It is not adamant, fluid, playful, sinful, holy, greedy, supernatural, vindictive, virtuous, nothing . . . love is neither possibility nor is it etched in stone. And whatever it is, it is not loyal.
If one is in love, what can they do?

Nand I do not agree with you.

Ahilya You are a learned man.

Nand I married you . . . I never even gave a thought to love.

Ahilya I owe a great debt to you, Swami. Marrying the daughter of a forlorn family, a girl of such young age, it is like giving her new life. Your benevolence knows no bounds.

You are in love with god, Acharya, and now, before your death, you are measuring the peaks of your love for me. Perhaps, it is also the reason why Shri Ram is taking his time.

Nand If I did not love god, would you have done what you are doing?

Sugriv *opens his eyes in shock, and begins chanting Ram-Ram again.*

Ahilya When Shri Ram met Ma Sita after fourteen years, he was called to the war zone. Shri Ram desired to meet Ma Sita in the presence of everyone, to say that, Sita, I was not fighting this war for you, but for myself. To proclaim to the society that nobody can abduct the reputation of the Arya dynasty. You may go with anyone.

Bharat, Lakshman, and if you wish, Hanuman . . . it is not my choice to make. Ma Sita experienced the revelation that she had left her lover Ram behind, but she had returned to find only the king in Ram. That he is solely a warrior now, nothing else.

Nand   You are talking only of Valmiki's Ramayana. The Ramayana has many versions . . . of many kinds /

Ahilya   Forgive me, Acharya. What the Brahmin teaches is what shall remain. (*Pause.*)

The Ramayana has many versions, you are saying this in Muktidham. The disciples of your temple believe that only one of them is as steady as their lock of hair. The day human beings become competent of listening to the denunciation of their gods, they shall no longer need god.

Nand   This is not the answer to my question. You know what I am asking you, Devi Ahilya.

Ahilya   The debate for the Mathadheesh shall be held today, and tomorrow, you have to announce your decision. And down here, in the town, your people are expressing their opinions . . . in conditions as grave as these, your mind is immersed in these thoughts?

Nand   Love is no less grave an issue, Ahilya. All this is borne of the scarcity of love.

Ahilya   Ram always somewhat delays every new gain . . . doesn't he?

Pause. **Nand** *sits on the cot.*

Nand   Ahilya . . .

Ahilya   Yes, Acharya.

Nand   Do I have no right to the complete truth?

Ahilya   About what are you/

Nand   In Muktidham, hiding the truth is also recognised to be a lie. Falsity has many forms, Ahilya, but the truth has only one.

Ahilya   What do you want to know, Acharya?

Nand   If I had to verbalise this question . . . wouldn't the value of marriage in the cosmos reduce?

Deprived of this knowledge, I will not achieve salvation. And if I ask the question, then . . . then I do not know what times may befall us . . . an era where everything is acceptable. Will you able to live in that era?

Do I have not even have the right, Ahilya, to expect a simple truth from my wife of so many years? Does the Nath Nand of Birpur not hold even that much value?

Pause.

Ahilya   If my answer shall allow you to achieve salvation, very well . . . Sugriv, why were you in love with Tara?

Sugriv I ... Devi, what do I know? I am just a Nat.

Nand Speak, Sugriv.

Sugriv Acharya, I? My wife is at home. My children would be sleeping. I am working to put food in their mouths. I do not have any such worries, my lord. How will I feed my family is all my mind is entangled in, my lord. How can I provide the answers to such perplexing questions /

Nand (*in a raised voice*) Did Sugriv love Tara or not?

Sugriv Yes, yes ... Acharya.

Nand Answer ... I want the answer. The moment I obtain it, I shall achieve salvation.

Sugriv You shall obtain it ... Acharya ... certainly ... (*He looks at* **Ahilya** *with fear.*)

Ahilya Sugriv, why were you in love with Bali's wife?

Sugriv What do I know, Devi ... she was beautiful. Forgive me, it was lustful longing perhaps.

Ahilya And what about your own wife?

Sugriv I would have probably harboured the same desire for her, Devi. I am a monkey, to whomsoever I am inclined ...

Ahilya You go to them ... like humans. You do not engage in a debate before your death. Am I right?

Nand Brilliant! Brilliant! This is fantastic ... May humans consume all the blessed fruits of the society ... and when their mind is weak, may they appeal to the monkeys ...

Ahilya The truth is bitter, Acharya ... will you be able to digest it?

Nand Now I am being questioned ... whether I shall be able to hear it not?

Ahilya Tara, Bali's widow ... after Bali's death ... immediately ... she was Sugriv's. She herself was in love with Sugriv. Every woman's love for a man is equal to a mother's love for her son.

Nand (*closes his eyes*) Ram ... Ram ... Ram ...

Sugriv Ram ... Ram ... Ram ...

Ahilya One individual loves in many forms, many love in one form, many love in many forms ... it is all agreeable, Swami. There is only love that is unacceptable ... loving one in only one form. That is why Shri Ram lost Ma Sita in the end.

Pause.

Nand Budhh abandoned his wife and child and left in the middle of the night ... he achieved salvation.

Ahilya   Yes, and so did his wife . . . only she was never heralded.

Pause.

I want to take your leave now . . . I have kept water. You are near the window, listen to the chaos of your people. They have spent so many years in their devotion to you. Now listen to the name of Ram from their mouths.

Nand   You are going down . . . to the disciples?

Ahilya   Yes, to *all* your disciples . . . they cannot sit down with their religious books until they have tasted the food made by their mother . . . today is the day of the debate, and all your disciples are eager. If it is what you desire, you may leave it all behind to achieve salvation, my lord . . . to this day, Muktidham does not allow for the salvation of women . . .

Pranam.

Ahilya *touches Acharya* **Nand**'s *feet. He gives her his blessings.* **Ahilya** *leaves.*

Scene Five

Down below, in the Buddhist temple of the lower castes in the village. **Bhikhuni** *stands before the idol of Budhh.* **Bhikhuni** *was a Nat, now she is a Buddhist monk. She is recognized to be Birpur's religious chief. With her is* **Nikunth**, *a young man. He is sitting in front of Buddh with his eyes shut. There are many weapons before* **Nikunth**, *swords, sticks, etc. Behind him stands* **Ghasidas**. **Guru Ma** *and* **Yuyutsu** *are standing at the door.*

After finishing her meditation, **Bhikhuni** *opens her eyes.* **Guru Ma** *wants to come in.* **Ghasidas** *picks up leaves and places them in front of her, so that she does not have to step on the ground.* **Ghasidas** *is on his knees.*

Bhikhuni   Come in, Guru Ma . . . here, everyone can enter inside.

Ghasidas   Yes . . . yes, Bhikhuni.

Pause. **Bhikhuni** *is silently looking at* **Yuyutsu** *and* **Guru Ma**.

Bhikhuni   Please sit.

Guru Ma (*sitting down*)   Please come up today . . . we have come to invite you /

Bhikhuni   This is also a house of God. Here too, the rule of speaking the truth applies.

(*To* **Nikunth**) The weapons feel less . . .

Nikunth   No, bhikhuni. Every household has been arranged to have a sword and a stick. And those brave-hearts who have volunteered to protect our temples have already armed themselves.

Bhikhuni   The messenger?

Nikunth   He is ready. He will leave as soon as he finishes his meal.

Yuyutsu This is between us. Sending a messenger . . .

Bhikhuni How is it between us? Causing the death of an unarmed artisan? Killing someone for absolutely no reason may be an internal matter for you, Acharya, but it is not for us.

Guru Ma It is possible that somewhere, someone must have committed a mistake. You think for yourself, on such an important day, why would anyone want any hindrance or violence?

Bhikhuni In order to function, politics relies on the memory of the ordinary people, Guru Ma. It is the significant days when violence is carried out, because it remains prominent in the memory of the people. Otherwise, what is the gravity of one man's death in Kalyug, where sin and immorality are the norm?

In your math, there shall be an argument today and after the decision is taken tomorrow, there is going to be a lot of change. Your sons must be telling the next generation something. You were not able to destroy the temples last time . . . this time /

Guru Ma It is not salvation that I see in your religion . . . I see politics. Do not forget that today, the king may be Buddhist, but for years /

Bhikhuni Guru Ma . . . after becoming a Buddhist monk, I am able to look into your eyes today . . . and do you know what I see?

Pause.

Solar eclipse . . . today is the day of the solar eclipse, is it not?

Pause.

Ghasidas We cannot cremate any corpses today, Guru Ma. We will have to keep it in the village.

Yuyutsu Whoever may be at fault, I apologize on behalf of that individual.

Nikunth We know who is the culprit.

Ghasidas No . . . we do not know . . . how can we know? Yes, we have speculated . . . but how can we know?

Bhikhuni The solar eclipse is believed to be very inauspicious in your religion. It is mundane in ours.

Guru Ma You are creating divides between my religion and yours as if you were never a part of this religion, Bhikhuni.

Pause.

Bhikhuni This stick was once a log of wood, and once a tree.

Guru Ma But you are forgetting that you /

Bhikhuni I am forgetting . . . that I was born a Nat. If even my shadow fell on your home, I was forced to eat dust and dung. And I could not even breathe in your direction, much less look at you. Here only . . .

Do you know why your sons are marching about the entire town in celebration? Because they have wanted the death of a Buddhist for years now. To portray themselves as powerful . . . and they were not able to do anything, because of the Nath Nand. It has been two days today that he left for Muktidham and look around you . . . this is not an isolated incident. It is the very foundation of your religion.

Guru Ma   I am sitting here in your house . . . I . . . Birpur's temple's Guru Ma . . . I have come here, into the village, to confer with you. This /

Bhikhuni   Give Guru Ma some water, Nikunth . . . she has come from afar.

Pause. **Nikunth** *takes water from the pot and gives it to* **Guru Ma**.

Guru Ma   I have no thirst.

Bhikhuni   You, Acharya?

Yuyutsu   Me neither.

Bhikhuni (*with irony*)   Nikunth, please make sure that every household has an adequate amount of water as well. They have swords and sticks already. But, serving our guests some water is an age old tradition of ours.

Pause.

Guru Ma   Please do not send your messenger . . .

Bhikhuni   Fear?

Guru Ma   None for myself . . . but the whole village.

Bhikhuni   What about this murder?

Guru Ma   If it is a murder, then Acharya . . . shall punish him.

Bhikhuni   Which Acharya?

Guru Ma   The Acharya Nand is at Muktidham right now and /

Bhikhuni   And salvation has no relationship with justice, right?

Yuyutsu   Whoever becomes the Acharya shall mete out justice . . . it is just the delay of a night.

Bhikhuni   And if he who becomes the Acharya is himself responsible for the death . . . Guru Ma, if we assume it is so, what if both the nominated Acharyas have a hand in this death?

Guru Ma   This is impossible . . .

Yuyutsu (*immediately*)   If I become the Acharya, caste will remain only in *varna* . . . in the realm of work. I even want to open the doors of Muktidham for all castes. In Sanatan Dharma, caste was meant only for professions. Today, the same /

Bhikhuni   I did not ask for history or condolences; I am asking for justice.

Nikunth   Even if you do not deliver justice, it is fine. We are powerful . . .

Guru Ma You are a child . . . what makes you think that just because you are standing with a few sticks and swords that you have the right to talk to your teachers in this manner? (*To the* **Bhikhuni**.) this is what you have taught them?

Bhikhuni You . . . have nurtured and looked after the residence of all the Acharyas with your own hands. Your sons block the entrance of the cave and cause the death of unarmed people . . . this is what you have taught them?

Guru Ma The stones could have fallen themselves. There is a hill. There are rocks. The stones can fall.

Bhikhuni (*laughing*)   the mountain is enormous, Ma . . . Buddha Dharma, Sanatan Dharma . . . older than all these and much bigger . . . the mountains are brimming with disaster, but they do not house historical anger. The rocks do not fall solely on Shudras, Devi.

Yuyutsu I understand your plight. But by sending this messenger, the Buddhist king will not be able to understand our harmony.

Bhikhuni Even I have not been able to understand it till today.

Guru Ma Your home also has its rotten fruits, Bhikhuni, and if they are not there today, they shall be born tomorrow . . . do not forget that Sanatan Dharma is one of the most charitable religions. You would not be able to leave any religion and then be able to make these statements that you making. We have always endowed others with value /

Bhikhuni Who are you to endow it? Who has taught you this history? The Sanatan Dharma has never been able to co-exist with the Aghori, the Aghori with the Mimamsakas, the Mimamsakas with the Shaivaits . . . haven't you laid destruction to math after math? Haven't you obliterated temples, only to build your own? Have you no knowledge of how many temples, how many Sanatan Schools have been wrecked by Sanatanis of different sects themselves? We have shunned your gods of mud, Guru Ma . . . your god's merits ar /

Guru Ma You are still not talking about religion. . . .

Bhikhuni What religion are you talking about, Guru Ma?

Guru Ma That religion, Bhikhuni, because of which today, you are able to envision a god who is only time, power and deeds. Who resides in mathematics, in melody, in the gap that resides between our breaths . . . the spiritual purity that you boast of today, is a blessing of our mud gods.

Bhikhuni And justice? Is there no place for justice?

Guru Ma Of course . . . there is, why wouldn't there be! Today, there is an issue. A grave issue . . . I am not saying there isn't, Bhikhuni. I never said that justice should not be served. I am also the Guru Ma of the temple of Birpur. I have seen thousands of religions birthed and then destroyed. Have some faith . . . and do not send this messenger.

There is nothing more hazardous for religion than a king. One day, it shall be your doom.

Guru Ma *begins to leave.*

Bhikhuni Guru Ma!

Guru Ma *stops and looks back.*

Bhikhuni What is god?

Guru Ma God . . . god is the knowledge which transmutes a human being from his bodily state towards the state of nothingness. Which transports one from the path of bearing fruits to fruitlessness. God is that knowledge, Bhikhuni, which frees us from every temple . . .

God does not live in a temple, Bhikhuni, neither mine, nor yours . . .

Bhikhuni Your religion is extraordinary, Guru Ma. Then why so many differences? If god is knowledge, then what space does caste occupy in this extraordinary religion?

Guru Ma Do you know what is god's greatest dilemma, Bhikhuni? Whether he should endow his creation with less power of recollection or more? (**Guru Ma** *takes the weapon from* **Nikunth***'s hands.*) If human beings have greater power of recollection, they shall not be able to live the lives of human beings. If human beings become aware of their every form, in all periods of time, they will become so full of fear that they won't be able to leave their mother's womb. And because their power of recollection is less, they have even forgotten that in reality, they themselves are god.

The day human beings are able to master their power of recollection . . . that day, they shall be freed of caste, religion, temples, Buddh, Ram, Keshav, Indra, Brahma . . . and they shall actually become one with god.

Guru Ma *returns the weapon to* **Nikunth**.

Whatever you may use this weapon for, child, use it wisely. For a long time, your actions shall define you, and unfortunately, you shall have no memory of today, of Birpur, of Mathadheesh's nominations and of this murder or death . . .

Guru ma *offers pranam and leaves. She insists that* **Ghasidas** *places leaves on the floor for her to step on.*

Bhikhuni Sadhu, Sadhu . . . there is no shortage of philosophy in your path, but your feet do not fall on the ground.

Guru Ma *looks back in anger.*

Guru Ma May god give you peace.

Bhikhuni Likewise. There is a big door between the village and the town, Guru Ma. Till it remains open, you and I can converse. You should make sure your son, in his fearlessness, does not shut them.

Guru Ma Even if he does so . . . he shall do it for his own protection.

Bhikhuni (*laughs*) We are monks, not *sanghis*. If the doors close, we will not be able to save you either. May the Buddha give you peace.

Ghasidas What do we do with this corpse, Bhikhuni?

Bhikhuni   Today is the day of the solar eclipse. We cannot do anything . . . tomorrow morning, he shall attain salvation in Muktidham itself. He has been killed at the hands of the Hindus. He shall depart from their door.

Scene Six

The artists, in the costumes of **Hanuman**, **Sugriv** *and* **Angad** *are standing between two poles and putting up a banner.* **Sugriv** *has climbed up one pole and* **Angad** *the other.* **Hanuman** *is standing below and watching them.*

Hanuman   You will get us all in trouble. What are you doing? Hold it straight . . . straight.

Angad   Is it the other way around . . . should we turn it?
Why is there a crowd there? Is someone coming?

Sugriv   Whoever comes . . . what is it to you? Put it up quickly . . . I am completely sure; it is like this only.

Hanuman   Sun . . . should it face the Sun or not . . . and this horse's snout should be towards the north, and that hawk . . . idiot! The hawk should be facing towards the east . . . what is all this crowd?

Sugriv   You will get us all killed . . . does the hawk ever take flight from west to east?

Angad   Why . . . why, father? Why doesn't the hawk fly from west to east?

Sugriv   Do not question me at every turn like a babbler, do you understand? When you don't know anything about something, you should just listen to the other person. The hawk always flies from east to west.

Angad   Then how does it return, father? Once it leaves, it never returns, is it?

Hanuman   I will give you one tight slap . . . both father and son behave like they are famous pundits . . . you are a pain in the ass, if I am telling you, it is the other way around, then it is the other way around.

Pause.

Angad   Something big is happening, I am telling you. This cannot be just about the debate, it's not possible only. Since when do people have so much interest in the debate?

Hanuman   Do not look that way. It is a political gathering of the higher caste. The people have come to express their rage . . . so, they will get provoked by anything, and they will beat up anyone.

Sugriv   Look over there!

Agnivesh *and* **Shrihari** *emerge on the stage, and address their sangh by putting tika on their foreheads.*

Agnivesh Today the day has come . . . when before us . . .

Sugriv Here it is . . . it begins . . .

Agnivesh and **Shrihari** *say something but they are not audible.*

Angad What are they are talking about?

Hanuman It is a speech . . . a speech. That too religious. We will not be able to hear it.

Angad Why?

Hanuman Because it is only for their caste . . . you do whatever I am asking you to do. Put up the banner.

Sugriv You let it be, please. Last time, when the Brahmins had asked us to place pots in the entire town of Birpur the night of the new moon, don't you remember what happened?

Hanuman Do not bring up old matters . . . let them go . . . then I /

Sugriv Yes. We placed the pots upright, we were supposed to put them upside down . . . for three months, we were banned from using the water from the pond. We had to walk such distances to beg for it /

Angad I am not putting it . . . not me . . . (*Begins to climb down the pole.*)

Hanuman Ay . . . climb up. Up, you climb up. Stop acting all high and mighty, refusing to put it up . . . what are you, a landlord . . . climb up!

Angad You will get us all killed . . . you . . . have grown old . . . look. It seems like Swamiji is angry.

Sugriv Religious speeches are always given in anger, son . . . watch, now one will be in a fit of fury and the other one will smile . . .

Shrihari *talks with eyes big,* **Agnivesh** *smiles.*

Angad Yes! But why?

Hanuman Because it leads to the birth of both, frenzy and compassion in the people at the same time.

Sugriv It is a peculiar combination of anger and inner peace.

Hanuman The moment two completely opposite emotions emerge together in the heart of an individual . . . you can be sure that that person is a foot soldier of a political gathering.

Angad But they must be talking about complex issues . . .

Hanuman Take any four words and keep repeating them in a new order over and over, the conversation shall become complex. What is so hard about that? Only the tone is grave.

The next sentences are spoken in heavy voices by **Sugriv** *and* **Hanuman***.*

Sugriv   The reflection of god is time.

Hanuman   He who is beyond time is a reflection of god.

Sugriv   Time is the cycle of mysticism emerging from the reflection of god.

Hanuman   Time belongs to the god who is dissolved in time like a reflection.

Sugriv   The only thing you have to keep in mind is that no one should understand anything properly.

Angad   But if you are speaking in grave tones, how is it invigorating?

Hanuman   One speaks in a sombre tone, and the other in an impassioned tone . . .

Sugriv   The sombre tone is for words of mysticism, and the impassioned for societal . . .

Hanuman (*in a sombre tone*)   Beyond time lies the reflection of God.

Sugriv (*in an impassioned tone*)   The lower castes and Buddhists have committed social injustices against you.

Hanuman (*in a sombre tone*)   Beyond God lies the truth behind the foundation of reflection.

Sugriv (*in an impassioned tone*)   The lower castes have fanned the flames of social injustice lit by the Buddhists.

The excitement of the people is heard.

Hanuman   Look, it is done . . .

Sugriv   What is being said makes no difference . . . you just have to keep beating around the same bush and speak in two distinct tones. One sombre, one impassioned . . .

Hanuman   If you interrupt him, you are dead. You shall put banners for others.

Amidst the hailing by the crowd, **Agnivesh** *and* **Shrihari** *put a tika on their forehead and exit the stage.*

Pause.

Angad   I'll . . . I'll become a Buddhist.

Sugriv   What . . . what did you say?

Angad   I'm telling you. I'll become a Buddhist.

Sugriv   Rascal . . . your generation should have their asses kicked. Do you think we are morons that we have been slogging away for years? Making others' chappals and cleaning up their dirt . . . we shall become Buddhists, I believe. Are the Buddhists standing with garlands to welcome you?

Hanuman   Oh, yes, speak even louder. Tomorrow, at the house of the Chamars, they will skin us only, you blabbermouth.

Sugriv Move, move . . . you focus on the work . . . is this fine?

Hanuman Now isn't the pig facing the wrong direction?

Angad That is why I say we should become Buddhists. Their *Jataka* murals paint the picture distinctly in one line . . . elephants followed by human beings. After human beings, monkeys. Even after a thousand years, the people will be able to convey the gist.

Hanuman This boy will get us all killed. Fool! Have you ever seen an upside-down pig?

Angad It is not as if we have ever seen a talking hawk or a flying horse. That is why we are saying . . . we shall become Buddhists . . . it does not have such complicated ideas.

Sugriv What is your problem, you keep saying the same thing over and over again . . . as if you are talking about a role in a cheap play, not becoming a Buddhist. We shall become, we shall become . . . you have found a lot to support your choice . . . have you gone mad?

Hanuman The elections should not be open to the youth at all . . . they do not have the age or the experience, but they have been given the right to choose.

Angad Yes, only the old should get the right to choose, right? Choose and then die . . . and the rest should have to live with the consequences of your foolishness . . . it is the time of the youth, do not forget. A new Mathadheesh shall be chosen. He will change everything.

Hanuman So then, stay a Hindu only. Why do you keep screaming, 'I shall become a Buddhist, I shall become a Buddhist'?

Everyone's banner has been set up, except ours. Our bones shall stand for the elections within the walls of the temple . . .

Sugriv Turn it upside down. I think everyone's is upside down.

Angad In the banners of the Buddhists, all the creatures are facing one direction . . . it's only our religion that is so very complicated. At every turn /

Sugriv It is a nascent religion . . . give it some time, they shall also end up in the same state as us.

Angad But they are not in that state now, are they?

Sugriv As of now, the Buddhist king is immersed in elevating his religion's status. If you become a Buddhist, they shall immediately send you off to war.

Angad Buddhists are non-violent . . .

Hanuman *and* **Sugriv** *laugh.*

Hanuman The youth cannot be helped . . . (*Laughing.*)

Sugriv (*laughing*) nothing.

Hanuman   If it is non-violent, how did it become prevalent in society?

Angad   With love . . .

Hanuman (*laughing, to* **Sugriv**)   Is your son an addict . . .

Sugriv   What can I say? All his friends are the same.

Hanuman   So, aren't we capable of the emotion of love? Make us act with love. What do you say? Make us! (*Everyone laughs.*)

Angad   Emperor Ashoka saw the Buddha after the battle of Kalinga . . . from then on, he became non-violent /

Hanuman   From then on, he became non-violent. (*Laughs.*)

Sugriv   And today's king. If he is also non-violent, why is he marching towards us with his army . . . what did you think Acharya Agnivesh's sangh is running around to prepare for?

Hanuman   The Buddha was also marvellous. Instead of making an appearance before the battle of Kalinga and saving two, four or even ten thousand lives, he decides to appear in the end! In the end when Ashoka sat down, grim, and looked back at the horrors he had committed. Why did I kill so many, how shall I burn them? Haye! In a flash, the Buddha appeared . . .

Sugriv *and* **Hanuman** *laugh.*

Sugriv   Their banners have been put up already. Only ours is left.

Hanuman   Listen to me . . . put it up as I say.

Angad   No, until I am a part of this religion, I shall live it right.

Hanuman   I shall give you a tight slap, do you understand . . . just because there is some sparse hair growing on your chest . . . you think you have become some enlightened man?

If we don't put up the banner before both the Acharyas go to meet the Nand, the mere act of sitting and standing shall become unattainable.

Angad   What if it is put up wrong?

Sugriv   We will not get caught and even if we do, there shall be some process of purification. If we don't put it up, we are in deep shit.

Hanuman   There are no purification processes in Buddhism, son . . . if you commit a mistake once, you have to face the cycle of karma . . . you will have to live your entire life with this fear. Oh goodness! I have committed a sin, now I shall have to bear the consequences. Should I leave all my work behind to dedicate my life to doing good?

Surgiv   Ours is better than this. Whatever comes to your mind, do it, as long as it is within the realm of your caste. There is a process of purification for everything and you will not be held responsible for any of your actions.

Every act is being carried out by god, all you have to do is listen to the Brahmins. Listen to everyone but do whatever it is you want.

Angad This is slavery . . .

Hanuman (*laughing*) In your age, everything is slavery. Young political revolutionaries never have any knowledge. But if they are both, revolutionary and religious . . . then it is very hard.

Wait and watch the state of the Buddhist religion in the coming years.

Sugriv (*laughing*) those who are not capable of anything, they become Buddhists to make friends.

Angad I do not agree with you.

Hanuman Don't believe us. If our elders had listened to their elders when they were young, we would not be here, putting up banners for the temple after leaving behind the work of Nats.

We were swept up in the wave of religion . . . and we were fucked.

Angad You cannot be blamed for any of it, right? You are merely the fatality of every generation!

Hanuman Son, we belong to the generation that was trapped in the middle. The one that neither changed the society, nor initiated revolutions . . . the one that came after a big revolution, and then before another big revolution, it became extinct.

Sugriv No one can help this generation. This generation will only put up banners for others and crack their knuckles.

You participate in revolutions. But, first, become something.

Hanuman You have neither Ram, nor Budhh. It is just said that Buddhists do not believe in caste.

Angad They do not believe in them . . . everyone knows that.

Hanuman Buddh was fortunate that he was born as a Kshatriya. You go ahead, leave your house and go sit under a tree, and then proclaim that you achieved nirvana . . . the people will make a door hanging out of your skin, I can bet my name on it . . . (*Laughs.*)

Sugriv The conch shell shall be blown any moment now . . . both the Acharyas are standing on the stairs of Muktidham . . . put up the banner. Tie it.

On the other side of the stage, both the Acharyas are taking their place.

Angad Acharya Yuyutsu says he shall open the doors of Muktidham to everybody . . . caste shall exist only within the realm of work, not religion.

Sugriv Acharya is talking as if, if he opens the door to everybody, Ram shall take everybody. This hawk, horse, pig . . . do you have any idea how old their pictures are?

Till they exist, nothing will change. Muktidham's doors may be opened, but who will free us from the bounds of the epics?

Angad   And if Agnivesh wins, then?

Hanuman   Who knows what caste he belonged to initially . . . but now he is the strongest voice against the Shudras . . . he shall make our lives hell! He is also young. He wants change, that is it . . . anything that shall give him the illusion of self-worth.

Angad   So, what is the solution?

Sugriv   Solution . . . the solution is not like a Brahmin's lock of hair that it stays forever.

Angad   It is because of your way of thinking that we are in these conditions today.

Hanuman (*laughing*)   Your children shall say the same.

Sugriv   And theirs too.

Hanuman   Besides, what does it matter what we think or feel? Their conch shells . . . their salvation . . . their debate . . . their king. . . . their Buddh and Ram . . . we are Nat by caste . . . they can make us monkeys today, demons tomorrow, gods the day after . . .

Angad   Is the solar eclipse beginning?

Sugriv   Here, tie the banner. We must not look in the direction of Muktidham during the solar eclipse. It is said that even Ram loses his power to reason at this point in time.

They tie the banner. The conch shells are blown. The solar eclipse begins.

Scene Seven

Slowly, darkness is descending. The birds can be heard as they fly back to their nests.

Guru Ma, *Acharya* **Nand** *and* **Ahilya** *are standing at their places. They are watching the eclipse over the water.*

Acharya **Yuyutsu** *and Acharya* **Agnivesh** *are slowly climbing up the stairs. They, having closed their eyes, are holding hands.* **Shrihari** *is standing in his place.*

Everyone is chanting Hari Hari Hari Hari Ram Ram Ram Ram.

Ahilya   Hey Ram . . .

She suddenly sees **Agnivesh**, *who has appeared as* **Ram**.

Ahilya   Who?

Ram   I . . . Ma . . .

Guru Ma   One should only pray during the eclipse, child.

Ram   I am already in prayer, Guru Ma.

Guru Ma What is this ... just a minute ago, you were on the stairs ... on your way to Muktidham, to attend your final lesson with Acharya, your caste ... if I open my eyes, that is what I shall see ...

Ram (*laughing*) Do not open them. You are a mother. Your love should be blind.

Guru Ma Are you in darkness or is it the eclipse?

Ram Time does not exist during the eclipse, Ma. Place, presence, they are all restless ...

Guru Ma Where is your brother? And what is your caste?

Ram He is climbing the stairs ... look there. He is almost inside ... I am there too, here too ... we shall announce the caste during the solar eclipse ... but a mother's love cannot change. Affection can't have a caste, Ma, can it?

During the eclipse, every caste becomes Ram. Ram becomes Buddhist or Buddh-like torturous Mathmahant ... the time is like this, Ma. It is all the time's fault. It is all time's play.

Shrihari Hey Ram,

   Give us the strength

   Give us the might to establish the reign of Ram

   Give us sticks, swords, daggers, knives, ropes, arrows, bows

Ram Son, why are you listing these things?

Shrihari Ram? God, you, in Acharya's form?

Ram You are all immersed in prayer, he was the only empty one so I took his form.

Shrihari We are preparing for war, god. Bless us.

Ram Take them ... what is there in blessings? Take two, or even four. By the way, have you thought about who you are going to battle against?

Shrihari I shall lay ruin to the Buddhist temples?

Ram Very good ... burn them to the ground.

Shrihari I shall take your leave, god.

Ram You believe in caste, don't you?

Shrihari Yes, yes, why wouldn't I? Everyone has suspicions about only your belief about caste.

Ram Why? Shambuk, Shabri, etc. etc ... what is the suspicion? Haven't you read the Ramayana thoroughly?

Shrihari No, the people say things, do you love everyone?

Ram The people have nothing at stake. Whenever, whatever is convenient, they say it. Which Ramayana have you read?

Shrihari Valmiki.

Ram Fool . . . in a few years, Tulsi shall come . . . read Tulsidas, have everyone read it . . . Tulsi is my own, the rest are all wild. They write just about anything.

Shrihari So, about caste /

Ram If I don't believe in caste, how will I stay king, fool? First, put some brains into these lower castes . . . there is no one worse than them.

Shrihari Why?

Ram Why are you asking questions? Are you literate?

Shrihari Yes, a little.

Ram Saale, I never studied anything beyond the bow and arrow, why are you studying so much? Engage in devotion, fool. Kill the lower castes or we will be in trouble.

Shrihari My teachers have told me /

Ram First, you do something about your teachers. They are bigger problems than the lower castes. The literates have no caste. First calm them down, then the lower castes, and then if you have time, the Buddhists . . . actually forget the Buddhists. In times to come, they will only make music. They are not capable of doing anything else.

Shrihari Jai Shri Ram.

Yuyutsu Hold my hand tight. If anyone falls, there will be one less Acharya. (*Laughs.*)

Pause.

Where is your hand?

Ram Here . . . is it not appearing clearly? (*Laughs.*)

Yuyutsu Not at all . . . are you here or not?

Ram Open your eyes . . . see for yourself.

Yuyutsu Opening my eyes during the eclipse. And should I lose them because of you?

Ram It is a strange worry. Bringing darkness to the dark . . . brother . . . I have become Ram now, so everything is not clear . . .

Yuyutsu *laughs as he climbs the steps.*

Nath Ram . . . Ram . . . Ram . . . You . . . I am your . . . He Ram (*He tears up.*) you have arrived . . .

Ram Yes, son . . . you have awakened, I had to come.

230 Muktidham: The Abode of Salvation

Nath   Grant me salvation, Ram . . . Ram, salvage me.

Ram *looks around.*

Ram   What do you want salvation from, son?

Nath   From this life, I /

Ram   Jump down from here . . . there, you shall have salvation.

Nath   You are chaffing your devotees . . .

Ram   So, Ram . . . does not joke around, is it? (*Laughs.*) Look at the entire Ramayana . . . there is only humour.

Nand   But you . . .

Ram   What?

Nand   You?

Ram   What?

Nand   You . . . just like Agnivesh . . .

Ram   Yes, yes . . . I had to appear in some form. It is his story, so I came in his form.

Nand   No no . . . you come in some other form.

Ram   This is great. Till now, everyone was begging to see Ram, now that Ram has come, you are complaining about this form and that form . . . hand them a towel and they grab on to the dhoti . . . useless!

Nand   Agnivesh . . . isn't he climbing up the stairs?

Ram   He is coming.

Nand   Then?

Ram   Then what . . . Ram can build an army of monkeys, he can vapourise witches and wretches by just reading a chant, then can't he be at different places at the same time? What happened to Ram is everywhere . . . he is here, he is there?

Nand   Yes, yes . . . grant me liberation from the circle of life and death.

Ram   From which circle?

Nand   Of life and death?

Ram   What circle is this?

Nand   My lord, you?

Ram   So, what will the final lesson be then?

Nand   I am in a predicament, god? Forgive me, I am hesitating in calling you god in this form of yours.

Ram (*laughs*)   What is the predicament?

Nand   I was planning to give the final lesson on non-violence, but I myself am so restless with this topic. And then, there are the people of my town, I did not know that they would all get so excited after one murder, all the while I was hoping to give a lesson on non-violence . . . what can I say, god?

Ram   Non-violence . . . it is a novel word. Think of something else.

Nand   God?

Ram   If I had walked on the path of non-violence, Sita would have belonged to Raavan, and I would have come home with Lakshman, crying, hesitant to say a word, my head bowed down.

Diwali would have been miserable.

Nand   But that was a war for justice, god.

Ram   Have you ever met someone till today, who believes that the war he is waging is for injustice? How did you get this far?

Nand   So, is there no place for non-violence in Hinduism?

Ram   Hinduism . . . this is also a novel word. (*Laughs.*)

Nand   Then what should I give my final lesson on?

Ram (*he thinks and then looks over at* **Ahilya**)   The girl is getting out of hand . . . clamp down on the women.

Nand   Meaning?

Ram   Meaning? Meaning remind them of our reputation. Make something up, but it should be harsh. It should sound important, that's it. It is your final lesson . . . say anything, but say it with gravity. Why are you spending so much time on the substance. (*Looks over at* **Ahilya** *again and again.*)

Nand   Why are you saying this, god?

Ram   This is how we say it. Don't shower me with your numerous traditions. Look, Ahilya is calling. I am going. There was one woman, I lost her too because of my entanglements with all of you.

Ram (*looking over at* **Ahilya**)   Ahilya . . . Ahilya . . .

Ahilya   God!

Ram   Yes, yes.

Ahilya   Give me love, god . . . only . . . love that is . . .

Ram   . . . everyone is on their own cloud in my name. Take this, take this. I am coming. (*Walks towards her.*)

Ahilya   You? I told you earlier . . . meet me only after the debate?

Ram   How will I give you love from so far away? Ram is in everyone. Now, take Ram.

Ahilya   Do not insult him.

Ram   Who?

Ahilya   Ram, who else . . .

Ram   How can Ram insult Ram?

Ahilya   You are Agnivesh . . . climbing up the stairs /

Ram   Yes, he is there too. The eclipse is about to occur. The directions are wayward. The mind restless . . . I am lost.

Ahilya   Only you can unite me with my love.

Ram   I have sabotaged my own love, in every part of the Ramayana, at least twice or even four times . . . how will I float your boat, tell me?

Ahilya   You are god, you can do anything.

Ram   Of course . . . you give in to temptations, and the moment dusk arrives, your cries for my help begin?

Ahilya   Look god, the entire town of Birpur desires to walk the path Agnivesh has chosen.

Ram   Of course . . . when a murder occurs, the illiterates of the higher castes immediately come out on the path . . . the illiterates of the higher castes always take out the anger they hoard for their forefathers on their neighbours, it is the rule.

Ahilya   Agnivesh is a scholar.

Ram   There is one scholar, oh beauty! . . . What about the group behind him? This is how it works . . . look at my story . . .

Ahilya   There were many revered scholars in your story, god.

Ram   Yes . . . one sends his son to the jungle for his wife, the second, alone in the jungle, sees a beautiful girl and cuts off her nose, the third keeps a pair of slippers at the throne and brings down the entire kingdom, and the people believe those slippers to be god and keeping paying their dues to Bharat . . . there were so many educated illiterates that the army had to be comprised of monkeys . . .

Ahilya   Oh, God, you . . . are . . . are . . . eclipse!

Yuyutsu *and* **Agnivesh** *reach the top. Agnivesh ceases to appear as* **Ram** *from hereon.*

Nand   What is this, Ram . . . the eclipse is not taking place . . . why this fury?

Yuyutsu   Why is the sun not covered completely?

Agnivesh   Did god change his mind too? Have we reached the peak?

Nand   Ram . . . Ram . . . Ram . . . where did you go? Against what times are you warning us . . .

Both Acharyas open their eyes . . . the **Nand** *stands before them.*

Pause.

Yuyutsu *and* **Agnivesh**   Pranam, Acharya.

Pause.

Nand   Pranam. (*Looks up.*) the eclipse . . .

Yuyutsu   It did not happen, Acharya . . . it is possible that after some time . . .

Agnivesh   Acharya . . . your health?

Pause.

Nand   I shall give my life, Agnivesh, do not worry . . . (*Pause.*)
Come in only after putting a coating. When youngsters enter, their life decreases.

Yuyutsu *and* **Agnivesh**   Yes, Acharya.

Nand   There are two vessels outside . . . turmeric and cow dung . . . Yuyutsu and Agnivesh . . . in that order.

Agnivesh *and* **Yuyutsu** *look at each other.*

Agnivesh   Acharya?

Nand   Brahmin's turmeric . . . and cow dung for . . . you, Agnivesh.

Nand *sits down. Both the boys quietly apply a coating.* **Nand** *keeps watching them.*

Nand   Do you wish to apply turmeric, Agnivesh?

Agnivesh *remains silent.*

Nand   Look, the entire of Birpur has their gaze fixed upwards . . . the entire region should have the knowledge of their Acharyas, either of whom may become the Nand . . . of what they are? What caste are they . . . how many gods and how many demons. Every people have this right . . . don't they?

Show everyone as you put it, Agnivesh. The entire town has knowledge of the caste of the son of the king's priest. Only yours has remained obscure.

Agnivesh, *shamefacedly, walks to the front.*

Nand   Look down, Agnivesh. In the direction of your people.

Agnivesh *stands there, trembling and wordless.*

Nand   Feeling shame over your own birth is a terrifying emotion, isn't it? If I had not received the message of your future in my dreams, this shame would have stayed with you your entire life.

You desire my death, don't you?

Yuyutsu *and* **Agnivesh** *stare at the Nath* **Nand** *with shock.*

Nand Are you going to take care of it yourself or is your sangh going to aid you?

The solar eclipse was essential. But Ram is all-knowing. He has knowledge of when human beings are following cosmic laws and when they are being led by their whims. I followed my own wishes. Ram came . . . he gave his blessings, and left.

I give you both my blessings for today's debate. Come in . . .

Yuyutsu *and* **Agnivesh** *begin to slowly walk in.*

Nand Muktidham still does not provide admittance to Doms, Acharya.

Agnivesh *quietly stands outside.*

Nand How can you argue from outside?
Take that broom. Walk on your knees and as you move forward, erase your tracks. And be careful that your shadow does not fall on any of us.

Agnivesh *remains quiet. Then he picks up the broom and begins to walk forward on his knees.*

Nand Sanatan Dharma is so benevolent that it is giving a Dom the permission to enter Muktidham and debate to become the Mathadheesh. And yet, people are not happy, they say we are merciless, that Sanatan Dharma is intolerant. On top of all this, what religion would give another this kind of status, only Ram knows . . .
What will a people, who become watchful after one death, do after a betrayal, you can gauge that for yourself, Agnivesh.
The final debate?

Yuyutsu *looks at* **Agnivesh** *with anger.*

Yuyutsu I am present, Acharya.

Nand Yuyutsu, are we all god? Are we all one, or are we mere creations of god and god is separate from us?

Yuyutsu Acharya . . . there is one god . . . the entire world is a reflection of god. We are all manifestations of god. But we are not god.

God gave us different kinds of work, he created castes, he gave human beings the realisation of humanity. He gave us the ability to see, touch, hear, and smell, so we were capable of perceiving all these differences.
We are all creations of god. But neither are we all alike, nor are we god.

Nand If we all are not created alike, then why do you wish to open the doors of the temple to every caste?

Yuyutsu It is a societal compulsion, Acharya. Even now, when I have dreams, there are only individuals of higher castes. There is not a single Dom, Chamar, Mahaar in my dreams . . . but I do not consider them insignificant.

Today, God has created such social conditions that there is no simpler way to avoid dealing with the idiocy of the Buddhists than this. Scoffing is the only means.

And, Acharya, it is not that by merely opening the doors, the Shudras shall start coming to the temple. They fear their history far more than they fear us. But yes, this mad scramble to become Buddhists, it shall stop.

Pause.

Nand   And you? Are we all god? Are we all one, or are we mere creations of god and god is separate from us?

Agnivesh   There is some god in us, but we are not completely god . . . like how filling a vessel with the water of the sea means the water in the vessel is the sea and it is not the sea. We are as much god as the water of the vessel is the sea. But we are not god . . . we are god and we are also not god.

Nand   You are a Dom. (*Silence*) The cast of those who burn bodies. I brought you here, from the crematorium, from your parents. Now, what will you say to your sangh? Will you become a Buddhist?

Pause.

Agnivesh   The necessity of my sangh has also been presented to me by the society, Acharya. If I was a Brahmin and you were a Dom, I would still appear in your dreams, and taking lessons from you, be extremely grateful.

And my protest is against those castes that are converting to Buddhists. Only because their king is Buddhist. A human being's religion is fated. Whether he may be religious or not, a believer or an atheist.
Spirituality is not a human being's choice; it is their foundation.

Till Buddhism pursues religious conversions, my protest will continue, because the preservation of this grand religion against an ordinary religion is also god's desire.

Nand   So, you accept that you are a Dom?

Agnivesh   You are my father . . . if you say so . . . I am and I am not . . .

Pause.

Nand   Have you ever committed a gross sin?

Yuyutsu *looks at* **Agnivesh**.

Nand (*with anger*)   Have you ever committed a gross sin or not?

Agnivesh *is quiet.*

Nand   You still have time to admit it, Agnivesh. Have you ever committed a gross sin? Even if you have, you shall not be punished . . . he who is below you shall receive the punishment.

Agnivesh   I am smeared in cow dung, on my knees, before my own Acharya. My classmate is in turmeric . . . who could possibly be below me, Acharya?

Nand   Women . . . women are below everyone else.

Agnivesh Women are creators, Acharya . . .

> Ma Kaushalya
> Ma Yashoda
> Ma Sita
> Ma Janmejaya
> the one who keeps Hari
> in Hari's attire, is in truth Radhika
> The one who became Ram
> is but Ma Sita in the garb of
> Ram . . . Love, warmth, desire, friendship
> The one who surrenders
> her attire for a pledge made by others
> . . . Who may be purer than
> Draupadi . . . (*Pause*)
> I have committed a gross sin and equally I have not.

Nand After the debate, the final decision rests with me. You had come in my dreams, Agnivesh. It is the reason I am giving you a final opportunity . . .

Agnivesh Even if I have committed a sin, Acharya, I would have to answer to God for it.

Nand The teacher is not God?

Agnivesh He is and he isn't . . .

Pause.

Nand So sin's /

Agnivesh Your salvation is paramount for the entire realm of Acharyas, Acharya Nand. If I unveil my sins, it may prove to be a hurdle in your salvation . . .

Nand Salvation . . . I shall achieve salvation. The solar eclipse shall occur. It shall certainly occur . . . I can hand over my math and my Birpur . . . to Buddhists, but not sinners . . .
Your army shall be awaiting my death with excitement?

Yuyutsu I have always told you, Acharya . . . that this group of Acharya Agnivesh is against our religious beliefs. If I become the Mathadheesh, I shall immediately have them banned.

Agnivesh And self-preservation? How will you ensure self-preservation in the future? The last time a handful of people had gone off to demolish the temple and how many priests had received the death sentence after? And the Buddhist king was weaker than he is now. If today, the Buddhists do anything /

Yuyutsu The key word in self-preservation is self, the soul, Agnivesh . . . not preservation. Human beings should be competent of preservation of the soul. Will Doms protect the Brahmins now . . .

Agnivesh   You hoard far more fury for the Shudras than I, Yuyutsu. You are merely keeping up this act to parade yourself as the bigger man. And anyway, you are the son of the king's priest. In your thinking, all devotees belong to the higher castes . . . you say there shall be no more castes, but all your dreams have only those who are of higher castes. A human being whose dreams and reality are dissonant, he cannot follow any policy, Yuyutsu. Your benevolence is merely falsehood in disguise.

Nand (*puts up a hand to stop him*)   The final debate ends now. Who does god belong to and who is he and who shall he be for the math of Birpur, I shall announce my decision after the eclipse is over.

Pause.

Both offer pranam.

Yuyutsu   What is the final lesson, Acharya? Today, the time has come for it.

Nand (*closes his eyes to think*)   Ram . . . He Ram . . . (*Sits down on the ground.*) the times are like this . . . whatever I say. (**Agnivesh** *approaches him to help him up.*)

Yuyutsu   Stop, Agnivesh. You cannot help the Mathadheesh while you are smothered in cow dung. The Acharya said it himself . . . you must keep even your shadow away . . . (*To the* **Nand**.) Come, Acharya. (*Gets up.*)

Agnivesh   Yuyutsu! Do not forget that I am like Nath Nand's son. I have grown up with his love . . . with his love, I have /

Nand (*looking at* **Agnivesh**)   the final lesson is on love. Love . . . any love, of any kind . . . do not do it unconditionally. Love is an unhealthy mind's reasoning. A weak body's effort. Human beings are not built for love . . . love is a unique flaw in human beings . . . (*To* **Agnivesh**.) in the final avatar, god shall eliminate this flaw as well.

Pause.

You have my blessings.

Yuyutsu   Pranam, Acharya.

Nand   May you emerge victorious.

Pause.

Agnivesh   Pranam, Acharya.

Nand (*with anger and sadness*)   get out of here, Agnivesh. Many years ago, Guru Ma had told me . . . Nath, fear your dreams. God sends warnings in our dreams. We mistake them for messages. I have made a huge mistake.
Get out . . .

Interval.

Scene Eight

After two days and two nights. The eclipse is still incomplete.

Ahilya's room. Ahilya *is giving* **Agnivesh** *a bath and removing cow dung from his body.* **Ghasidas** *is standing before them with a giant potli.*

Ghasidas   It is still not coming off? It is tough. It went inside me . . .

It has been two days and two nights . . . the incomplete eclipse can still be seen in the water, Agnivesh . . . this eclipse is not going to end anytime soon.

Ahilya   How did you come here?

Ghasidas   With great difficulty. I slipped in before the doors were closed. I know another path through the mountains, I shall leave from there. Will you come along, Agnivesh?

Agnivesh *remains quiet.*

Ghasidas   The last group of Shudras is leaving in a bullock cart, Agnivesh.

Agnivesh (*to* **Ahilya**)   you leave it, I shall do it myself.

Ahilya *gazes at him quietly, and then begins bathing him again.*

Ghasidas   Your sangh has declared war on the Shudras and the Acharyas of the temple. The doors are shut. Down there, the army of the Buddhists is approaching. The town has been engulfed in pleas for help. If we are caught . . .

Agnivesh   My sangh does not take any action without my permission.

Ghasidas   You no longer hold the same power as you did until the final debate, Agnivesh. In Sanatan Dharma, the definition of god is uncertain, but the definition of Shudras is singular. It is absolutely certain! Please, you tell him, Devi, that he should leave from here.

Agnivesh *looks at* **Ahilya**.

Agnivesh (*to* **Ahilya**)   I told you . . . I will do it.
What of the leadership of the sangh?

Ghasidas   Shrihari is taking care of it. They have murdered Ved Pashupati, set fire to the hut of the teacher of political science, Acharya Raghunandan, and Acharya . . .

Agnivesh   Yuyutsu?

Pause.

Where is Yuyutsu?

Ghasidas   At the market square . . . he was blinded . . . a twelve-year-old child of the sangh gouged out his eyes, in front of everyone. It cannot happen in a mere two days and two nights . . . you all must have waited years in anticipation and prepared.
Look . . . (*Shows the potli.*) whatever I could acquire from your hut, I have got it along.

Agnivesh   What? Who let you in?

Ghasidas   I shall tell you all that . . . you /

Agnivesh You should go now, Ghasidas. There is still a lot of difference between you and me. I shall not run away from Birpur. My time has just come. Have you seen the stars? There have been changes in the eclipse. This is my time, it is written in my horoscope. (*Laughs.*)

Ghasidas You are laughing, Agnivesh? At least, I am a Nat. You are a Dom. They will hesitate to even burn your body. You will lie rotting on the bank of some river.

Agnivesh (*screaming*) Ghasidas!

Ghasidas Say whatever you want. If someone had not bathed you in Acharya Nand's hut, the Brahmin children would still be throwing stones at you.

Ahilya Let us go . . . I shall also come.

Pause.

Yes . . . I . . . there is nothing holding me back in Birpur now . . .

Ghasidas I have heard that it has been two days that you haven't even served water to Acharya Nand?

Ahilya Acharya Nand did not ask me for water in twenty years, Ghasidas . . . and even you would have never bothered to ask your wife!

Ghasidas You are saying this out of anger. Forgive me, I cannot take you with me.

Ahilya Why?

Ghasidas You do not belong to our caste. Our bullock cart will not be able to carry the weight of a higher caste.

Ahilya But /

Agnivesh Nobody is going anywhere, Ghasidas. My disciples are taking longer to come here today, but they shall come. You save your own life . . . if I call the others, you shall be put to sleep here itself.

Ghasidas So, you are not coming along?

Agnivesh No.

Ghasidas Fine, don't come with me. It is fortunate for me. But do not leave this hut. If you saw the cosmos from the eyes of my caste, you would not need the map of the sky to read the changes in the constellations.
I shall take your leave, Devi.

(*He begins to leave, but then stops.*) And yes, Agnivesh, if you are forced to leave for some reason, drink an adequate amount of water before you do. The well for the Dom caste is four villages away.
Pranam!

Ghasidas *leaves.*

Ahilya *quietly sits in a corner.*

Agnivesh Ahilya?

Ahilya Why are you being stubborn?

Agnivesh Just two nights ago you were saying . . . that I shall become Nath Nand and marry you. And today, you want to leave Birpur?

Ahilya For our marriage, we do not have to stay in Birpur, and you do not have to become Nath Nand. Even if we leave here, we can be married by merely exchanging garlands before God, without any priests or witnesses, a *Gandharva* wedding.

Agnivesh You are a Brahmin. That would be immoral.

Ahilya If staying in a dreary, ethical marriage is more worthy of a Brahmin than sincere love, then I am a Dom like you, from today . . .

Agnivesh But how can I leave my home out of such fear? I, Agnivesh . . . Birpur's math's . . .

Ahilya A man hears his name so many times in his lifetime that he begins to believe it . . . isn't it?

Pause.

I do not want to leave out of fear, Agnivesh. But out of love . . . the love I have always had for you. Anyone could have found this love. I have heaps of it . . . if you are deserving of it, then accompany me. Otherwise, I shall leave alone. This Birpur has nothing to offer us anymore.

Agnivesh We shall remain incomplete if we leave this town. Will we be able to love if we are incomplete?

Ahilya Love is birthed in incompleteness, Acharya Agnivesh. It is in incompleteness that Shri Ram fights wars for Ma Sita, in completeness even a washerman can obliterate an entire dynasty.
Will you come with me?

Agnivesh My heart tells me that my disciples will come . . .

Suddenly, the loud melody of drums and conch shells is heard.

Ahilya It seems like the Buddhist king's army has arrived at the door . . . it is possible that the Buddhists still keep up the pretension of non-violence. Here, that pretension is no longer needed.

Scene Nine

The same night. In Muktidham. **Guru Ma** *is serving the* **Nand** *with water.*

Nand His education was provided by you. By you only /

Guru Ma Have you eaten something?

Nand No, there are some actors who perform the play of Ram. When they come to chant, they bring along something to eat. Because of this eclipse, all food would have been left over from days on end . . . anything . . . today, even they did not come.

Guru Ma You come with me to the door of the town.

Nand Why? I have given up everything to come here. To enter an eternal trance.

Guru Ma The Nath himself talks to the king . . . isn't it?

Nand There is no Nath in Birpur at the moment. The king shall have to wait.

Guru Ma He is already waiting. But the pier that lies inside the town, it is under your watch. What about that?

Nand This is not my responsibility; it did not happen in my time. (*Pause.*) No, not in my time /

Guru Ma It did . . . it seemingly did.

Nand When did I give the education that made this destruction possible?

Guru Ma Did you not impart it? This violence, isn't it overflowing in the education imparted at the math? Sub-caste, caste, havoc, blame, aren't these all forms of violence?

Nand You are talking like Buddhists . . .

Guru Ma Nath . . . Nath! Here . . . look here, at me.

Nand You are aware that I do not look at you. My wife is /

Guru Ma You do not look at her either . . .

*The **Nand** turns around to look at her.*

Guru Ma We were classmates, Nand. We took education from the same Acharya since we were four years old. Then one day, you became the Nath and you stopped asking after me.

Nand You were more knowledgeable than I . . . that is why you became Guru Ma.

Guru Ma Now, just this once . . . listen to this one thing I am asking you to do, Nath. Come, let us go down. Peace shall descend on the town. And at the door, we shall hold a conversation with the Buddhist king. The culprits shall be awarded punishments, and then . . . then, you can enter your eternal trance.

Nand The next Nath?

Guru Ma Yuyutsu . . .

Nand But if I go down, my salvation /

Guru Ma Ram grants salvation, Nath. He does not receive it . . .

Angad *comes running in, and he throws his crown and tail on the ground.*

Angad Take these . . . enough.

Nand In the divinity of Muktidham /

Angad Are you all fools? Or were you in a deep slumber all these years? If I don't find my father . . . I shall, with my own hands, burn Muktidham to the ground.

Guru Ma Angad!

Angad This is not my name! To feed myself, I was slaving away for you. But enough is enough . . .

Nand Wherever your father is, he is safe.

Angad You are all-knowing, aren't you? The stairs to Muktidham have been dyed red with blood. If anything happens to my father /

Guru Ma What . . . what has happened . . . tell us properly.

Angad He was coming here, to him only, to chant Ram for your salvation. And it is your group of followers that attacked him.

Nand That is my not my group of followers.

Angad How is the math's group not yours?

Nand You won't understand . . .

Angad Of course, how can we understand? We are illiterates, isn't it! I had told my father to become a Buddhist or espouse the math's sangh. But no. He said that neither one of those were a part of our religion.

Nand He was right.

Angad When Acharya Yuyutsu was assailed in the residence of the Acharyas . . . father set off to save him . . . he has not returned since.

Guru Ma Yuyutsu?

Angad Yes, Ma.

Pause. **Nath** *and* **Guru Ma** *are worried.*

Angad This is all your fault.

Nand If you say such things, you will go straight to Hell.

Angad After burning everything, and I will take everyone with me.

Hanuman *enters.*

Hanuman Pranam, Acharya . . . (*Hitting* **Angad**.) pick it up . . . pick up everything. Forgive us, Acharya, forgive us . . . pranam, pranam, Guru Ma.

Angad Where is he . . . did you find him?

Hanuman *stands silent.*

Angad What?

Hanuman Forgive us, Acharya (*Pulling* **Angad**.) we shall come when night falls to recite the legend of Ram.

Someone else will take Sugriv's . . .

Nand Where is Sugriv?

Hanuman *stays quiet.* **Nand** *closes his eyes and recites a prayer.*

Angad Where is he . . . where is he?

Hanuman I shall tell you downstairs. We cannot give an account of a Shudra's agony here . . . come down.

Nand Angad.

Angad What has happened?

Nand Angad . . . come here.

Angad *runs to him, as if* **Nand** *is about to show him something. The* **Nand** *embraces him.*

Nand What condolences can I give you, son? Forgive me.

Hanuman (*runs and pulls* **Angad** *away*) Move back, back . . . leave him . . . move back . . .

He pushes back the **Nand**. *The* **Nand** *looks at him in surprise.*

Hanuman Don't touch him. Your life shall decrease.

Nand *and* **Guru Ma** *look at him with shock.*

Guru Ma What are you doing . . . you illiterate . . . Shudra. (*Assists the* **Nath** *in standing up.*)

Hanuman No, Nath, now that you are terrified of death, you want to steal our age from us?

Nand What are you blabbering, like an absolute fool!

Hanuman We will not give you a part of our life. We shall come in the night to recite the legend. We do your work for you, but we will never give you our children's lives.

Nand You are all illiterates. Absolute illiterates. . . . barbarians . . . that is why you are becoming Buddhists . . . and those who are not converting are even greater illiterates. Perish, each one of you . . . you are a Shudra in this lifetime, you will be an insect in the next. Who die as soon as they leave the soil . . . and they thrive in cow dung. All of you. Only insects.

Angad *wraps his hands around* **Nath**'s *throat.* **Nath** *begins to choke.* **Hanuman** *and* **Guru Ma** *run to break his hold.*

Hanuman Leave him. He wants you to touch him . . . leave him . . . (**Angad** *is on the verge of killing the* **Nath**.)

Hanuman Leave . . . leave him . . . if your lifespan reduces, what will we eat? Fool, even my father is no more . . . if you die, we shall all starve to death. You are insane . . . leave, leave him, I say . . .

Angad *turns around and taking* **Hanuman**'s *head in his hands, powerfully hurls him on the* **Nath**'s *cot. Blood flows and* **Hanuman**, *covered in red, falls.*

Nath *and* **Angad** *sit down on two separate sides, panting.* **Guru Ma**, *in complete shock, takes* **Hanuman**'s *bloodied body in her hands and looks at him.*

Angad What do we do . . . what do . . .

Angad *wraps himself around* **Guru Ma**'s *feet and begins to wail.*

Guru Ma *picks him up. She sits down on the ground and puts his head in her lap.*

Guru Ma Will you still refuse to go, Nand . . . is your salvation still so alluring? Is this salvation? Making an individual so helpless that he is liberated of his humanity . . .

Nand What could I have done, Guru Ma? I, myself /

Guru Ma (*as she speaks the next few lines,* **Guru Ma** *removes* **Angad**'s *ornaments*) salvation is achieved by a lone soul, Nath . . . but atonement is accomplished by a society. This is religion.

Now, **Angad** *is in an ordinary man's clothes.*

Go, child . . . you are now free from the Ramayana. Do not look back. There is no place for you here.

Scene Ten

Shrihari *enters* **Ahilya**'s *room.*

Agnivesh *smiles upon laying eyes on him.*

Shrihari Pranam, Acharya.

Agnivesh Pranam, pranam, disciple . . . the sweet sounds of the revolution have reached my ears . . . (*Looking at* **Ahilya**.) I told you . . . my disciple will come . . .

Shrihari It is with your blessings, Acharya.

Agnivesh Did the Buddhists retaliate by attacking us?

Shrihari We have shut the doors. The Buddhist king is waiting for the succeeding Nand outside.

Pause.

But we shall destroy our biggest opponents.

Agnivesh Who?

Shrihari The intellectual Brahmins and the lower caste Sanatanis of Birpur.

Agnivesh What? What are you saying? You are killing your own people?

Shrihari Lord Shri Krishna has said . . . everyone is ours. In war, a brother does not spare his brother. This is religion.

Agnivesh Why are you talking like a fool, Shrihari?

Shrihari Those Acharyas who have taught us non-masculinity for epochs. Their bodies have been hung on every intersection. First, we must sanitise our own faction. The Buddhists shall fall on the right path on their own.

Pause.

Ahilya Get out of here. This is the hut of the head of the math.

Shrihari I have called women like you my mother in this math . . . my religion has been corrupted to some extent owing to it.

(*To* **Agnivesh**.) Acharya?

Agnivesh I just have to utter a sentence and your people, you know what they will do, don't you, Shrihari?

Shrihari You are a Dom, Acharya? What will they do? There is no one above God, and god is not Buddhist. Keep your caste in mind when you talk.

Nevertheless, I have told this awakened army that you could be a twice-born Brahmin man. One of your births can be in the Brahmin caste.

Agnivesh *walks to the window and looks out.*

Ahilya Let us go, Agnivesh. I had told you earlier, there is no religion left to salvage here . . .

Shrihari You have been a part of many religions . . . no? You are aware, aren't you /

Ahilya Let us go, Agnivesh. No one will lay a finger on you. We shall open the doors and become the Buddhist king's refugees. Let us leave.

She begins to leave with her parcel. **Agnivesh** *stands frozen to his spot.* **Ahilya** *returns.*

I . . . I am with you, Agnivesh. Who do you fear? There is no need to hide anything anymore. You shall never be alone again.
This. What is this? He is neither Sanatani, nor Buddhist. He is a leech. A bloodsucking leech . . . a stain on the name of Birpur.

Shrihari *slaps* **Ahilya** *hard. She falls.*

Agnivesh *gestures for* **Shrihari** *to stop. He goes to* **Ahilya** *and helps her up, and he props her between* **Shrihari** *and him.*

Agnivesh Manusmriti part two. The rules for the wife of the teacher and the disciple. The woman who loves the disciple of her husband should be fed to the dogs. Yuyutsu is no more . . .
Do you have any dogs?

Pause.

Shrihari Acharya Agnivesh is our consciousness, Manusmiriti our guide. Jai Shri Ram!
Come, Devi.

Ahilya *quietly stares at* **Agnivesh**. *She goes near him and spits on his face. Outside, the barks of dogs can be heard.*

Ahilya There is only one path to salvation in this town of Birpur now, Agnivesh. And that is becoming food to the animals . . . I thank you!

The barking of dogs increases.

Scene Eleven

Yuyutsu *is tied to a giant wooden pole. Blood is pouring out from his eyes.* **Agnivesh** *stands before him.*

From afar, the barking of dogs can be heard. **Yuyutsu***'s blood is dripping slowly.*

Yuyutsu If you let me go, these people will blind you too, Agnivesh.

Agnivesh I never wanted to kill you, Yuyutsu. I never /

Yuyutsu My blood will flow till dusk . . . you won't have to murder me, Agnivesh, the sun's first ray will do that. When the sun is visible again . . . if it ever is . . . do not offer water to the sun god. You are not worthy.

Agnivesh *tries climbing up the pole.*

Yuyutsu Get down. Get down. One of us has to be here, it is necessary.

Agnivesh I cannot leave you here, like this, to die, Yuyutsu.

Yuyutsu I will die. But I will not be saved at the hands of a Dom. Stay away from me.

Agnivesh What are you saying, Yuyutsu? I am trying to save your life.

Yuyustu What is there to save, Agnivesh? Even if I lose my life, I will take birth elsewhere. Think of your conscience. In the end, think only of your conscience.

Agnivesh Let me help you, Yuyutsu. You are like my brother. I never even imagined this moment.

Yuyutsu Nobody could have imagined this moment . . . but I will not take my final breath in the arms of a Dom. Have some mercy. Leave.

Agnivesh I will stop this revolution.

Yuyustu It is not yours to stop.

Agnivesh I will become the Mathadheesh, I can put a stop to it.

Yuyutsu Nobody will listen to you.

Agnivesh Why . . . why will they refuse to listen? I will re-establish normalcy. Presently, the constellations are such that /

Yuyutsu Lover, friend and teacher, after murdering all three, what normalcy will you return to Birpur, Agnivesh?

Agnivesh Who have I murdered, Yuyutsu? I was creating an army against the Buddhists. All this /

Yuyutsu What can you see around you? Look around and tell me.

Agnivesh *looks around and then closes his eyes.*

Yuyutsu Can't bear to see it? This is your punishment. In the days to come, your vision will not let you sleep . . .

Agnivesh *opens his eyes again to see.*

Agnivesh I have been subjected to great injustices, Yuyutsu. Why am I receiving this punishment?

Yuyutsu You set in motion all those injustices when you misused your stream of knowledge. The discipline has nothing to it. It has been written by ordinary people like you and me. Their envy, their greed, their dreams, and in reality, wouldn't there have been disputes?

We have not merely comprehended the knowledge we have wielded it. It is the reason why today my eyes are spouting only blood and your eyes will not let you sleep.

Agnivesh *looks here and there.*

Look. Now, just look. You will beg for death, but this vision will not let you . . .

Yuyustu *suddenly quietens. Pause.* **Agnivesh** *takes out a dagger. He is about to stab himself in the eyes.*

You are committing the same mistake again, Agnivesh. The convenience of violence again.

Agnivesh *stops and looks at* **Yuyutsu**.

If you gouge out your eyes . . . you will keep imaging this catastrophe. And that illusion will be far more frightening than reality . . . religion and vision reside within, not outside.

Agnivesh You are erudite. But you would still give up your life rather than let a Dom touch you.

Yuyutsu I am helpless . . . my religion has taught me only fear . . .

Pause.

Agnivesh?

Agnivesh Yes . . . talk.

Yuyutsu Who is this boy?

Agnivesh Who?

Yuyutsu Shrihari?

Both begin to laugh.

Yuyutsu That one . . . who was scared of heights?

Agnivesh (*laughing*) Yes . . . and who, out on the porch, ate mud.

Both laugh loudly.

Yuyutsu What did you teach him . . . that this is /

Agnivesh His father had died /

Yuyutsu Yes, yes . . . he had gone off to destroy the Buddhist temple . . . (*Both laugh.*)

Agnivesh When you find someone in their childhood who happens to be a coward, you should make them courageous.

Yuyutsu Otherwise, he will grow up to be a snake.

Agnivesh You have beaten him up several times too.

Yuyutsu Of course, I would have hit him. If he was still under me today, I would have given him two hard slaps.

Agnivesh I would have done it myself . . . but /

Yuyutsu The Buddhist king is standing at the door . . . and the entire town of Birpur is under his control?

Agnivesh Nobody can triumph over foolishness, Yuyutsu. One time, you had asked this Shrihari . . . (*Laughs.*)

Yuyutsu To fetch water from the well . . . and he had fallen in! This is the same one, isn't it?

Agnivesh Yes . . . it is him . . . the eccentric mixture of fear, foolishness and servitude.

Yuyutsu As if we are extremely clever. (*Both laugh.*) One blind man and the other Raavan.

Agnivesh Raavan . . . you are calling me Raavan . . . (*Laughs.*)

Yuyutsu Obviously . . . you are going to get yourself killed . . .

Agnivesh We are all fools.

Yuyutsu And those who shall repeat our story years from now . . . they shall think of themselves to be extremely clever too.

Agnivesh And moral, and faithful and valiant. (*Both laugh.*)

Yuyutsu But even their dreams and realities will be flawed.

Agnivesh And when they shall be telling our story, precisely at that moment, their Shrihari will be up to his antics outside.

Yuyutsu   Because his dreams and actions have no dissonance . . . (*Both laugh.*)

Yuyutsu   When I die . . . will you cremate me?

Agnivesh (*looks at* **Yuyutsu**)   Yes . . .

Yuyutsu   Where is Shrihari?

Agnivesh   Salvation . . . he has gone to Muktidham to accord salvation.

Yuyutsu   You did not go?

Agnivesh   No one can create hurdles in his path now. He has decided that once he achieves salvation, he will declare me as the Nand. Then, I shall open the doors.

Yuyutsu   Then, go, become the Nath. What will you say to the Buddhist king?

Agnivesh   We have seen the enlightening ways of Buddha. We shall no longer bear arms. (*Both laugh loudly.*)

Yuyutsu   May God grant Nath Nand salvation. (*Pause.*) Will you be the one to set fire, to my mortal body . . .

Agnivesh   Yes, certainly. But I am a new Dom, you will burn inconsistently, at places soft and at others hard . . . alright?

Both keep on laughing.

Scene Twelve

It is the third quarter of the night.

*Acharya Nath (***Nand***) is sitting in Muktidham with his eyes shut.* **Shrihari** *stands behind him with a sword.*

Nand *looks at him. Smiles.*

Nand   Ram?

Shrihari *is surprised.*

Nand   Bring it . . . bring it to me . . . bring the paste.

Shrihari *pushes forward the cow dung. Acharya* **Nand** *begins to coat himself with it.*

Nand   Eat your food . . . it will give you strength. After the day we have had, anyone's body is liable to break down.

Shrihari   I cannot eat your food.

Nand (*laughing*)   you have been eating my food for years, child.

Shrihari   Do not call me child.

Nand   That is enough . . . should I put more?

Shrihari   More . . .

Nand   As you see fit.

Pause.

Shrihari   You asked me to, so I am consuming a morsel of food. (*He eats the food.*)

Nand   Certainly . . . you should not stay without food in your youth. Your stomach will fill up with bile.

Shrihari   Your body shall be hung at the square . . .

Nand   It is better . . . if possible, please ensure I am facing south . . .

Shrihari   Yes, it is.

Nand   That is good. Thank you, my lord. Thank you.

Shrihari   You are not applying it properly.

Nand   I have grown old . . . (*Laughs.*)

Shrihari   Should I do it?

Nand   Yes, you do it . . . it shall be easier for me.

Shrihari *walks to the* **Nand** *and begins applying the coat of dung.*

Nand *starts to move away in horror at* **Shrihari***'s aggressive advance. Suddenly he stops and notices him carefully.*

Nand   Shrihari?

Pause.

You should also recite a prayer. After my death, Ram will definitely come to take me with him. You will only take my body down to the town. Recite a prayer. Thanks to me, Ram shall hear you too.

Shrihari   Yes, Acharya.

> He Ram.
> The mighty, the prosperous.
> The great being, the first incarnate.
> May people beat the drums in the name of Ram.
> May people shower praise on the name of Ram.
> May people do so until the era meets its end with the name of Ram.

Nand *gives* **Shrihari** *his sword.* **Shrihari** *stands with the sword in his hand.* **Nand** *sits before him. Eyes shut. He is smiling as he listens to* **Shrihari** *recite the prayer.*

Shrihari   In the name of Ram /

Nand   Are you reciting the prayer for yourself or for Ram?

Shrihari   Acharya?

Nand   No, no . . . forgive me . . . continue your prayers . . . chant the name of Ram. I am here by the way . . . whenever you deem the time appropriate. Proceed without hesitance.

Shrihari Yes, Acharya . . . .

> He Ram
> Bestow upon this world light.
> Bestow upon this universe freedom from the eclipse.
> Bestow upon this world wisdom to escape ignorance.

Nand At least recite the prayer with your heart in it. See how the eclipse has been going on for so long now? It means there is something wrong.
Why are you praying for light? It is an eclipse that you must seek. An incomplete eclipse is horrific.

Shrihari Yes, Acharya . . . He Ram . . . Bestow upon me the eclipse . . .
Bestow upon me the power of the darkness of the complete eclipse.

Nand Aahaa.

Shrihari Bestow upon me . . .

> Bestow upon me the strength, the courage,
> the taste of the final triumph.
> Bestow upon this world
> the name of Ram
> the . . .

Nand I am here, child . . . Do not hesitate . . .

Shrihari Yes, yes, Acharya . . .

> He Ram
> He Ram, the great . . .
> He . . .

He is about to wield the sword a couple of times during the prayer but he is not able to go through with it. **Nand** *opens his eyes. He looks at* **Shrihari**. *Pause.*

Nand Do not converse with Ram . . . only take his name. It will be easier . . . (*He shuts his eyes and sits down once again with a smile.* **Shrihari** *looks at him.*)

Shrihari Siyavar Ram Chandra . . . (*Screams.*) Siyavar Ram Chandra

He is about to wield the sword when he stops again. **Nand** *opens his eyes and smiles.*

Nand Banish Ram from your mind, child. Keep him only in your throat. With peace . . . without any emotions . . . without any doubt . . . with an attentive mind . . . with a cool head . . . do it like an animal.
This is the future.

Shrihari *looks in his direction.* **Nand** *closes his eyes and recites his prayers. Offers his pranam.*

Both are silent. Acharya is seated. **Shrihari** *is standing with the sword. Absolutely quiet. Nobody is moving.* **Shrihari** *raises the sword and without any emotion, kills* **Nand**.

The moment the Acharya's body falls to the floor, the sound of the conch shells is heard. With the conch shell, **Agnivesh** *becomes the* **Nath**.

The moment **Agnivesh** *becomes the* **Nath***, the eclipse becomes complete.*

Glossary

Acharya Teacher at the math (Hindu monastery)

Bhikhuni A female Buddhist monk

Chamar Members of the Shudra caste, the lowest rung in the Hindu caste system, who work as tanners

Chura Members of the Shudra caste, the lowest rung in the Hindu caste system, who work as sweepers and manual scavengers

Dom Members of the Shudra caste, the lowest rung in the Hindu caste system, who cremate corpses

Gandharva One of the eight classical types of Hindu marriage. This ancient marriage tradition from the Indian subcontinent was based on consensual acceptance between two people, with no rituals, witnesses or family participation

Ganjika Marijuana

Mahar Members of the Shudra caste, the lowest rung in the Hindu caste system, who are responsible for the disposal of animal carcasses

Manusmriti An ancient Hindu text of laws (Dharma-shastra)

Math A Hindu monastery

Mathadheesh Also known as the Nath, the head of a Hindu monastery

Nat Members of the Shudra caste, the lowest rung in the Hindu caste system, who work as actors

Neelkanth One with a blue throat. Hindu god, Shiva

Pranam A form of formal greeting by joining one's hands and bowing

Sanatan Dharma The orthodox form of the religion of Hinduism

Sangh An association of followers of the math

Sanghi A follower belonging to the *sangh*

Varna The Vedic system of social hierarchy which mandates profession in accordance with one's family lineage, broadly divided into Brahmins (priests), Kshatriyas (warriors), Vaishyas (businessmen) and Shudras (menials)

Vishnu Hindu god, Krishna

9 Kinds of Silence

Commissioned by PlayCo, New York

9 Kinds of Silence opened at PlayCo on 17 September 2023 at 122CC, Second Floor Theatre, New York City.

Presented by PlayCo

Founding Producer	Kate Loewald
Executive Producer	Robert G. Bradshaw/
Written and Directed by	Abhishek Majumdar
Set and Costume Design	Jian Jung
Light Design	Emma Deane
Original Music and Sound Design	M. Florian Staab
Dramaturg	Jocelyn Clarke
Casting	Victor Vazquez (C.S.A., X Casting)
Production Stage Manager	Siena Yusi
Production Manager	Andy Sowers
Line Producer	Durra Leung
Props Supervisor	Natalie Carney
Associate Production Manager	Sarai Frazier
Assistant Stage Manager	Julie Cai
Wardrobe Supervisor	Sara Vandenheuvel
Audio Engineer/Sound Operator	Jimmy Kavetas
Company Manager/House Manager	M. J. Lugo

The Cast   Hend Ayoub, Joe Joseph

Characters

Mother: *Mid-60s to 70s OR late 40s. Identifying Female. The character is from a minority community, wherever the play is performed. The actor may or may not be from that same community depending on the place where it is being performed and its own sensitivities and limitations around casting*

Son: *About twenty to twenty-five years younger than mother. Identifying Male. The character is from a minority community, wherever the play is performed. The actor may or may not be from that same community depending on the place where it is being performed and its own sensitivities and limitations around casting*

Note

a. The opening production imagines the Prophet from a particular theology. This can change depending on the context. The description of 'form' and 'formlessness' is to change accordingly. The minority identity can be racial, gender orientation, caste, class or faith related.
b. A *Silence* lingers

   A *Pause* is a block in thought. The actors should not linger on the idea of the previous lines but be stuck for how to take the conversation forward. A pause is also shorter than a silence

   . . . ., indicates a lingering unlike a pause but the absence of complete silence unlike a *Silence*

As the audience walks in, a woman sits at a desk, with a typewriter. She has a small cassette player and an old microphone connected to a loudspeaker in the room. Much like the radio studios of yesteryears.

She has a bunch of bags kept around her desk.

There is a blackboard in the room.

A round dial telephone on her desk.

The room is full of sand. A window and two doors. Curtained. The window is translucent to start with, though through the performance it can be transparent / opaque as specified.

In another part of the room a translucent partition. A man sits on the other side of the partition. Not visible clearly to the woman. Audience can see him and that he wears dark glasses. The partition is suspended and covers him up to his waist. His legs are visible. Softly, the sound of the ocean.

The phone rings, she panics and picks it up. She is quiet. The person on the other side speaks although we do not hear them.

She keeps the phone, makes her gaze stronger on the person on the other side of the translucent partition. He is unperturbed. Sits absolutely still. In some time the phone rings again and the above sequence of actions is repeated.

Other than the soft sound of the ocean, there is no sound. Silence in the audience is desirable.

An unlit bulb in the room.

It is early evening. High tide. The sun is setting. Appropriate to the time, light comes in through the window.

A couple of dogs bark ferociously outside. She goes to the window. Opens it. The sound of ocean and the dogs increases.

Throws pebbles that she has at them. They run away.

She shuts the window. The room gets quieter.

She turns around. Looks at her desk. Looks at the partition.

She goes to her table and picks up a grey folder kept on her desk. On top of it six stars that are from a uniform. She looks at them intently. Puts them back on the desk.

Silence.

Mother   I've got to. (*Stops.*) You've

You've got

To.

Yes. You've got to.

Pause.

Speak. (*Silence.*) Sitting here and . . . and (*adjusts her desk*) . . . this . . . dead air. Making no sound. (*Pause.*) Can't get you. (*Breathes.*)

Silence. In some time we begin to hear the room more clearly. The small sounds that are present in this room.

She changes the mood deliberately.

(*Looks at a file.*) G97Sector13North. I wish they gave us a map of these places you come from. (*Laughs.*) Never quite sure what this means. Sector 13 North. (*Laughs.*)

Paradise? In Paradise are there sectors? Is there North, South? (*Laughs.*)

You want to talk? About Paradise?

She picks up grapes from her table. Eats.

Have some. (*Points to the bowl of grapes on his desk.*) Paradise, apparently will have . . . FRUITS. Grapes most likely. (*Laughs.*). I don't know. People say.

Smart people.

People who know. God. God says I think. I read somewhere. Or did my great aunt tell me? Grapes in Paradise.

Do you want to talk? About grapes?

Long silence.

G97 . . . You are a hero. (*Pause.*) We sleep in peace because of you.

(*Smiles.*) I really mean it. We Salute you. (*She salutes him.*)

But now. The phone has already gone Brrrrr (*Laughs.*) twice. And you don't want that. No No No, Sir. Not that phone to ring. (*Laughs.*)

On the other side of that door (*Pointing to the exit.*) there lies, lies, HOME.

Smiles.

(*Silence.*) Speak.

Let it all out, before you get back in to the motherland again.

Relieve yourself of the. (*Pause.*)

Of the you know, the. (*Looks at her manual.*) Negativity, yes that's the word, ne-ga-ti-vity that you are carrying.

Your Hurt, pain, sorrow, fear, right here in this . . . womb. (*Referring to the room.*) With a mother. (*Smiles.*)

> *A two- to three-minute sparse soundscape plays. She picks up the folder again. A movement sequence with him moving very slightly but in discrete actions. With her opening the folder. Holding the stars and going to the window. These three minutes are a snapshot of what happens to them in a real time of fifteen minutes of waiting. Choreography which shows the woman's state of mind at this point. It also gives us*

a sense of the different positions in which the man remains silent. The choreography enhances our sense of silence in the soundscape and how the characters are feeling when quiet.

Long silence.

She types. Reads.

Silence. S. .i. .l. .e. .n. .c. .e.

Erases it with her eraser. Types again. Reads carefully by putting on her reading glasses from the desk.

Two Os, Four Es, Three Ts . . . no Qs.

'The Subject does not speak'

Pause.

'Subject'. (*Looks at him. Pause.*)

Peeps outside of the curtained exit to see if anyone is overhearing. Comes back on noticing that no one is there.

Bloody official language. Never liked it. (*Looks at him and smiles.*) You're not a subject. You are our children.

Some things about these government types. I just do not approve of. At my age. No.

Going back to her normal tone.

The government is great of course.

(*Changing her tone again. In order to develop a false sense of intimacy.*) But some of these people. Call over and over . . . keep asking 'Has the Subject spoken'?

(*Pause.*) Subject? Do you think Heaven has subjects. Does Heaven have waiting? (*Thoughtfully.*)

Silence.

The musical silence of listening to another. (*Smiles.*) In my village, I learnt to sing. And my teacher, may he be blessed, a pious man, said, god lives between the notes.

Listen . . . listen to the gaps.

Shuts her eyes, listens to the silence.

He sits as if he is about to pray. She looks at him. He stops.

You cannot pray here. I am sorry. Not. . . . not in silence.

She takes out a folder from her drawer. Exactly like the folder she already has on her table. She looks at the first folder again. Touches the stars. Looks at him.

My child. (*Silence.*) It is an essential step. (*Silence.*) You speak. (*Silence.*) I give you some basic guidelines. (*Silence.*) To get back to the motherland. (*Pause.*) Basic. (*Pause.*) Guidelines. Nothing forced.

Just simple ways to get back.

You follow them. I give you . . . this. (*Pause.*) This ticket to meet your mother.

You go out of that door and they'll check this folder before entry. If they find the yellow card, you can go home my child. If not, if by any chance I have to give you the red card, you'll go there thinking you are going home and they'll shoot you, right between the eyes.

With the red card, my child, you will have no way of escaping a sure and certain death. I am not supposed to tell you about the two coloured cards but I am telling you because I care.

She looks at him intently. He does not shift. She goes to the window. Lifts the curtain. The sound of the ocean increases in volume. In some time sounds of a dog barking. She shuts it immediately.

Dogs. Bloody dogs. Animals of the devil. Greedy as fuck. All this bullshit about loyalty. Bones. Bones. Bloody bones. If humans didn't have bones, they wouldn't give a damn.

That's what they are after I am telling you my child. The bones. You give them bones all your life, and in the end they will wait on your corpse, to suck some of that marrow from your spine. And us (*Pause.*) god-fearing humans, good people, are such lumps of emotion I tell you, we watch them watching us and make up this entire fairy tale about . . . about them dying at our grave. Pathetic. .patheticcheap emotion when all they are after . . . (*If needed, a gesture.*)

Pause.

In Heaven, there will be birds . . . birds I am told . . . They don't come here anymore . . . sit far away . . . I keep calling. But they never . . .

The light slowly changes at the window, as if a ship is arriving and its lights are falling on it. The sound of a foghorn from a distance.

(*While the foghorn plays.*) The other day, as I slept at home after the long (*emphasising on 'long'*) night shift here, I had a dream that the Prophet. (*Pause.*) That the Prophet had sent his messenger. His own beloved messenger to tell me something.

He had beautiful eyes. The eyes of my son. He walked up to me and sang a song of lament. He was missing what he had destroyed. He cried at what he had shot. He looked me in the eye and said, the Prophet is coming. The Prophet is coming?

Silence. A lingering sense, as if something of the messenger is still in the air.

One must live till the Prophet arrives. One must do one's work for the nation.

Silence. The lights on the window go away. Back to harsher light in the room. Fade in back to the sound of the room.

She looks at him intently. No sound except the soft sound of the ocean.

The phone rings again. They are both startled. She picks it up.

– Sir. (*Stands up.*) Yes. Yes. (*Pause.*) I . . . I understand, sir. No. I understand. Please. Yes, sir. I will. He. He will. Yes, sir. Long live/

The call is disconnected from the other side.

She picks up a manual from her desk.

OK.

OK I get it, you are – huh, just my luck. One of those unavoidable. Bloody hell.

God's work.

Looks at the phone.

The shits. Huh. Sit in your decorated offices in the legislative. And leave us here with –

(*Calms herself. Counts. In the language of the actor.*) 1. 2. 3. 4. (*Breathes in and out to calm down.*)

In Paradise, there is a government office where women have chairs with cushions and men sit on tattered spring boards. Where women have telephones that make calls and men do to receive orders.

Smiles. Pause.

My child. I don't think you understand.

Eats a grape.

Have a grape.

He doesn't.

(*Eats more grapes and talks while eating.*) There is no (*takes out a grape skin from her mouth*) silence out there.

Out THERE. Out of that door. Nothing. Zero. Buzz. No, sir.

It's been a long war. For you. For us. For the motherland

We have our voice at the top now. Our man in the – let's say – the father in the motherland.

Strong, decisive, not afraid to cut it to heal it. A surgeon. A shearer. A great builder.

Building us back, my god, building us back from – from war, you know, this distant yes but war nonetheless is what's the word, what's the word. The word for.

He suddenly makes a sound as if he were about to say something desperately. Stops.

Silence.

I know, I know that when you had left, there was a different supreme leader. Another father at work. And then there was the supreme contender. And now the supreme contender is the supreme leader. And there is a new supreme contender for the new supreme leader.

Things move on, your motherland gets new visionaries. New saviours to protect us from the brutal, god hating world outside. (*Pause.*)

You have trouble speaking, my child? Trouble, breaching the silence within you?

No problem, the motherland has just the answer . . . the alleviation . . . the antidote . . . right that is the word . . . antidote for your trouble. We understand . . . We . . .

Shows him the manual.

Simple. Documented. Professional manual for training returning soldiers to belong . . . belong? . . . (*Mumbling in Arabic.*) to speak . . . to make sounds . . . to . . . (*Pause.*)

Nine. (*Pause.*)

Nine kinds of sound. That help you speak again my child. The government approved remedy for silence. (*Pause.*)

I appreciate the, the sound you made just now. (*She repeats the sound he made to bring us back to context.*) That's good, it's a beginning. Everyone starts differently.

Once you learn these sounds well, you will be ready to speak again.

Looks at him.

OK ready?

Goes closer to her table. Switches on a control next to her microphone. Takes a tape out from her drawer and plays. Motivational music plays from the loudspeaker in the room. A melody with a rhythm getting faster, like a running song. She starts to speak into the microphone which also comes out so that she can perform with it standing away from the table. Between the song the focus transitions to **Son***'s movements. The director is free to transition whenever it seems suitable to them.*

Repeat after me my child.

Sound #1. The song of encouragement that helps us all build the nation together.

Looking at the manual.

Song lyrics (plays on tape)	Mother's text (sings live)
Aaaaah Aaaaaah Aaaaaah Aaaaaah *Aaaaah Aaaaaah Aaaaaah Aaaaaah*	Aahhaa, yes . . . aaahhaaa. Simple . . . syllable after syllable Aahhhaa aaahhha Add a little nasal tone to it And go for it Unhhaaa
Together through the war and siege *Glory to our people's prestige* *Getting up and dusting off the dirt* *Embracing martyrs with gaiety and mirth*	*Together through the war and siege* *Glory to our people's prestige* *Getting up and dusting off the dirt* *Embracing martyrs with gaiety and mirth*
Aaaaah Aaaaaah Aaaaaah Aaaaaah *Aaaaah Aaaaaah Aaaaaah Aaaaaah*	Aaahhaa aaahhaa Unhaaa Unhaaa
Starting a new day for each other *Passing on the great flag* *from brother to brother*	*Starting a new day for each other* *Passing on the great flag* *from brother to brother*
Aaaaah Aaaaaah Aaaaaah Aaaaaah *Aaaaah Aaaaaah Aaaaaah Aaaaaah*	Unaahhaa aaahhhaaa Come on my child you can do this Sound #1: Song of Encouragement
Every morning from six to seven *Gather in parks round tanks and planes*	*Every morning from six to seven* *Gather in parks round tanks and planes*
TRANSITION TO SON'S PERSPECTIVE	**TRANSITION TO SON'S PERSPECTIVE** *(Mother is silent.)*
Grab your trophies, teeth and bones *Wear them* *Hang them* *Tear them out of the savage*	
Glory to the civ'lized in us all *Glory glory to our nation* *Glory to the civ'lized in us all* *Glory glory to our nation's soul*	
Glory to the civ'lized in us all *Glory glory to our nation* *Glory to the civ'lized in us all* *Glory glory to our nation's soul* *Glory glory to our nation's soul*	
TRANSITION BACK TO MOTHER'S PERSPECTIVE	
Aaaaah Aaaaaah Aaaaaah Aaaaaah *Aaaaah Aaaaaah Aaaaaah Aaaaaah*	Aaahhaa aaahhaa Unhaaa Unhaaa

He sits absolutely unmoved. Unfazed. The music plays. She looks at him. She is quiet and so is he. She goes to the knob on her table. Reduces the volume slowly. As she reduces, he moves slightly. She looks at him. . . . Her breath is heard.

She reduces the volume. She begins to walk up to his side of the partition. Stops midway. Looks at the other side perplexed. She is quiet.

Silence.

The. (*Pause.*)

Dumb silence

Of

Of slumber

Or worse still

Apathy.

Silence.

I hope you don't think, I'll let you huh. (*Counts.*) 1. 2. 3. 4. 5. 6. 7. Phew. (*Breathes in. Breathes out. She touches her folder with the stars.*)

I hope you are not one of them. Them, who come from godless families.

Them. (*Pause.*) Who don't believe in Heaven. Them . . . them who don't believe in the nation or God. But you are a believer. You just prayed.

(*She prays.*) Because of people like you, we get a bad name. You do not speak and we are questioned. Our sons are also out there you know. They are also. . .

She turns around, walks to the other side of the room. Switches on the bulb in the room. She notices that nothing is written on the blackboard. She walks up to her table. As she walks closer to the microphone, the sound of her feet are amplified. She takes a piece of chalk from her desk and goes back to the blackboard.

Writes. Sound #1: Song of Encouragement. *The sound of writing with chalk is amplified. Check marks it with her chalk. She turns around to look at him. Silence.*

He appears uncomfortable and fidgety as the chalk sound is amplified. She maintains it. He is fidgety.

He interrupts the sound of the chalk with a sound similar to the song of encouragement. It seems like he will speak. She waits at her typewriter. He explores the sound very softly and then stops.

She looks at him, hoping he will speak. She makes the sound twice again. He shuts his ears and eyes as if he is going to explode. He is quiet. She looks at him. Silence. She types.

Three Us, three Gs, seven Es. That's unusual. I must have used the same word twice.

(*Reads out.*) 'Subject is encouraged by the song of encouragement'.

(*She looks at it closely. She pulls out the red card from her drawer. Looks at it. Thinks. Pushes it back into the drawer. Looks at the sentence she has typed again.*) It's been years since I read a complete sentence. Read two today? (*Breathes in. Pause.*)

It drove me to insanity when I did early on.

The women who read what they typed in the early days, God bless them, threw themselves under buses that took them home.

They went back to town, and often heard a familiar voice.

In a market or during prayers, making us . . . us . . . struggle to forget something we knew about this person that they themselves wanted to forget. We live the war thrice over. Once on our own, once with you, and once again becoming the memory of the war.

Then. (*Pause.*) The Ministry of Empathy, as always, came up with the measure of relief. It added a paragraph in the manual, instructing us to record without registering, typing without troubling ourselves with meaning.

The heroes said words, we typed alphabets.

Alphabets, for even words could have residual meanings which could drive an entire town full of women to abject madness.

I mastered the art. Of recognizing no meaning. The perfect recipe to build a great nation. A society of love and . . . and families of forgiveness. We say what is given, what is approved by the nation. The meaning is in the form.

Pause.

The messenger, the messenger, when he is sent by the Prophet in my sleep . . . talks and talks and talks throughout and insists on meaning in the words. (*Pause. Touches the stars.*)

Pushes meaning into my dreams after an otherwise meaningless night of listening to others. (*Pause.*)

(*She looks at the stars on her desk.*) This is why, perhaps . . . they warn against our god. The war against a formless god of meaning in the time of living a meaningless life of form. They, their god, the god of many. And us, our god, a god of the few. A tenant god, inhabiting the home of a landowner god. Does our god own his own patch in Paradise? Or will we have to prove our loyalty everyday there as well? (*Pause.*)

Silence.

War is a good thing.

We send ordinary people, we get back heroes.

Pause.

You are a hero but the government . . . the government cannot recognize silence, my child.

Pause.

Last year three quiet ones, shot people. (*Pause.*) Old people and little children in three separate incidents at the market square. (*She nods her head disapprovingly.*)

Came in . . . quiet. And bang bang bang. Then two of them shot themselves. One in the skull, one in his mouth. (*Mumbles prayers.*)

And all of them were the silent ones. (*Silence.*)

The silence of the young, when it fails to make sense of its time. Nothing more dangerous than that in the world. (*Silence.*)

    To be our glorious selves again, our dear leader, has eradicated the silence inside us.

    Silence.

    Prayers. (*Pause.*)

    Prayers for instance.

    The Supreme Leader, one night, on radio announced that anyone who supported the troops, who loved the nation, would no longer pray in silence.

Silence.

    I get it. If you pray in silence, how do we know what are you praying for? This is how it begins. Always. Violence in prayers. Then violence in market square. Bang bang.

    Imagine a country which declares that the war is won and yet allows the spread of such a contagious disease.

Silence. She goes very close to the translucent screen . . . Stands there. Both of them breathe at each other from two sides of the screen. This is heard loudly.

He turns to her. Gets up. Picks up his bag. Ready to leave through the door. he came in from.

Leave. (*Pause.*)

Some are like you. Who go out of *that* door. (*Pointing to the one they would have come in from.*)

Silence.

When we return the next day, they are not here. Not one of them. (*Pause.*) They haven't gone to the city, they are not on the shore, where are they?

Silence.

They clear the entire shore of everything. Food, clothes, body parts.

Spotless.

They don't go back anywhere, don't enter. The city. The ocean. Where do they go?

No one knows.

No one

Pause.

Silence.

Next evening when we arrive in buses and wait for the boats . . . I can tell you . . . we can feel a peculiar silence. The silence of . . . the missing.

The sound of the ocean is amplified.

He stops. They are both quiet. In anticipation.

He returns. Music sequence. Passage of time.

Alright, my child, let us try again.

Sound number 2.

From the manual. The sound of infectious laughter.

> To recover from the silence within you try . . . try laughing, my child.
>
> *Takes her microphone. No track potentially this time.*
>
> *Laughs.*
>
> The laughter of comfort. Of returning home to safety.
>
> (*Laughs.*) The laughter of recognition. Of knowing that there is at least one other person who understands you and your particular kind of laughter and where it comes from.
>
> (*Laughs.*) Responsible laughter.
>
> (*Laughs.*) The wild laughter of childhood.
>
> *Pause.*
>
> Very different from
>
> (*Laughs.*) Irresponsible laughter of comfortable youth.
>
> Very different from
>
> (*Laughs.*) The mad laughter of a mob.
>
> (*Laughs again.*) The crazed, triumphant laughter of a mob on finding in their midst the one who does not belong.
>
> Laughs again.
>
> *Silence.*
>
> *Laughs. Laughs. Silence.*
>
> *Laughs.*
>
> *Silence.*

Long laughter.

Laughs till she has tears in her eyes.

You must understand, it is mandatory in the country now.

This is not a choice anymore. Happiness. If you love your country, you absolutely have to, have to be happy, have to be, have to have to, laugh . . .

He remains quiet.

She picks up a star. Goes close to the window. Points it up and looks through it into the sky.

What rank are you? How many stars do you have on your uniform?

(*Pause.*) Stars . . . my mother used to say that we are all star dust.

One night, I sat here on my chair. While typing letters. As the soldier spoke. I fell asleep and the Prophet himself appeared to me. I could not see him clearly but I knew it was not the messenger. He said something, about the sound of Heaven. Everyone always reveals what it looks like in Heaven. But he was telling me something about its sound. (*Pause.*) Although . . . I . . . I heard him. Registered nothing. Just As, Us and Ps.

Since then I have tried every night to sleep here. Even if it were for a second. Hoping he would come again. And this time, I'd perhaps not just type but for God's sake comprehend, what is he saying.

When I woke up the soldier was crying. And then he went silent. The thick . . . silence of a mind that has relieved itself of what should be other people's guilt. He got up, took his yellow card and went home. I wasn't sure if the Prophet had come for me or him.

Silence.

I am not giving up on you. Because you served in the military. My husband was in it. (*Takes out a picture from her pocket.*)

Silence.

Our wedding photograph. Good man. Went to the last war. Didn't look back.

Never returned.

Never said my prayers for him. The nation needed us, not to mourn the martyrs. Never did.

Pause.

(*Takes out another photograph.*) My son. Brought him up. Sixteen years by myself. Saw him look like his father and be like me.

Silence.

Suddenly we were at war again . . . A new threat was away they said. We could not see it but we knew it was there. A new enemy. A bad enemy. Them. A new 'Them' outside. The worst of its kind. Hated our life. Our children.

Gave up a . . . the . . . the only son. (*Silence.*)

Three months. We were told. On radio. No choice.

Pause.

Does Heaven have choices? Does God forgive or we have to do the forgiving there as well?

Silence. She looks at all the pictures again.

My life. (*Pause.*) In three pictures. Three quiet images . . . Husband, son and the only one of them together.

Silence. She looks at the pictures. He takes out some pictures from his pocket slowly and brings them very close to his eyes. Long silence. She looks at her pictures while he feels them. A possible silent choreography here playing with patterns of how they look at their pictures. He tears the pictures.

Loudly.

Silence.

This one.

The silence of resentment. My mother called it. Why are you doing this to me? I am a mother too.

The phone rings. She is terrified. She gets angry, picks it up.

Screams loudly into the mouthpiece.

I am doing it! I am doing it! (*Pause.*)

Changing her tone.

Sir . . . Sir. He is talking. He is talking non-stop. I am typing page after page. Yes yes. I am sorry. I was just . . . I am sorry, sir. I apolo/

The person on the other end cuts the call.

Long silence.

We do not have much time, my child. They are beginning to notice that you have been long.

If we do not end before dawn, they will storm the tent. Both of us will be shot dead. Is that what you want? Will that be a suitable end to a mother and a child of the motherland?

Pause.

Do you want dogs to eat us? Are you just watching me with your soldier's cold steel eye and judging me with disdain? Who are you? How can /

When the messenger came to see me, he always had eyes I knew. With the eyes of my son, father, mother, teacher and . . .

There must be meaning. There must be some meaning to our love, for our people, for . . . for what we know, what. what we say, what we do . . . for the motherland . . . no? There must be . . .

Pause.

Silence. He sits with his head in his hands.

You are doing this again.

Looks at him. Silence.

You are changing the silence.

From the noisy silence of disgust to this claustrophobic silence of accusation.

Accusation . . . why the silence of accusation on me? What did I . . . You are ruthless, you'll make me kill you, you ruthless . . .

She seems very fragile suddenly. She opens the manual. Pause.

Sound number 3, the song of the nation.

The wrong tape plays.

Sound number 3, the song of the nation. You know this, my child . . . I know you know this. You buried your brothers with this. You've heard it, lived it, sung it.

Beat.

She starts to play it. He immediately stands up. She plays it for a few seconds. He gets up from his place. Walks towards the tap on his side. She immediately switches off the anthem. She notices that he is blind and wears dark glasses.

He starts to wash his face without taking off his glasses. Goes breathless. She is nervous looking at him.

You . . . you cannot cross the curtain. We are not allowed to see you. (*Pause.*) You are not. (*Silence. He opens the window. Sound of dogs.*)

You should be reported. (*Pause.*) No questions. (*Pause.*) They should bother about your kind of cases. Not me. Why me? (*Silence.*)

Can you shut the window? The draught, it'll kill me. And the noise. God help us. The noise. (*Insert Arabic phrase.*)

What were you expecting? You'll come back and run into your mother?

Pause.

How blind are you? Can you see a little? (*He turns in her direction.*) How many fingers? (*She is showing her fingers.*) Here (*she moves three, shows him*) and now? (*She moves them again. Shows two.*)

God. God. God is with you.

You walked into the tent of a mother with a son out there. Out there in that noise.

They remain facing each other in silence. Only the sound of the ocean.

She goes close to his face. She is shivering. She holds his face. Shuts her eyes. She touches his face. He is shaking like a leaf.

She holds him. She takes his glasses out slowly. Feels his eyes. There are two dead eyes in there. Completely lifeless. Vacant. Perhaps even just two holes.

She touches his face.

Long pause.

They sit down holding each other. The sound of the ocean goes up.

They sit in this way for a few minutes.

(*She kisses him on the forehead.*) I had a boy. A son.

(*Hands him the stars.*) These are his stars. Just like yours. Can you feel them?

She touches the stars on his uniform.

He holds her hand and takes the stars from her.

Mother (*looking away from him helplessly*)   Speak, my son. Speak. Please . . . I can't have you die here, my son . . . please . . . please, my son.

He starts to dig the earth as if he is going to bury something. **Mother** *notices him gradually. He gently places the stars in the ground. Covers it. And recites the prayer of the dead. She looks at him surprised that he can speak, as he completes the prayer.*

Silence.

Mother   You . . .

Silence.

Mother   Are you the . . . the messenger?

He sits in silence.

Mother   Have you seen my son? Is this really him? They gave me these stars, this morning. From another tent, of another mother. (*Pause.*) Could be anyone right? The dead return. It has happened before. Why should this be him. I lost my . . . we won the war . . . there must be some . . . some meaning in. (*Pointing at the grave.*)

Pause.

Mother   Are you the /

Son No.

Silence.

Mother How do you know /

Son Paradise. I heard Paradise the moment I lost my sight.

Mother My son . . .? Did he?

Son Paradise. In Paradise there are no. (*Pause.*) Grapes. No fruits.

No oasis. No garden.

Pause.

Mother (*in panic*) Then?

Son The sound of a large field.
Over-crowded but speechless.
Us. Eternally looking for our loved ones.
Looking. For meaning in our looking.

A quiet place sometimes.

Where we search but aren't allowed to take the

Names of those we love.

Pause.

Mother Hell? Did you hear Hell?

Son Yes.

Mother And?

Son Louder. Same fate as Heaven, except us celebrating our condition.

Mother Isn't that better?

Son Cheerful but devoid of all meaning.

Mother Why?

Son Shame. We are ashamed of what has been done in our name and we are unable to face what we have become. The sound of loud emotion that covers up for shame. of a people surviving on their own noise.

Pause.

Our greatest fear in Hell is to find our own.
And for them to see who we really are.

Pause.

Silence.

Son Who are we? Really?

Mother   We are what we do when no one

   Is watching

We are what we think
When we are truly quiet.

Pause.

Mother   Did you hear . . . my son?

Silence.

Son   You want to know where?

Pause.

Mother   No.

Pause.

Mother (*in desperation. Loudly*)   We won the war. You are back.

Silence.

The phone rings loudly. **Son** *keeps sitting next to the grave. The woman goes towards the phone. Looks at it as it rings. She breaks its cord.*

She walks up to him next to the grave. She takes out the rest of the pictures and buries them too.

Mother   I wanted you to speak.

Son   I did.

Silence.

Mother   Is the Prophet coming for us again?

Son

Mother   You . . . you heard him?

Son   No

Mother   No?

Son   He was quiet.

Mother   His messenger? Are you his . . .

Son   He came, he saw. He left without words. I don't know why.

Mother   Either there are no words as yet or there is nothing left to be said.

Pause.

Mother   I know.

Son   What?

Mother   He wants me to listen. Listen again.

Son   To?

Mother   To this. (*Long silence.*) To the silence between us. (*Pause.*) Even my dreams are not mine anymore.

Son *holds her hand. She embraces the grave. She looks at him.*

Silence.

She goes to her table. Takes a yellow card. Puts it in a grey envelope and walks to him.

She holds it out for him.

Mother   You have spoken, my son.
Take this. Go. Go home to your mother.

He waits. Facing her. Holds the envelope. Gives it back to her. He removes the shirt of his uniform. He hands it over to her. She holds it close to herself. He waits. He turns around. Picks up his bag and leaves through the curtain that opens on to the shore. The sound of dogs is heard loudly.

The mother sits at the grave holding the uniform. She covers the grave with the uniform. She starts to recite the prayer of the dead aloud. She takes a pause. Defiantly says the rest of the prayer in silence.

The sound of birds gathering in large numbers. As the prayer comes to an end, the birds create a cacophony as if they are flying in large numbers over her head. Silence.

Lights out.